Don't Be Late for the Wedding

Charles L McCuen

authorHOUSE®

AuthorHouse™
1663 Liberty Drive, Suite 200
Bloomington, IN 47403
www.authorhouse.com
Phone: 1-800-839-8640

First published by AuthorHouse   11/19/2008

ISBN: 978-1-4343-8749-3 (sc)

Library of Congress Control Number: 2008905448

Printed in the United States of America
Bloomington, Indiana

This book is printed on acid-free paper.

A side of the Lord that nobody talks about, and the times that we are living in; "The End of Times". Are you ready?

DEDICATION OF THIS MANUSCRIPT!

I have to dedicate this book to my wife, Joanie; of now forty-three years of marriage. She not only has lived through my time in hell but has always been there for me in the worst of my experiences. She has been faithful and given us two wonderful children; Shawn and Michael. Both are sons and both have been a blessing to have around us, also to this world. She has somehow endured by having been consumed over the last fourteen months in the writing of this book and the second book which I have just completed. When I say consumed that is exactly what and the only word that could adequately define this experience. I feel blessed that our Lord found me to be usable and that He has saw me through all of my difficulties and I do Glory in my tribulations.

There is one other person who I also dedicate this book too. On April the seventeenth, 2008, two days before my first involvement with a Prison Ministry I pleaded with the Lord to just give me one ear. Just one who would reason with me and who would listen to me. I was in tears before the Lord wanting desperately for just one ear explaining that I didn't need three ears nor did I require a Minister or a Pastor. Two days later He seated me at a table beside an inmate named, let's say Howard; at ISP or the Indiana State Penitentiary. Howard is a pseudo-name but Howard knows who I am writing too or speaking about. You are blessed Howard and the Lord has just given Himself a voice inside of the Prison Walls, through you and your servitude to our Master. Thank you and God Loves and will provide for you always.

The last person who I want to dedicate this book too is a friend, a distant relative on my wife's side and lives in California. His name is Larry and he has given this work of our Lords a grand review and has also been a good ear in letting me vent as to some of my frustrations in the writing of this manuscript.

For those of you who are or were lost and just happened to stumble across these works of our Lords. I hope that you will find hope, strength, guidance and peace as a result of reading its contents.

PREFACE

My name is Chuck Mc Cuen; I have a problem with the news media of today.

They have a tendency to slant their views to align with their political agenda and this book is not about Politics or Religion. It is about our God, not my God, but our God! My heart and my desire are to make God real and believable; someone you will want to find in your life. I write this because the end of times is not far away and it's time to make a choice and the correct choice I hope and pray. There are many who don't know the Lord and many who are lost or in bondage. I do not want that anyone should miss the boat, so to speak.

This book is written with the intention of giving Christians some information on issues that you may not have considered yet and hopefully revealing a side of the Lord you may not know of. It is also intended to be an instrument in which you will share with a family member or a friend who is bound up in addictions or does not know the Lord and is lost. It is fundamental but yet very revealing. I'm writing about life, about living and about dying. I'm writing about something we all seem to have a concept of but don't seem to be in agreement on. I'm writing to everyone and I mean everyone. I don't care if you're male or female, if you're English, Russian, Chinese, Japanese, American, Arabian, Turkish, Pakistani, French, Canadian, African, Iranian, Jewish (Israel) or any other nationality. We are all brothers and sisters, living in this world under one God and that's what I'm writing about. A God who is divine, Holy, who is the Creator of all things that are living, all things; the earth, the universe, the sun, the moon, the stars, the ocean, the mountains, the rivers, the trees, the forests; all things.

A God, who is Love, is forgiving, is understanding, who knows no sin and will not look upon sin which I will explain later in this book. Yet we are all sinners, every one of us; though some of us understand and try not to sin, we all fail. Even Paul the disciple of Christ wrote, (Rom. 7:19-20); "The things I ought to do, I do not do and the things I ought not to do, I do. Woe is me, it is not me that sins but the nature of sin that is in me that sins." There is only one who is without sin and that one is God; "Jesus Christ." I changed the title of the Book which was "Conversations With God" And "Prophetic Visions" to Don't Be Late For The "Wedding"; (Mat. 25:1-12). That was a result of the prayer I prayed Sunday night 12/23/07 asking the Lord if there was anything in my book that shouldn't be there or if there was anything that I needed to add or change. If you don't believe in answered prayers then read the last paragraph on the Section coming up which is titled Introduction. This book has taken on an additional concern and that is are we ready for the "Seven Years of Tribulations?" I must tell you at least five times in this book that the date that the Lord will return is really irrelevant. What is relevant is; do you know where you're going to spend eternity if you die tonight and if you live and if He does return are you prepared for the worst? He is "Love," I mean everyone and He does not want that one soul should perish, not one. I hope that I can open some new windows of consideration for your life now and your future eternal destination. Good reading, I would love to hear from you and I left my E-Mail address on the last page. Even if you think I'm crazy I would still enjoy hearing from you.

CONTENTS

SECTION ONE
Conversations with God

SECTION TWO
Revelations of the Holy Spirit & Prophetic Visions

SECTION THREE
Poems & Quotes

INTRODUCTION

I have inserted this in the beginning because of what I have seen and heard, felt in this last nine months since I started writing this book. I will admit that I have been obsessed with what the Lord has revealed to me but I cannot keep to myself the goodness God has revealed. All that I want to do is to open your eyes to the possibility of what may lay in front of us and maybe not that far into the future. There are two words that we have, in my opinion, totally abused, one of those words is the Church and the other word is Religion. The Church is not the building that you go to on Sunday mornings to hopefully worship God; the Church according to scripture (The Bible) is the body of Christ. The Church is Christians or believers in Christ. According to scripture, Jesus Christ is the head of the Church and we as believers are the body. When you hear people use the word Church in today's speech they are talking about the building not the people and all of the buildings that call themselves Churches do not worship Jesus Christ as Lord and Savior, that is part of the reason that Christianity has not been as desirable as it really is. Show me another God who preaches Love, Forgiveness and Life Eternal if you will receive Him and believe Him.

The other word Religion is one that I really don't like, when someone refers to me as being too religious I almost want to scream. Religion is the biggest problem that we have had in the body of Christ. Religion in all practical purposes is mans laws around Gods Word. Religion has allowed man to put God in a box and leave Him there only to visit occasionally on a Sunday morning and for some that is only on Easter Sunday. I am a Christian, who believes that the Holy Bible was hand written under the inspiration of the Holy Spirit, Gods Word. I also believe that the Bible was written for anyone and everyone to read, it is God's love story between Him and creation, us. It was written for anyone in the hopes that they would know the truth and receive Him and believe Him. The Bible was not meant to lie on the shelf and collect dust and that you were to go and learn everything from the minister at the pulpit on Sunday mornings. If you don't know what God said in His Word how do you know if what you are hearing is the truth or a distortion of the truth? There are demonic, religious spirits that work their way into some Christians, some Parishes and cause all kinds of distortions of the truth. Our asylums are filled with demonic problems and religious spirits, I believe that if you were to play softly Christian praise and worship music over the PA systems in asylums that you would find people within a couple of years start to lay down their medications and walk out freed from bondage.

There is another word that can cause you problems also and that word is intellect or intelligence. There are some who know so much they are dangerous. They can give you the answer to any question you might want to ask but give them a hammer and a nail and they could tear a house down in less than one week. Too much intelligence or not enough can distort reality. I say that because either God is; either a reality to you or a myth, a mythical dream character? In my walk in life I thought that God was for the dead or dying, that He was someone you got involved with at the end of life, not during the growing or working stages of life. There is one last word before we begin and that word is most critical that you keep it on the front burner of your mind; that word is "believe." I said just shortly before would you receive Him and "believe" Him? The Bible says in Mark 9:23 "Jesus said unto him, if thou can believe, all things are possible to him that believes."

I was reborn and found God on my knees in South Georgia starting at midnight of Sept. 10th, 1986. He carried me for I know the first year if not two years of my sobriety. He carried me out of South Georgia back home in Indiana to a Rehabilitation Hospital for chemical addictions and then took me to the tables of Alcoholics Anonymous. I was three years sober and well into my walk with God and the Bible before He put my spiritual mentor Clint into my life and Clint took me to a place where he and his wife went to worship God, (Church) Clint's wife Martha, the whole male side of her family was in the ministry and the Church was started by her father. He called his Church "The Word of Life" and referred to it as a step down Pentecostal Church. It was Non-Denominational and full Gospel, definitely "Spirit" filled.

I have taken the time to tell you this because my walk with our Lord has been different then what most people has been. What you are about to read you could never convince me that it is not true but I am not asking that you believe everything that I've written. I am only asking if you will consider and give Christ a chance. That you will consider what may be sitting just over the horizon of time and those questions that I raise. I pray that what is put on paper will open some new windows of consideration in your walk through life or give you a different perspective of life. No; I am not against Ministers, Preachers, Pastors, Priests or Evangelists, Religion. I am just saying that all are not Spirit filled and minister the Word of God, Christianity and the Word of God is all about Jesus Christ. The Bible is all about the Blood, about God, Jesus Christ. The Bible says that; "Life is in the Blood," John 6:53. If you follow the Blood trail from Genesis to the Cross then you will understand what Jesus did when He shed His Blood, His life for you.

It's now Christmas Eve. and we have just returned from the 7:00PM Candlelight Service at the Church. We closed the service with candles lit as we sang "Joy to The World" and this prayer came over me as we sang. "Lord; With all that You have blessed me with and all that You have revealed to me I can't stay silent. To stay silent and take this book to the grave with me would be so that I could neither live with You or with myself. If I could walk out and just breathe you onto others, I would do it. To think that maybe just one will read what is written herein and come to receive you, whereas they may have come to their end and cry out; "Why didn't someone tell me!", I couldn't endure Lord knowing that as a possibility. I ask Lord that you will go with these words and touch those who are without, who are lost or have lost their way; free those who are held in bondage. Let them be still Lord as they read and let them hear your heart beat as the words pass through their minds. Lord; bless them with everything that you had in store for me. Just to know You and to have been touched by You is sufficient for all of my needs. Father; Hear my prayer, for it is in and in the Name of Jesus that I write and pray. Amen. Good reading and God Bless!

SECTION ONE
CONVERSATIONS WITH GOD

CHAPTER ONE
THE BEGINNING

I opened the way I did because that is what He says it is. He says in (Eph.6:12), "We wrestle not against flesh and blood (each other) but against principalities and powers of darkness and spiritual wickedness in heavenly places. In (Rom.3:23), "We are all sinners and have fallen short of the Glory of God", in (Rom.3:10), "that none of us are righteous", or in right standing with God." None of us! I would like to start with August 10th at 7:30 PM in a motel room, I believe room 107 in the middle of South Georgia, US, in the year 1986. I was 45 years old, a plant manager of a small distribution warehouse for a large Corporation up north in Indiana. On August the 10th, Wednesday evening at 7:30 pm I had just entered my room. I sat on the end of the bed I slept in and turned on the television set and the sound off. I had fixed a stiff drink and set it beside the television set on the dresser. I was trying to pull myself together. I had already had my after work seven or eight martinis but I was very sick, physically exhausted and mentally tormented to the brink of insanity. Usually I would fix a couple of drinks, get cleaned up and go back out for the evening only to find myself totally intoxicated and pass out or wonder back to my room around 3:00am in the morning. My drinking career of thirty one years had climaxed into one half gallon of vodka (approximately) for the last two months and that was due to the sins of my flesh and what I felt I had to do to survive in South Georgia. My normal daily consumption of alcohol was a fifth of vodka which I mixed with diet Pepsi to change the taste and discolor the alcohol so no one would know that

I was drinking, so I thought. I had my first swallow, one swallow of vodka, when I was fourteen years old and now I was drinking a half gallon a day. For years I drank beer because I didn't want to have a problem with alcohol. It got to where three cases of beer wouldn't get me through the weekend so I was not only getting a beer stomach but the expense was getting out of hand. You see I was also smoking five packs of cigarettes a day. That's thirty five packs a week or 100 cigarettes a day. I figured it out one time and you would have to light a cigarette every ten minutes for sixteen hours and forty minutes every day. It doesn't even leave you eight hours to sleep.

Well this night I just couldn't go on. I was at the end of what I know today was spiritual torment. It would start early in the morning and last until I could get about eight martinis in me. The negative thoughts or lies would just race continually across my mind and it was impossible to stop them. They would start with "What If" to "It Was" and then "Oh! What am I going to do?" My mind would just race and the tension would build until it felt like I had a 1000 LB weight strapped to my chest. I would just pace the floor going from room to room, out to the warehouse and then get in my car and go check, supposedly on the other warehouse. There would be times that I felt like stopping the car, getting out and running as fast as I could and when my legs and lungs screamed from the pain of not getting any rest or enough oxygen I would just run faster until I would just fall face down in the dirt and die. Just Die! The only other problem I had was that I couldn't stand to sit alone so I hadn't eaten a meal in over six weeks. Well you drink like that, smoke like that, don't eat anything and just run all day long you do get very sick both mentally and physically. Evidently I figured if I could just relax a few minutes and get my breath I could get cleaned up and continue on. I must have laid down and passed out. When I woke up it was totally dark in the room with the T.V. still on and no sound so I rolled over and turned on the light and looked at the clock thinking it was probably about 8:00 PM. It was 11:40 at night, now I was really in a mess, what was I going to do? I had already slept more than most evenings and had next to nothing to drink yet, so to speak. I thought about getting something to eat but that was out of the question. By the time I got cleaned up and over to the restaurant it would be closing or closed for the evening. I thought *about just putting on some shoes and going over to the lounge but that was not an option either. Where I stayed they had a band and at that time of night during the week the only ones left were redneck drunks just looking for either a woman or someone to pound on. I obviously didn't qualify for the one and I certainly wasn't up for the other option. All I could do is sit in my room and drink until morning and probably drive myself totally insane. I was in a hopeless situation with nothing to focus on or do and I knew any minute that door was going to open and in they would come (demons) and I couldn't take another battle another beating. My first Spiritual experience! HE spoke! HE said, "Chuck you never tried, you never gave life a chance!" I knew it was true I had hid in my problem for the last thirty-one years, ever since I was fourteen years old. HE then said, "Son, your time is up, the team has been chosen and you never showed up for the first practice!" HE has a way of saying things so you will understand. You see sports were my forté. What that said to me was I was not going to see the dawn of the next day and if there was a place you went to after this one I wasn't going there! Well I don't know what you might do in that situation but what that did to me was it drove me to my knees between those two beds, hands clasped together, my face buried in my hands, kneeling over the other bed and you would have thought someone had opened the flood gates on a dam. I cried at age 45 for the first time that I could remember since I was fourteen years old. I cried for at least fifteen or twenty minutes. My hands and the bed was sopping wet from tears. I cried until there couldn't have been a ½ ounce of liquid left in my body. The only words that came out of my mouth and if I said them once I cried them out at least twenty times. Every time a thought of something I had done that I hated or regretted doing I cried out, "God Help Me!" Today I will tell you that is the most powerful, international prayer you can pray. You don't tell him what to do, how to do it, or when to do it. You simply say if you're not there and won't help me, I'm dead! God answers prayers like that, though I wouldn't advise testing that statement if I were you. In that fifteen or twenty minutes I died; the person He picked up off his knees, sat on the bed was not the same person who had just gone to his knees. I sat there exhausted, spent; no life in me and with my head hung down staring* at the floor and that was the last thing I remember. I was now what was known as a New Creation, a new creature in Christ.

The next thing I remember was being awakened in the morning. My eyes opened and it was light outside. I was lying in the center of the bed on my back; my head was in the center of the pillow, the covers pulled up neatly across my chest and my arms were on the outside lying across my chest. I looked over and it was 7:00 o'clock in the morning. Having to use the facilities as the normal first thing in the morning, I pulled the covers back, got out of bed and headed for the bathroom. I hadn't gotten ten steps and I knew something was different. I didn't figure out what it was until later. What it was that was different was the battle was over. It just didn't matter anymore, nothing mattered. If my wife left me, hopefully when things got better I could get her to come back. If I lost my job, well when things got better I would find another one. Nothing mattered! I got to work early for a change, I went around and talked with employees in the warehouse that I hadn't said two words to since I had been commuting down there. I went in the office and talked to my secretary about her family life. I'd never done that before. I finally ended up in my office just sitting at my desk with nothing to do. I had been so busy dealing with my problems and spiritual battles I hadn't even begun the first project I had come down to accomplish. I started to feel a little anxious and I didn't want that to start again so I decided to call back up north to my wife. I just wanted to hear her voice and know that the world had not come to an end. She was happy to hear from me and after about ten minutes of conversation she asked me, "why did you call me?" Listen to what I said. I said, "I just wanted you to know that I was coming home a week early to get help for my drinking." She started to cry; I could have bought her a two carat diamond and it wouldn't have meant as much as those words I just spoke. She was the only one who knew. She had begged me to get help a year earlier when I chose to take severance pay and leave an employer of sixteen years. But, no, I had to find a job. If that was going to happen it would be later; besides I didn't have a problem. My problem was they just didn't pay me what I was worth. Well, when everything settled she said to be sure and call her when I knew the flight schedule and she would be there to pick me up at the airport. I wasn't scheduled home for another week and three days.

We said goodbye and hung up the phone and I just sat there staring at the wall. That is not why I had called her; as a matter of fact the thought had never even crossed my mind let alone considered getting help for my drinking. What's more amazing yet is I really didn't have a problem considering getting help. It was Wed. /Thurs. I was on my knees and it was now 8:30 AM Thurs. I spent the rest of the day debating on how I was going to explain to my corporate office that I was coming home early. You see I had laid out a complete schedule of time elements through the completion of this project of making that branch profitable, where I would hire a full time branch manager, train him and return up north to continue on with the project of managing the computer system I had cost justified and was going to be purchased Jan. 1987. I would be done in Georgia in late Nov. 1986. I waited until late Fri. at 4:30 PM to call back up north. I got the boss on the phone I felt the most comfortable with and announced I would be returning home a week early. He obviously wanted to know why and I told him that I was sick. We had a long conversation about changing the flight plans due to the expense. The tickets had already been purchased based on my schedule. He finally got me to agree to make it through the weekend and call back on Monday morning and let them know how things were going. If it got too bad I could go to the emergency room at the hospital down there that it would be covered under my insurance plan. I was disappointed and so was my wife but that was the best that I could do for the time being. I again left work and went straight back to my motel room just like I had done Thursday evening. I never left the motel room until Monday morning at 7:30 AM. Thurs./Fri./ Sat./Sun. I ordered room service and forced, forced myself to eat dinner. It was almost nauseating but I managed to get some of it down. I drank in total moderation. The most I drank was five or six mixed drinks of diet Pepsi and vodka. It had to be less than 1% of my previous daily consumption. I watched T.V. some (sporting events) and slept a lot. Monday morning I was at work early, rested and called immediately up north and got the other boss on the phone. I explained the same thing to him; I was sick and was coming home a week early and nothing had changed over the weekend. He tried to reason with me to stick it out and stay on schedule due to the expense of changing flight plans. I finally just blurted into the phone - I'm not going to die in South Georgia! He said! "Gosh if it's that bad get home." So I gave my tickets to my secretary who just came in and asked her to get them changed to fly out of Atlanta no earlier than 1:30 that afternoon. I called my salesman off the road and told him to cancel his appointments for the afternoon; I would need his help driving me up to Atlanta and returning my company car back to the branch. I didn't know how long I would be gone but I didn't want to pay parking expense if it was over a week. If necessary he could come and pick me up when I returned.

The flights were changed and I was to depart out of Atlanta at 2:00 PM Monday. I told my salesman to pick me up at the motel at 10:00 AM and he could get my secretary to go with him to pick up his car when he returned from Atlanta. We would drive my company car to the airport. I left to go get cleaned up and packed. I took a long shower and got dressed, cleaned up, shaved, etc. and was packing my luggage when I started to perspire profusely. I had to get undressed, take an ice cold shower, dry off and get new clothes out to wear. About the time I was half packed my salesman showed up to pick me up. I threw everything in the suitcase and made one last scan around the room; said let's go; and we were off. I threw the luggage in the trunk and asked him to drive. We had to stop at the motel office and pay my room charges and expenses. When I left the motel office and went to get back into the car to leave my knees gave out on me just as I grabbed the car door handle. Somehow I got the door open and pulled myself into the car and tried to get turned around and set upright. We hadn't gone 75 yards and I told my salesman that I couldn't make it; to take me to a doctor or the emergency room at the hospital if he didn't know one. He knew a doctor so we went there; I told him to wait; it would just be a minute because I was not going to miss that plane. I went in and told the receptionist I had to see a doctor immediately. I had a plane to catch in Atlanta and didn't have much time. I apologized but if it was not possible to see someone, please let me know and I would go to the hospital for help. She excused herself and the next thing I knew she was at the entrance door and told me to come on back to a room; the doctor would be with me in just a minute. When he showed up, I told him everything, how much I drank, how long I had been drinking, my problems with other women, everything. He took a blood and urine specimen and asked me to wait for the test results to come back in. I said I couldn't that I had a plane I had to catch. So he went over to his desk and wrote out a prescription. For what, I don't know. He returned and stood with his hands together, head slightly angled, staring at me. Finally, he said, "Son, you are very sick. I don't know where you are going but wherever and whenever you get there go directly from the airport to the hospital. Don't go home, don't rent a car, don't get a motel room, call a friend or get a taxi just go directly to the nearest hospital. You are very sick." I agreed so he handed me the prescription he had filled out; told me to get it filled and take one immediately that it would help me with the anxiety. I thanked him for his service on such short notice and assured him I would do as he suggested. We got the prescription filled and headed for Atlanta. I slept most of the way to Atlanta (around one hundred and fifty miles). I only woke up once to a radio commercial that was a little girl pleading with her father to stop beating mommy. It was on alcoholism! That fortunately was not one of my problems. I was more of a verbal abuser if you would get on my case than I was a physical abuser. I never did strike or threaten to strike my wife and we are still married today. Well we made it to Atlanta, I said goodbye and said that I would probably be back in about two weeks just to proceed as normal and north I headed.

CHAPTER TWO
RECOVERY

I arrived home around 6:00 PM and my wife greeted me, happily at the airport. We went home and I spent the evening with the assurance that tomorrow I would go and get help. Tomorrow came and I was sitting up when my wife left for work. I then laid back down to think things over. Mistake! Only to awake sleepily at 10:00 AM. I proceeded to make myself a soft drink and went out in the living room to wake up. It's now 12:15 and I'm sitting in the living room in my underwear with my back to the front porch, blankly staring through the dining room into the kitchen at the side of the refrigerator. My wife on her way to lunch passed the house and saw my car sitting in the driveway so she stopped in to see what had happened at the clinic. As soon as she passed the refrigerator she saw me in the front room still not dressed. She walked to the edge of the living room, stopped and said, "I thought you were going to get help?" I said, "Oh, I am. I'm going this afternoon!" She turned to leave, took five steps, stopped, turned around and you could see the tears in her eyes. She said, "If you're still here when I get home tonight, I'm leaving." She turned, stomped out, slammed the door, and left. Well that was the end of my debate. You see I was starting to convince myself now that I was home, in a couple of weeks everything would be smoothed over and okay and I could just return to Georgia. Now I had to at least go speak to a counselor in the local treatment facility and convince them everything was okay. I lied something terrible; I'm not sure if it was my vital signs that gave me away or if my wife called and said if I showed up for an interview and they let me out, didn't admit me, she was leaving. One of the two had to have happened because no matter how hard I tried I was there for the full thirty day program.

They kept me in detox for three days before they let me out into the open wards. I found out later they couldn't get my blood pressure down from a 196/120 (stroke time). As a matter of fact if it would have gotten any worse they were going to move me to intensive care. I had reduced my drinking so much my body was literally going into shock. All I remember is being on an IV and falling in and out of sleep every four or five hours. On the third day, they let me start eating non solid meals like Jell-O's, ice cream, cereals, liquids, etc. While lying in bed with nothing to do, I would reflect back on what had transpired since I had fallen to my knees in South Georgia. The only scripture I thought I remembered anything about had something to do with a "valley of shadow, death". When I got out of the detox room I asked the nurse or someone if that rang a bell with them and they said it sounded something like they thought was the 23rd Psalm. I asked if there was a bible anywhere that I could look it up. There was one in the sitting room outside of the detox room where you could smoke. I found the Bible and opened it up to guess where...one page from the 23rd Psalm. It was Psalm 22. I'm telling you when He gets involved, or we let Him get involved, things happen. I have long since put that Psalm to memory and cannot forget it. I know I went for ten years without saying it, quoting it, or longer and I still had not forgotten it.

The same day I got out of detox into the open ward the first person I ran into said something that became a cornerstone in my walk with the Lord. We accidentally ran across each other going the opposite ways and she stopped to introduce herself because she had not seen me there before. She had just finished the thirty day program and was leaving and I was brand new in the open ward. So we spoke to each other and wished each other well, success. When she went to leave she said, just remember; "If you ain't prayin, you ain't stayin; fake it 'till you make it!" I'll tell you how that entered my warped mind. That said I didn't need to read the whole bible first; all I had to do was believe there was a God I could talk to and start talking to Him. As of that night and ever since that is exactly what I did. Every night, and sometimes for hours, I would just talk to Him. I guess I was blessed I was raised in the United States. You see my parents, God love them, had me in Church every Sunday from before I could walk until I asked if I could not go any more. I had to sit in the main sanctuary with the adults because they didn't have nurseries or ministry programs yet for the youth. So the only God I had ever heard about was the God of the King James Version of the Holy Bible, the God of Abraham, Isaac, Jacob and Moses etc.

Three days out of detox, they gave me a complete physical and I mean complete. The only thing that showed up was there were some signs on my liver that said I was a heavy drinker but in time they would go away and you would never know that I had a drink in my whole life. The doctor in South Georgia was so concerned when he got the test results back, he wrote me a letter telling me what they had found and again insisted if I had not been to the hospital to go immediately without delay. My wife brought me the letter he had sent and I read it and took it to the physician who had reviewed my physical with me. I asked him, showing him the letter, what happened to these things? He shrugged his shoulders and said, "He obviously doesn't understand alcoholism!" Either that doctor in South Georgia gave me a miracle bottle of pills or another miracle had just happened in my life.

I could go on and on about sobriety itself but that's enough for that story for now. I haven't had a drink in twenty-one years and I haven't smoked in many years. I very seldom drink coffee; I don't watch television, listen to the radio, other than ministry programs or Gospel Tapes, CD's. I haven't subscribed to a newspaper for over twenty years; in all honesty, I really don't want much to do with world events and all the lies, the politics. I want to tell you about my walk with this GOD I did not know. Before I start, I want to tell you what I now know for sure. I know everything I've already told you and everything I'm going to tell you for sure, but this I want you to know before I start.

1) God is Love!
2) He wants to be a part of everything - your needs, your concerns, your dreams, everything. He wants to walk with you and talk with you daily.

3) *Ask Him and He will forgive you your sins and look upon them no more.* *"He will wash you white as snow" (Psm. 51:6-9). "He will throw them as far as the East is from the West" (Psm. 103:12). "Forgive that you may be forgiven" (Luke 6:37). The question is "will you forgive others?", "will you forgive yourself?"*

4) *GOD in the flesh is JESUS CHRIST, there is no other!*

It says in the Bible that (Pro. 9:10), "The fear of the Lord is the beginning of wisdom." He wrote for me the speech I was to give several weeks ago at the Michiana Great Banquet #31 (MGB#31), a three day spiritual retreat. What He wrote was.

Fear - Is the dedication of time and thought!

I just heard a good one the other night;

Fear --False evidence appearing real!

CHAPTER THREE
INTO ACTION:

I said in the last chapter I just started talking to God. As of that night and for a long time I would go to bed at night, flat on my back with my hands clasped together and thank Him for that day and then just lay there and talk to Him. I'd tell Him about the things I understood, the things I didn't understand, the things I liked and the things I didn't like. I would just talk to Him; ask Him questions, sometimes for hours.

I'm now going to tell you why God has done everything He has done in my life from the time I went to my knees in South Georgia through today which is May 8th, 2007. The new birth Sept. 10th -11th 1986, the things He has spoken to me, the visions, the revelations, everything! The Bible says in (Heb. 11:1-6), "Now faith is the substance of things hoped for, the evidence of things yet seen and without faith it is impossible to please God because you must believe that He exists and is a rewarder of those who diligently seek Him", must believe that He exists and is a rewarder of those who diligently seek Him. Question! Does not what I did on my knees in South Georgia qualify for that definition? I went to bed at night, every night and talked to God for hours at a time, does that not qualify for that definition? Why would you talk to God for hours if you did not believe that He existed and would someday, sometime, somehow start talking back or responding? You may not have consciously thought that through but is not that only reasonable? I'll be real honest with you; I did not figure that out until after the second or whatever number miracle happened in my life on Aug. 6th,

13

Sunday, 2006 at 1:15PM in my easy chair at home. I'm telling you now so that you don't think as I write on, that I have just lost my mind. I'll tell you about Aug. 6th, 2006 later on. What I am going to do is to tell the things He has done for me in the order in which they occurred.

I got released from the hospital thirty days later. I returned to work and inquired if I could return to Georgia to complete what I had set out to do and knew that I was capable of doing. We had a meeting and my main boss did not understand; he apologized but seriously he didn't understand and that was okay. I understood his problem and concerns. I told him it was okay that I understood the way he felt and thought. I told him that today I could do a much better job for him than what I had ever been able to do before. Well I wasn't going back to South Georgia. It was now almost Nov. 1, 1986 and I was also not going to be allowed to install, train and run the new computer system, software I had cost justified, which was being purchased on Jan. 1, 1987. He agreed he would provide me with a job for as long as I wanted it but as far as growing with the corporation that would not happen. So as of Jan. 1, 1987 I went from salary back to hourly pay, punched a time clock and worked on the UPS bench in the warehouse. I enjoyed not having the pressure and it is much easier to find another job if you're employed. In mid February an ad appeared in the paper for an outside salesman with a company who sold the same products as the company I was now working for and the other company I had worked for over sixteen years. I must have driven my soon-to-be new boss half crazy. I called once, if not twice, a week to see if they were taking interviews yet. He would laugh and say not yet, but to go ahead and call back later in the week to see if things had changed. Well I was interviewed, hired and began work on May 8, 1987. Our Chief Operation Officer (Corporate office Ft. Worth, TX), came into town to do the interviews. I sold them on the fact I didn't have direct outside sales experience, but I had twenty years working with the same products they sold (two of their competitors) and I had spent most of my career selling my concepts and ideas to the Division Managers and employees in which I was very successful. What locked the job for me was number #1 my persistence in calling about the job and number #2 I gave as a reference a personal friend that was Branch Mgr. out in Pennsylvania for their competition where I had worked for sixteen

14

years. I gave them his phone number. They asked if I would step out for a minute while they called. It wasn't long they called me back in and gave me the job. The manager they called in Pennsylvania, when asked if he felt I could handle an outside sales position, answered, "If you hire him, don't send him out here. I do not want to compete against him!" It's good to have a good relationship with others who you worked with at prior employers.

My first experience in outside sales. . . I worked four weeks in the warehouse getting familiar with the warehouse employees and their way of doing things. I worked one week in the office and then went to the boss, my manager. I said that everyone was running full steam ahead and the sales guys really didn't have time to drag me around. If he didn't have a problem, I felt comfortable in getting started. I might have to ask some direction questions first but the rest should be easy. So he gave me my list of accounts and the company car I would use and off I went. The first afternoon I only planned on seeing one account just to get my feet wet. I had to ask exactly where they were located but the rest was easy. I found myself up in the back hills of a small city that sets to the North and West of where I was going. I was on a dirt road trying to find a shortcut. This dirt road became one of my favorite spots just to sit and meditate or pray to the Lord. Well this day, first day, I'm up on this dirt road and I caught myself playing a mind game I used to always play. I called it prediction and control. I would try to figure out the questions or problems they might bring up and then how I would respond. I never won that game - someone would lie and everyone would believe him and not me. Well here I am playing this stupid game with someone I had never even met. I pulled the car over, put it in park and looked up through the front windshield up into the clouds. I said, "Lord, I really believe you gave me this job and this is where you want me to be. But I'm going to tell you, Sir, if I have to drive around all day and play this stupid mind game, I'm driving back tonight, turning in my keys and walking home; I quit! You either take it from me or I'm gone!" Thank You Lord! That was the last time I ever played that mind game. My car became my sanctuary for the next sixteen years. I spent every minute I was in the car with the Lord. I had praise and worship tapes, I had teaching tapes on spiritual issues, and I had radio ministry programs I liked to listen to. Sometimes I would just meditate on the Word and preach or teach in my mind. I even used to have communion with the first sip of a new diet Pepsi and I would tear off a piece of a fresh doughnut which I bought for the occasion. I would not touch either one until I was at the cross ready to honor that which the Lord did for the world; "Gave His life." I would ask the Lord to forgive me for what I was using but when I tore a piece out of the roll or doughnut it was the flesh that I was eating and when I would take the first sip out of the drink I had not drank from yet, it was the blood I drank. I know this sounds a little foolish or disrespectful maybe but in reality it's not. Where your actions are, there is your heart also. It's your heart the Lord wants. He loves you so much He gave His life (Blood), for you, He died at Calvary Hill so you could live again in righteousness (right standing) with Him both here in this earthly outfit and in heaven with him. Disrespect is to never go to the cross and partake of communion. God will honor your heart. There is a lot of scripture that talks about your heart. The bible says:"What comes out of your mouth is the overflow of your heart," (Luke 6:45). Be careful what you say, you just might get it!

1) "It's not what goes into a man that defiles him. It's what comes out of a man that defiles him", (Mat. 15:17-18).

2) "Life and Death are in the power of the tongue", (Prov. 18:21).

3) "My Words are Life, they are health to all your flesh", (Prov. 4:20-22).

4) "Out of the overflow of the heart the mouth speaks", (Mat. 12-34).

5) "Set a watch over my mouth put a guard over the door of my lips", (Psm. 141:3).

6) "Heaven and earth will pass away but my Words will never pass away", (Mark 13:31).

7) "In the beginning was the Word and the Word was with God and the Word was God. He (Jesus) was in the beginning with God and all things that were made were made through Him (Jesus) and nothing that was made was made without Him (Jesus)" (John 1:1-3).

8) "To love the Lord your God with all your Heart, Mind and Soul", (Mat. 22:37).

Mind = All encompassing - heart, spirit, soul, programs of interpretation of your senses, work area and history files.

Soul = Is everything in your brain, your mind, your heart, your history.

Heart = The essence of - your beliefs, your feelings, the fruit of who you are, your will, the center of, command center, thoughts and intents, your emotions. It's is the mind of your spirit man.

Spirit = Is the workhorse - retrieves new and old information, actions, it's what moves you (in your head and body), your words.

Spiritual = Thoughts, beliefs, words, tears, emotions, feelings, action.

Will = Is what you do!

I really didn't plan in getting into all of that at this time but what's the problem, maybe I'll change my mind when I get this all finished and revise it then.

I became top salesman for awhile after three years on the job. When I would get to an account, I was totally at peace, nothing on my mind, 125% for the company I worked for. I would talk with the receptionist and share testimonies of what God had said or done. When I would get into the purchasing agents office I was more interested in him, what he liked. You can just glance around their office and know where their heart is. I would talk for twenty or thirty minutes on what they liked . . . sports, fishing, golf or families, whatever. I could sell my product or let them know I wanted to be a supplier of the products they used in less than five minutes, so they would always see me. I had purchasing agents that I could take to lunch that never went to lunch with anyone. The reason I was successful was because I broke the boring, monotony of their daily tasks. I let them talk about what they liked and I really enjoyed it because I was at total peace with myself. I quickly learned who I could share the Lord with. So anytime they had a problem or a need, guess who they would call?

CHAPTER FOUR
FIRST VISION:

I remember the first vision the Lord gave me. I was in my car (sanctuary) and I was questioning if I was really going the right way or if things were so bad at the end I would believe anything rather than going back and dealing with those problems. It was really kind of a foolish question because those problems are gone, they're behind me. But the Lord gave me a vision - I was reaching up with my right hand holding onto a right hand/arm that was extended down out of the clouds. My left arm was extended down behind me and someone was holding onto my left hand. All I could see was my mid-section, my two arms and hands. Then the vision left. I said, "Wow!" I was going the right way, I was holding onto a hand above me extended down out of the clouds and there were others there; I wasn't alone. Now here is a newborn baby question. The only thing I'll tell you first is, God says, "There are no stupid questions"! I then asked the Lord, "How many are in front of me and how many are behind me?" He answered; "Some days your right hand is in mine and other days no one is holding on to your left hand!" The interpretation He gave me was - When my right hand was in His hand and someone was holding on to my left hand was when I was in fellowship with the Lord or sharing my testimonies, faith with others. When nobody was holding onto my left hand was when I was out in what I called the wheat field. When I was out of fellowship dealing with what I had to take care of, my responsibilities. You know you can spend every spare second with the

LORD and function better in life than you can if you're trying to do things on your own.

The more I grew in the Lord, the more I hungered to know Him, what He said, His Word, who we are, what is it I'm supposed to do, and what I shouldn't do. Over the first two or three years the Lord did so much. He put a spiritual mentor into my life. He put other people in my life that helped me. My sponsor taught me how to laugh, relax, and have good wholesome fun, how to enjoy life. He took me to a special Church that nurtured me spiritually. I was there for over seven years until my friend, the minister, and his wife transferred and moved to another location in Indiana, which was too far for me to travel on a weekly basis. I know he is participating in a Christian Jewish Church which has always been where his heart was and he is probably teaching which he always said was what he was called to do and participating in the music ministry. I think I was still looking for that first church and about two months ago I found the church that I really believe is where the Lord wants me. He will let me know if it is for only a while of that I am sure.

You see I'm hard to minister too, I'm particular and demanding. The minister above that I spoke of was younger than I am but what a servant of the Lord. He set a standard that's hard to match. The Church was non-denominational, no Church traditions, strong with upbeat praise and worship music, Spirit filled, full scripture and he taught straight out of the Word Of God, Bible. He had many great connections; he knew a lot of Jewish people who had converted to Christianity. They're on fire; there is no holding them back. A lot of people do not know or believe this, but the Jewish people (Hebrew) are God's chosen people and Israel is the Promised Land. It was in the beginning (Old Testament) and it is at the end (New Testament). The minister, Mark, had such a love for people. He felt everyone had a calling and it was his job to help you find your calling. There were always a lot of alter calls, no time limit of services or praise and worship. You see God works through all things, everything for His good purpose. Everyone has a Church home that was meant for them and some of us are still searching or Church hopping you might say. God works through animals, bushes, stones, anything, all things like I said. We just aren't spiritually intoned (some are) to His ways, His voice. You do know that we are a spirit, that has a heart and a soul and we live in our earthly (temporary) bodies and we live in a spiritual world. We need to start thinking about what we are thinking about. I always like to ask the question; "Do you think that every thought that goes through your mind is yours?" If it isn't, and it isn't - then where did it come from and whose is it? I wrote a poem, He wrote the poem, and it's in the back of the book, it's titled Wisdom.

When I really went on my search for God, I couldn't get enough. I bought book after book, pamphlet after pamphlet, tapes and CD's attended classes on spiritual warfare and bible study groups. I have spent more time getting mentally tormented until I finally proved it was spiritual and learned how to stand, how to fight. We have the victory. I used to go to bed early so I could read and some nights I would read the Bible until as late as 3:00AM. I could hardly hold my eyes open I was so tired. I would reach over and turn the light off, lying on my back and I would take the Bible, close it, standing it up on my chest and take my two thumbs, cross them. I would let each of my thumbnails touch the inside of the back and front covers. I would slowly drag my thumbs back over each other until the tips of my nails touched. I would then dig in and open the Bible back up, somewhere in the middle of the Bible. I would lay it open, face down on my chest and clasp my hands together on top of the Bible and pray thanking the Lord for the day and then I would pray, "Lord while I sleep tonight, I'm going to ask You to write your Words on my mind and in my heart so that I might know God", Thank You - Amen. Did He do that? I don't know, but my ability to retain and recall things has been magnified considerably. All I know is the Word says, "Whatever you pray and ask for, believe that you receive it and it will be yours?" (Mark 11:24).

CHAPTER FIVE
THE LORD SPEAKS
THROUGH A STONE:

*I*n my search for the Lord I found myself on my favorite dirt road up in the hills and was ten minutes away from my next call. John the purchasing agent was punctual. He left for lunch at 12:00 Noon sharp and was back at his desk at 1:00 PM. It was five minutes to noon so I couldn't get there before he would leave and I wasn't hungry. So I just pulled the car off on the side of the dirt road and decided to spend some time with the Lord. I know for about the first fifteen minutes I was in prayer and meditation. That day I just wanted the Lord to reveal Himself someway. Just to do something so that I would know that I knew. Just something! When I had finished I sat back relaxing and lit a cigarette. The Holy Spirit started nudging me to get out of the car. I didn't know why (now I do - the number 3 is perfection for man and the number 7 is perfection for God), but the number three always seems to show up when God wants my attention. I know it was the third time the Holy Spirit nudged me and spoke softly to get out of the car. I looked around and I'm up in the hills on a dirt road, no traffic and I can't see any houses where I was located. So I got out of the car and started looking around, I thought maybe He would just appear by a tree and then disappear. So I looked at ever tree and bush that was around me and there was nothing. I knew it was the Holy Spirit that was telling me to get out of the car. The Holy Spirit in me is a soft, quiet voice that kind of rises up from within me and the Holy Spirit kind of nudges me or pushes me to do something. When the Lord speaks, it is always inside but His voice is just like I would be talking to you and His voice seems to come from up - down into me.

It was obvious I wasn't going to see anything and I knew it was the Spirit so I thought maybe there was something that I was meant to find. So I went over to the edge of the dirt road where everything had been kicked to by the passing cars. It had rained earlier that morning so the road was still damp not heavy mud but wet. I must have walked forty yards down the one side of the road. I would see something that would look different so I would bend over and pick it up, look it over real good only to throw it away. I finally picked up one stone that definitely wasn't precious but it was different. It was heavier for one thing and it was more rectangular in shape. It was well covered with mud so for some reason I just hung on to it. Well after thirty or forty yards I crossed over to the other side of the road heading back towards the car. I would see something interesting, bend over and pick it up and sometimes I would almost throw away the stone I had been holding onto and keep the new stone. But at the last second I would change my mind and discard the stone I had just picked up, holding on to the old stone. I don't know how many times I almost threw away the stone I had been holding onto and changed my mind and kept it. I had probably walked eighty yards up the other side of the road and hadn't found anything. I looked at my watch and it was twenty five minutes after one. I had been up there for an hour and a half. So I immediately headed back to the car to get back to work, it was obvious I wasn't meant to see or find anything. I opened the car door, took several Kleenex to wipe the mud off the brim of my shoe and the stone I had been holding. I got into the car and set the stone on the top of a portable console I had between the two front seats. I closed the door and turned to start the car and my eye caught that stone sitting on the console. I laughed at myself and said, "What a fool - who are you to see God!" I will tell you exactly what was spoken into my mind as I looked at that stone. He said, "Am I not the Alpha and Omega, the Beginning and the End? Am I not all things and in all things? If with all your mind, heart and soul you really want to see me can't you see me here in this stone?" (Rev. 1:8). I started to well up and tears were running down my cheeks. That stone has since been cleaned up as well as I can get it and it never leaves my night stand by my bed. If I ever have a need to feel close to God, I just reach over and grab my stone and sometimes fall to sleep just holding on to it. He says, "He will never leave you or forsake you", (Heb. 13:5). I've been told and believe the reason for the bad times is to bring you closer to Him. I know He will never let you suffer beyond what you can bear, (1Cor. 10:13).

CHAPTER SIX
MORE TESTIMONIES, LOGIC

Things just kept happening to me. I know He carried me for the first year if not three years. It was about three years before I started having to deal with spiritual attacks again. It seems like for twenty or twenty five years before I was on my knees in South Georgia, I would have to get beaten so badly I couldn't function. I would get driven almost to the brink of insanity. The attacks would last for about six weeks until they would prove to be a lie and then they would go away. I would lose thirty five to forty pounds; I couldn't eat, couldn't sleep and the anxiety and the fear. I would get going about a 1,000 miles per hour with a 1,000 pound weight strapped to my chest. I couldn't hold a thought; my mind would just race with all the negative thoughts. I honestly thought they had been caused by drinking because for the first three years sober I never had another attack. He tried to prepare me for what was about to come again but I was caught totally off guard. Like I said, I thought they were behind me. I'll tell you about it when I get there. I was still in the process of learning and to be honest I don't know but what I will always be in the process of learning. I am convinced that we are a work in process and the process will not end until we get there, if it ends then.

Well I was in my sanctuary, (car), one day and the Lord spoke! He said, "Chuck I'm unreasonable." I said, "No, Lord, it's me; I'm the one who is unreasonable!" He then said, "No; What I'm telling you is that I am beyond your ability to reason." I said, "Thank You." I then looked down and said, why did I say that? I don't even know what He means. I didn't have to think long and I had to say yes! He is beyond my ability to reason. All I had to think of was life eternal, infinity. I know what it means but I can't reason it or see it. I have absolutely nothing to compare it to. Everything I know or have seen has a beginning and an end. How can you reason or comprehend something you have nothing to compare it to? Later I wrote MGB#31

1)   The Lord did not say "Come let us reason together!"

    If you read in the book of Isaiah, the Lord does say, "then come let us reason together," but if you read the whole chapter; the Lord is speaking to Sodom and Gomorrah and He told them not to send up their burnt offerings (for forgiveness, anymore), you either do what I told you to do; then come up and I will listen to you and forgive you your sins or then "come let us reason together".

2)   HE said, "Come and believe me!"

    You see everything HE teaches you is for a purpose - so that you will understand.
    Another time the Lord spoke and said, "Chuck; write your name in my Word!" I said, "No Lord, I can't do that, that's Your Word from the first word in Genesis to the last word in the book of Revelations. I know that man pushed the pen but it was all under the inspiration of the Holy Spirit and it says in your Word woe to the person who changes one thing - so I cannot and will not change your Word" (Rev. 22:18-19). That might sound a little mouthy or arrogant, but after I thought about it I said no that was a pleasing answer to the Lord because I was standing on my faith in His Word. He then said, "Give me a scripture that has meaning to you." I didn't think long; I said, "Luke 1:37 says "With God nothing shall be impossible." The Lord then said, "Look in your Bible. In your Bible it says, Chuck, nothing is impossible in me." What I'm telling you is to make it personal, I wrote it for you. So I'm telling you when you read God's Word let Him speak to you - He wrote it for you! God has done absolutely nothing for me that He will not do for you. Nothing!

If you struggle hearing the voice of the Lord, try this. Tonight, go to bed early and lie on your back and get quiet, real quiet. Try to stop all thoughts and see if you can find yourself in a field. A big field that is peaceful, there may be flowers, the grass or growth may be short. When you find yourself in the field, look for the Lord, He will be wearing a white robe and He will come to you. When you are in His presence ask Him one of two questions:

1) Do you Love me?

2) Is there anything you want to tell me?

Only ask one question and He will speak clearly and more than likely repeat it. Once you know what He said have a pen and a piece of paper handy and write it down. If you don't understand ask Him, tell Him you don't understand. You may have to try this several times before you get an answer or find the Lord. This is an exercise in Faith and I know it will work if you're persistent about it.

I was in a meeting one night and the Lord using my hand wrote this with a ballpoint pen on the side of a Styrofoam empty coffee cup.

1) "You can't have what you have unless it comes from Him, Who is true."

2) "You can't keep what you have unless you give it away."

3) "You can't give what you don't have."

I sat the cup in front of my sponsor and a few minutes later he picked it up and read it, turned, smiled and said that's good. When the meeting was over I threw the coffee cup away. I wasn't concerned about remembering what He had written; I knew that I wouldn't forget it. Three days later I was with my spiritual mentor and I wanted to tell him what the Lord had written on that coffee cup. I tried and tried, for two days and I could not come up with one line He had written. Now eighteen years later I'm trying to put together my talk at the MGB#31 which was from March 1- 4, 2007. I wrote my speech four or five times only to tear it up and throw it away to start all over again. The fifth time I wrote it, it was now my time to give my preliminary presentation in front of my peers to critique what I had written. I knew it wasn't any good so I got before the Lord before I went out to speak. I told Him what I had written was me not the Holy Spirit, so I wasn't ready. He was going to have to help me because I was going to wing it. I fell flat on my face. I had a resentment I hadn't dealt with and gotten rid of yet. I went out and opened my mouth and what came out was the resentment I was still struggling with. When I left the room I almost ran to the prayer room to ask for forgiveness. That was only the second time I had ever done that. Just a point of interest, you have to deal with resentments. Let them go, speak forgiveness towards them, they're a cancer. The Bible clearly states "FORGIVE so that you may be FORGIVEN", (Luke 6:37). That also means that you have to forgive yourself. First make your amends and if they're received or not, you have done all that is required of you. Now you have to forgive yourself and then ask the Lord to forgive you. It doesn't work any other way. Unforgiveness will keep you out of miracles and in bondage. If you're not willing to forgive you are the person who is held in bondage, not the person that you won't forgive. They probably don't even have a clue that it is bothering you; just trust me on this one.

That evening my wife and I babysat for our grandchildren. I was seated in the front chair by the TV and she was behind me on the couch playing cards with our granddaughter. So I was thinking on my talk which had flopped that afternoon and I started with a scripture I had come across by accident and it showed upon four of the five times that I had written my talk. Well I was meditating on that scripture and the Lord gave me a vision and as the result of the vision I was given another scripture. I slept on it and the next day I got up and wrote my talk in one half of the time it had taken me before. I never changed a word and as I read it, trying to put it to memory, so I could talk openly rather than read it at the Banquet. Every time I read it I got a deeper understanding on what was written on paper. Guess who wrote it! I can't write something and read it and get a deeper understanding out of it. If I write it then it would be what I know, what I believed. I may choose to change a word or two or maybe restructure a sentence for clarity, but I couldn't get a deeper understanding of what was written. I'm telling you all of this because after reading what was written I was making some notes on paper, thinking about the things I like to ponder with. As I've already mentioned, heart, mind, soul, and spirit! God the Father, God the Son and God the Holy Spirit! Guess what I came up with? Those three lines I had written on that coffee cup eighteen years ago. The lines I couldn't remember three days later. At the end I'll tell you about my speech you will get a chuckle out of that. I'm going to start my preaching for just a second. I sometimes get upset with the things that supposing intelligent people come up with. A thing like my ancestry goes back to an ape. Things like man only uses 17% of his brain and look at what we have done with 17%. Just imagine what we could do if we would use just 25% of our brain. We probably could transport ourselves through time and space and recompose on a spot on Mars or something, just like in Star trek. Just so you understand how I feel and think. God does not make junk. You have exactly what you need to have to survive on earth and there are no extra parts or space in your minds. The 83 % of your brain you never use looks something like a computer disk after you compress the disk. The 17% you use is the work area, the processing area, the programs of interpretation of what you see, hear, taste, and feel in your heart. The 83% you don't use is like a disk on a computer it's just a warehouse of file after file. Everything you have ever said, felt, tasted, read, heard and seen. Everywhere you have ever been or everything you have ever done, everything is there. From the time you were born, if not from the time you were conceived in your mother's womb. If that is not true then how is it that people who have a near death experience, they are pronounced dead and then come back to life. They always seem to say there was a tunnel of light and their whole life just flashed by in front of them. Is God a peeping Tom with a video camera? Not my God! Where were those three lines I had written eighteen years ago? Why, under hypnosis, can they take a person back in time and they can tell you the license plate number on a car they only saw for a fraction of a second? You don't have to believe me on the 83% of your brain; you don't have to believe me on anything; but, I hope you will bear with me and maybe see some things a little differently than what you used to. The testimonies and the scriptures I cannot make up so if nothing else, please, just hang on to them. The other things just make sense if you believe the bible and Gods Word.

CHAPTER SEVEN
WORDS/ FAITH/ TESTIMONIES:

Well you now know my beginning and hopefully why things have happened in my new life and why they have happened. You see, there is another scripture that I like - it says, "If you lack wisdom ask God for He freely gives wisdom to all that ask. (Jas.1:5)" He freely gives wisdom to all who ask! I don't know about you, but if God is giving something away I'm going to be somewhere in the front of the line and be sure to get some of it. You know I used to have a problem with the scripture that says, "That the fear of the Lord is the beginning of wisdom, (Pro.9:10)," I would always ask my spiritual mentor, Clint, why does the Bible say to fear the Lord. I wanted to love God not be afraid of Him. How stupid of me, if you only knew how I have treated the things I love over the years you would understand. My friend would tell me that another word I might use would be respect. That was better but it just didn't give me the understanding I needed. It had probably been eight months since I had asked him that question and we had stopped after a meeting to get a sandwich and a cup of soda. That night the question came back up again and I apologized because I knew he had told me something but I couldn't remember what he had said. So I asked him again and just as soon as he started to answer me the Holy Spirit started to speak. I held up my hand to try and get him to stop talking and I turned and looked down trying to hear the Spirit. The Holy Spirit said, "How did you handle fear when it set in?" I said in my mind, "It more or less controlled me. I couldn't get my mind off the fear. I like dedicated all my time to it." The Holy Spirit said, "Isn't that what God wants?" Years later I told you that I wrote Fear = Dedication of time and thought. There is good fear and bad fear. Remember we live in a spiritual world and the fear of the Lord is good fear. The fear that is created by darkness, demons is bad fear. There is a way out of bad fear and I will explain that later.

The company I worked for had four of us who were pretty well grounded in our beliefs. One day I was in the office and was going from the warehouse back to the sales area and one of the purchasing agents heard me talking and asked me to stop in for a minute. I went to see what he wanted and he asked me where I was going to Church and if they spoke in tongues out there. I told him where I was going and that yes sometimes someone would stand up and speak in the Spirit and others during prayer time would pray in the Spirit. Why? He told me to be careful because one of the other guys, who were a friend of mine, one day, would ask me and to be careful how I answered him. That he thought that was Old Testament and if you spoke in tongues you had a demon in you. I said, okay and left to go back to work. I forgot all about what he had told me just as soon as I left because it didn't bother me one way or the other how other people felt. It was about six months later and we were sitting in the sales office and my friend popped the question. He looked over and asked me where I was going to Church. I told him and described the Church as being non-denominational. He then asked me if they spoke in tongues out there. I told him that I didn't but they did. He then said what did I think about that? I turned and answered him. I said, "Well, I know what the Bible says, it says that speaking in other tongues is a gift freely given by God and it also says that another gift was the interpretation of tongues." I said, "Every time someone has stood up and spoke in tongues, when they sat down either another person or sometimes the minister would stand up and give the interpretation of what had just been spoken. So I get the benefit out of what was said and I don't have a problem with it." That was the end of the conversation. You see if you get grounded in the Word you don't have to worry. If they don't agree with the Word of God then they're the one who has the problem, aren't they? It also says that speaking in tongues should only be done where someone has the gift of interpretation otherwise it is for your own personal prayer closet and should not be done in public. It was about four or five months later I had to drive sixty miles over to the university my oldest son was attending. I was about half way there and it was like I just couldn't hold it back. Like I was sick at my stomach, so I opened my mouth and out it came. I got so excited I spoke in the Spirit all the rest of the way to the college and I couldn't wait to head back home. I rattled in the spirit the whole trip. Since then I do pray in the Spirit sometimes because I'm not sure exactly how or what to pray for. The Spirit knows my heart and my needs. If you look back at my answer, which by the way, I hadn't even thought about it, that was an answer of faith in God's Word and I was rewarded for it. You know, I don't remember where, but someone ministered or said there is as much power in one verse of scripture as there is in the whole Bible. I don't know for sure but I do know sometimes I would feel almost guilty. Just look at what I did with the first forty five years of my life and what all He is doing for me. My oldest sister was in Church every Sunday for it seems most of her life. A very sincere Christian, tithes, and is on prayer chains etc. and very active in Church her whole life. She gave her life to the Lord when I believe she was seventeen years old. I left the Church when I was eight year old wanting to return when I could go to a class like my older sisters were. I just couldn't get comfortable in those wooden pews and I couldn't understand what the minister was preaching on and it seemed like eternity. So I asked if I could wait until I was older and then come back. The problem was I never came back. My oldest sister, who used to scare the heck out of me when I was in the world, I am probably closer to her than anyone in my family. She never left the Church, she gave her life to the Lord and has been a faithful servant, believer most of her life. She and her husband went to Church with our parents for least ten to fifteen years. I always go and tell her what the Lord has said to me or the visions He has given me. She doesn't seem to tell me about those things happening to her. I sometimes, like I said, felt guilty. It's like if anyone deserved it, she certainly did, why me? I don't go there often and I don't stay long at all. I'm blessed to have the experiences I have had and wouldn't trade them for anything. I just know what God has done for me He will do for anyone. I am not special; blessed, yes, but not special, but then I guess we all are!

I've gotten over that, you see after August 6th, 2006, (The Black- Box), I now understand things that I could never understand before. I think you will enjoy that story. You see I now believe that nothing, absolutely nothing happens in God's world by mistake. There are no mistakes, no accidents or no coincidences. You have a free will to do or believe what you choose. He will not force His way on you but regardless He loves you and wants you to love Him in return and honor His ways, for He is God. He will always be there for you. All you have to do is surrender and turn to Him and don't be surprised, just like me. He will be standing right beside you when you turn. He is the Alpha and the Omega, all knowing, all seeing and all things and in all things. He wrote the end when He wrote the beginning. You see I had to go where I have gone so that I can do what it is that He wants me to do. Writing this book is part of it but I know that's not all, it's really just begun.

CHAPTER EIGHT
SPIRITUAL WARFARE:

I told you that I spent a lot of years for periods in a living hell. I got spiritually beat up, tormented to the brink of insanity at least two or three times a year for five or six weeks at a time. The problem I had was that I did have a heart and there were things I would not do, they were against my moral fiber. But I would get drunk and be in the wrong place at the wrong time and here they would come with their lies, lusts, anger, etc., and drunk I had no defense, I couldn't say no. Then I would have to wake up the next day or two and sooner or later the reality would come to what I had done which I had promised that I would never do. Now I would have to look at it, the reality. So the battle was about to begin. Because they will come with all their lies and tell you what is going to happen and the next thing you know you are in fear, deep fear and you can't shut them up. The only other option you have is to lash out at the problem in anger and destroy it or blame something and justify your actions. If it is against your morals you can't do that no matter how hard you might try. The only other thing you can do is go back and get drunk again so you don't have to look at it.

After you start thinking on the first one, the next one will come and he is worse than the first one and it just keeps building and building until you can't shut them up. The Lord carried me for the first year if not three years. Nothing could come at me during that period but when He sat me back down even though He had taught me I still hadn't caught on or practiced taking a spiritual stand. You need to understand a couple of things. Number one, think about what you're thinking about. Kick them out before they get a foothold. Number two, they do not know what you're thinking or what you believe but they can see what you do and they can hear what you say. Why do you think the Bible says or God Wrote, "to set a watch over your mouth to set a guard over the door of your lips"? Remember what I had said earlier - (Prov.18:21) "that life and death are in the power of the tongue", and (Mat.12:24), "what comes out of your mouth is the overflow of your heart." My oldest son at about the same age as I did decided or got persuaded by the neighbor's son to try the same path that I had taken only worse. It wasn't long until my faith would run out and I would grab a hold of the situation, run to save him rather than letting him be responsible for his own actions. I didn't want anyone to go where I went, especially my family members, friends. They could see what I was doing and they could hear what I was saying. Here they came again with their lies. The next thing you knew, they would have him in prison, raped and then murdered. Same problem all over again! I sought prayer counseling, tapes on spiritual warfare, went to class Wednesday evenings on spiritual warfare. I was never clever enough to do what He told me to do in His Word. To put on the spiritual armor in preparation for battle before you go into each day. They would get me going 10,000 miles an hour mentally before I even knew what was happening. Usually it would last for four to six weeks before it would prove to be a lie and come to an end.

I was in the middle of getting unmercifully tormented and the Holy Spirit said, "You need to be baptized." I drove thirty miles straight home. It was a Friday afternoon and I had just finished the last call I had to make that week. I called my special pastor whose Church was about fifteen minutes from where I live. I got him on the phone at home and said, "Mark I need to get baptized!" A long pause on the other end, he would always try to hear you spiritually so he would know what to do. He then said we could get that done Sunday at Church. It wasn't scheduled but it wouldn't be a problem. I said. "I need to be baptized sooner than that, do you know anyway?" Long pause again. Then he said, "Can you be here by 6:00PM tonight?" He and his dad were going over to a friends Church to listen to a speaker that evening. It was a Pentecostal Church and they have baptism before every service, the pool is always ready and he could get me baptized there. I said, "Is there any way I can get baptized before then?" Long pause again, and then Mark spoke and said, "Can you be here at the Church by 3:15 this afternoon?" I looked at the clock and that gave me about forty minutes to get there. I said, "Yes I can be there!" Mark said it was only dad and him that were home but he would have his dad start filling up the horse trough behind the Church. The water would be cold but if I was there by 3:15 they would get me baptized. So I was baptized in a horse trough out back of the Church at 3:15 on a Friday afternoon. I met them at the Pentecostal Church that evening for the service and I remember hearing Mark tell his dad, laughing, that I was about to go out in the Spirit, "down". Well that was the end of that battle! By the way this is no longer a problem. They don't come around anymore, not since Aug. 6th /2006.

I did get to a point one time that I just couldn't take much more and I got up the next day and I found time to think for a bit. I decided that I must have drunk too much that I had damaged something in my head. There just shouldn't be any was this should be bothering me this way. It wasn't that big of a deal. I called my sister who has a degree in Psychology and working for a treatment center to deal with those problems. I asked her if there were any Christian Psychiatrists that she knew who worked there. She wasn't positive but she was pretty sure that she knew one, who was very good and gave me his name. I called and made an appointment for that afternoon. I told the doctor I had to stop the anxiety; I was going a thousand miles an hour and not going anywhere. It was like I had a thousand pound weight strapped on my chest and I couldn't slow down enough to reason things out. He wrote me a prescription and set another appointment to see me again in the next three days. I got the prescription filled, went home and took one pill. It knocked me off my feet. I never got off the living room couch until about midnight. I forced myself up and struggled back to the bedroom and was out for the night. The next morning I awoke and thought that I had been wound so tight that the medication being the opposite of the tension had just knocked me out. That today it would be better. I took another tablet and the same thing I spent the whole day on the couch except around noon I forced myself to get up and see if I could drive and maybe it would be better.

I went two blocks and turned around and went back home I couldn't even focus on the road. Back on the couch again only to force myself back into the bedroom around midnight.

I woke up the next morning, thought about things and I made a decision. I decided that the problem was not mental it was spiritual. I threw the pills in the waste basket, got dressed and went out got into my car and drove forty miles over to a small city that was to the east and south of where I lived. There was a nine hole golf course just south of that city, it was in the woods and nobody would be there at that time of day on Thursday. I rented a pull cart which I never used I always take an electric golf cart. I paid for nine holes and went out and by the time I got to the first tee I was getting hammered so bad I had tears starting to roll down my cheeks. I drove my ball, hurriedly went to the ball, hit it again and did the same thing until I finally got to the green, then I think I six putted just to get to the next hole. The second hole turns 90 degrees and about thirty yards down the fairway you enter the wooded area. I had tears just running down my cheeks by this time. I hit the drive and just about ran to the golf ball. When I got to the ball I was behind the trees where no one could see me from the clubhouse and nobody else was on the golf course. I picked up my golf ball, put it in my pocket and with one hand pulling the cart, my other arm stretched up towards the heavens and my head turned up - I'm really getting hammered by now. Every verse of scripture I knew that I could stand on came out of my mouth. "Greater is He who is in me than he who is in the world" (1Jn. 4:4), "I can do all things through Christ who strengthens me" (Phil. 4:13), "God did not give me a spirit of fear but of power, love and a sound mind" (2Tim.1:7), "No weapon formed against me can prosper for greater is He who is in me than he who is in the world" (Ish. 54:17). - I would look down, turn and say - "Leave!" "In The Name of Jesus!", "Leave!", "You Cannot Stay!", "You Have to Leave!", "In the Name of Jesus!", "Go!" I would look back up into the heavens and repeat everything all over again and again. They seemed to shut up for a second and then started all over again. You see they know they cannot stay in the Name of Jesus but they don't know if you really believe what you're saying. I cut over to the back of the golf course which has a long par five and then a par four. I turned and played a par three before

I turned to cut over and go back to the clubhouse. To see you out there you would have to be looking with a pair of binoculars, well I kept doing what I was doing and when I got to the middle of the fairway on the par five it dips down and there is a pond and a small clump of trees on the side and a woods on the other side. I let go of the golf cart and put both hands up in the air and I'm almost screaming the scriptures out of my mouth and telling them to leave. I don't remember how long I just stood there doing that but finally I found myself on the fairway heading back up towards the clubhouse. By this time my legs are burning from walking, I'm almost out of breath from screaming the words, my throat burns so I just cut across everything and went back to the clubhouse. I tuned the cart in, took my golf bag out and put it in the trunk of the car. I unlocked the car door and almost fell in the car I was so exhausted. I started the car and drove a ¼ mile down to the stop sign where I had to turn. By the time I had looked both ways everything had pretty much settled down and back to normal. Guess what! "No More Noise – It's Gone", and it didn't come back anymore. I kept my appointment with the Psychiatrist and told him that I would no longer require his help, that the problem was spiritual not mental. You don't tell a Psychiatrist that because you will immediately put him in orbit. I finally got him back down and convinced him that I wasn't insane. I told him I appreciated his help but I wouldn't need to make another appointment, if things didn't work out I would call him.

I had to continue to fight hard to make them leave but I would always win. If I was in my car I had a tape that the last song for the last two or three minutes the lead singer says Jesus! Then the whole choir and the whole congregation, three balconies, are on their feet, arms up in the air and they say Jesus! The band starts to play and they just stand there shouting the name of; "Jesus! - Jesus!" "Jesus! - Jesus!" for two or three minutes, you can't stay seated in the car. I'll put that tape in and fast forward to the end; hit rewind and count off seven seconds then hit play and turn the volume up. I'll just keep doing that until I have it going full blast. I'm holding myself up off the car seat by the steering wheel and I'm out singing the song. You would have to think I'm nuts if you were to see me go by or pass me. When I'm exhausted I'll sit down and turn the volume down, relax and guess what,

"They're Gone!" You see they were so used to having their way with me I had to prove that I was not backing down that I knew what I was saying and believed it. I know I've spent a long time talking about spiritual battles but I know how many people don't have any idea about the reality of what I just told you. We live in a spiritual world, God is Spirit, words are spirit, and thoughts are spiritual. That's why they can't see any activity or signs of usage in the 83% of your brain. Demons are spiritual beings, they cast negative thoughts that just gets whispered in your ear, or they can be in you depending on where you are spiritually, and they just sit on the work table of your mind and if you pick them up and think on them the next one that comes is worse than the first one. I said it before, we need to start thinking about what we're thinking about. We need to start slowing down and watching what comes out of our mouths. Did you know that the scripture, Bible, says "To call those things that aren't as though they are and believe in your heart and not doubt with your mind and they will be." What are you saying about your sons and daughters, your family, friends? I mean it's time to get real, to get serious about God, about Jesus. To read His Word and believe Him! God is Love! His Word is alive! Jesus Christ died for the sins of the world (the whole world). His Blood, His Life, He gave for the atonement of the sins of the world! We are in right standing (righteousness) with God, Who is Christ Jesus in the flesh. That's why the only way you can go to the Father is through the Son (Jesus Christ)! Read John 1:1-5 and John 14:6-11 then John 14:12-24! Why? Because He; is in Him.

CHAPTER NINE
THE GREATEST STORY:

Let me tell you a story about my wife's grandfather. My wife's grandparents were more than special people to her. My wife at the age of fourteen had to do a lot around the house for her two younger sisters and younger brother. Her mother had some severe problems when my wife was fourteen. Her father traveled a lot. My wife could usually keep things moving and under control during the week but when her father would come home on the weekend's things would get worse. No matter how much he tried to help it just seemed that in order to get things settled down he would have to ask her grandparents if they could watch the kids. Her grandparents had a lot to do with the raising of her and her brother and sisters. After we got married and moved to Florida only to return a year and a half later, we seemed to get together on Sunday afternoon to eat and play dominoes or cards together. We always had fun together and I ended up calling them my grandma and grandpa; they were beautiful people. As they grew older and grandpa could no longer drive or take care of the house, they sold their house and moved into an apartment. One day grandpa spoke to my wife; he couldn't see or hear very well at all and he always thought he would be the first one to go and he didn't want to be put up in a nursing home if he got to the point his wife couldn't take care of him. So he asked my wife if there would be any way he could live with us and she said it wouldn't be a problem at all. She said something to me about their conversation and I agreed, I told her to tell grandpa not to give it another thought. As it ended up his wife ended up

43

in the nursing home. She got to the point she couldn't cook, she couldn't get dressed, couldn't take a bath or shower without help and she really needed someone to walk behind her while she struggled with her walker. Grandpa's son, Burt, was retired and he served meals on wheels as a service for those who were in need. He had grandpa on his list and would make him his last stop. So in the morning he would come and pick grandpa up, take him to breakfast and then to the nursing home. He would spend some time with both his parents then leave to deliver lunches. My wife or I would go over after work and spend a little time with both of them and then tell grandpa that it was time we were going to have to leave in order to get home in time for dinner. We would wait in the lobby for about ten minutes, grandpa would come out and we would get him back to the apartment in time for supper.

I remember the day that my wife got tied up, called and asked if I could go get grandpa. I did and we ended up in the van headed back to his apartment. Grandpa just sat in the passenger's seat, silent with his head hanging down, staring at his lap. I knew he was about in tears so I tried to talk with him to pick him up. He was almost non-responsive so finally I looked at him and I said, "Grandpa!" Just think of the fun the two of you are going to have together. He cocked his head, looked at me, you could see the tears in his eyes and said, "Chuck, she doesn't have much longer to live." I chuckled and said, "I don't mean here, I pointed my thumb upwards and said - I'm talking about up there." I didn't know it but I planted a seed that day.

Well grandma passed away and grandpa got to where he couldn't hardly see or hear well enough to be on his own so he asked if it was still okay to move in with us. We said we would love to have him and he had about six or eight weeks left on his rental agreement and that gave me time enough to build a room in the basement, carpet it and finish it off for my oldest son to sleep in. We cleaned and fixed up the center bedroom and when grandpa's rental contract expired he moved in with us. Grandma was ninety when she passed away so grandpa was going on or was ninety one years old when he moved in with us. There was one Saturday afternoon and everyone was gone and I was working out of the front porch and grandpa came out. Grandpa, except for meals, spent most of his time in the bedroom where he had his T.V. and tape player with head phones. We would rent books that were on tape and grandpa could play them, put the headsets on and turn the volume way up so he could hear what was being said or he would sit in front of his T.V. at news time and sit about two foot away with the volume up, door closed so he could try and see the T.V. set. When grandpa came out that Saturday afternoon, I knew he wanted to talk so I started a conversation with him. I don't remember what we talked about, but I do know in answer to some of the things I would tell him what the Lord had done or what He had said and shared some of my testimonies with him. I always do, as a matter of fact if you were to call me today and I didn't even know you, if you would open the door a crack and not stop me I would probably have you listening to me just sharing an update on what the Lord was doing and has done in my life.

Time continued to pass and grandpa was now I believe around ninety four years old and his cancer which was under control and stopped in his mid eighties had started back up again. When his son took him to the hospital, they discovered the news and made the decision that if they were to try and stop it again at his age it would probably kill him. It was a very slow progressing cancer and they felt that he would surely pass away before the cancer would ever get to be much of a problem. If he experienced any pain, they could treat that with medication. So the decision was to just let it go as if everything was okay and keep a watch on it. It wasn't much later and my wife told me that grandpa had told her that he was ready to die. Life had become a burden for him, he couldn't hear so he quit listening to tapes and I would find him with his face about four inches from the T.V. screen just trying to see the difference between light and dark figures on television. Grandpa had reached a point where he had a catheter which my wife would clean up each evening.

So grandpa could barely see the difference between light and dark, he couldn't listen to his tapes anymore because he could barely hear. Everyone he had grown up with had passed, so life like I said was a burden. Even though he loved the grandchildren, he couldn't enjoy them because he could barely see them or hear them. The only thing he had was our little fluffy mop, Winston, a Yorkshire terrier dog. That little rascal would jump up on a 30" barstool on the other side of the kitchen counter from where grandpa sat and eat the food off his plate. Grandpa couldn't see him. The dog would stand on his back legs and lay over the counter, stand on his toes and stretch and he could get to the plate on the other side. He followed grandpa everywhere. They were the best of buddies and grandpa didn't have a clue as to why. But they sure made good company for each other. Well it had been about six months since grandpa had told my wife he was ready to die and I had come home, Sunday, after Church, changed clothes and was out in the living room just sitting and meditating. I had turned the T.V. on to the Chicago Bear's pre-game show and had the sound turned off waiting on the show to start. Grandpa came out and sat on the end of the couch about three or four feet from me. Like I had said when he would come out where I was I knew he had something on his mind and wanted to talk. Everyone else was gone, the wife was shopping and the kids were down at the park playing ball. So I started a conversation with Grandpa. I had to talk louder than normal so that he could hear me. As we were talking the Holy Spirit said, "What's keeping grandpa alive?" His cancer was back affecting him and I knew he had told my wife six months earlier that he was ready to die but grandpa was a wonderful man, he had a soft heart, he was caring and had a mind like a steel trap. I used to love to hear him talk about their lives back during the depression. Grandpa had turned ninety five years old and it was now I believe 1990 or later. Well we talked for just a while longer and that question was just laying there on my mind. We reached a point that it was a good time and I said, "Grandpa, have you ever given your life to the Lord - asked Jesus to come and be Lord over your life?" Grandpa shook his head back and forth and said "no." He had seen Billy Graham on television a couple of times but had never done that. I asked Him, "Would you pray that prayer with me and accept Jesus as Lord over your life?" He said he would so I turned where we could hold hands together and told him I would speak the words and he needed to repeat them after me. I would only say six or so words and then let him repeat them. We prayed what is known as the sinner's prayer together. He asked Jesus to come into his life and be Lord over him. That he believed Jesus died on the Cross and on the third day God raised Him up from the grave and seated Him at his right hand and made him Lord over all the Heavens and the Earth.

When we finished grandpa thanked me, he said that he had seen the changes that it had made in me and they were good, he was happy for me. I welcomed him into God's Kingdom and told him what the Bible says. "If you confess the Lord Jesus Christ with your mouth and believe in your heart that God raised Him from the dead. You will be saved" (Rom. 10:9). It also says in John 3:14, "God so loved the world that He gave His only begotten Son and whosoever believes in Him shall not perish but have everlasting life." I told grandpa there was one more thing he needed to do and that was, if he was angry with or holding anything against anyone - he needed to let go and forgive them. Then he needed to ask God to forgive him his sins, the things he had done wrong. I told him, we're all sinners, every one of us and we seem to hold on to our anger when the bible says, "not to go to sleep on your anger." Grandpa asked me if he needed to tell me and I smiled and said "No, you need to tell Him." When it's getting late tonight just go to bed a little earlier and do that then before you go to sleep, just don't forget to do it. Grandpa then said, "You know, Chuck, I only have about six months left to live." The Holy Spirit said, "He has two weeks." We talked just for a short while longer and the game was on T.V. so grandpa left to go back in his bedroom to watch and listen to the game.

The next day (Monday), my wife got a phone call from Burt, grandpa's son. He said that when he came to bring grandpa lunch that he was still in bed and couldn't get up, he was sick and in pain. So Burt got grandpa up and dressed and helped him to get to the hospital. Grandpa was admitted so they could run some tests and do blood work to determine what the problem was. My wife went up to see him when she got off work that day, returned home with no additional information on his condition but he seemed to be more comfortable then she expected. When Burt had left him at the hospital he told them that grandpa stayed with us and if there was any news on his condition to call my wife. He gave them both her work number and our home number. That night around 4:00AM in the morning we got a phone call. It was the hospital and they informed my wife that the slow moving cancer he had, had just exploded, it was all through-out his lower and mid-section. They told my wife if there was anyone who would want to see grandpa alive, she needed to contact them and let them know that he wasn't going to live much longer. That he could go at any time. They kept him on medication to help and to reduce any pain he might be experiencing but there wasn't anything else they could do. Well my wife immediately called Burt and they together came up with a list of people that each one would take care of contacting. Of course my wife was there with grandpa as much as she could be. She even took a week's vacation to be with him at the hospital.

Well I held grandpa up in prayer, I said, "Lord, selfishly I do not want to lose my grandpa, I love him, but I know he's coming home to be with you and I can't ask for more than that. The only thing I ask is that you take him in peace, that he doesn't have to suffer and that you let him be alert to know and speak to the people when they come to pay their respects. Thank You Lord! AMEN!" What an answer to prayer, my wife would come home from the hospital and tell me who had come up that day and that he knew everyone by name and talk about things they had done years ago together. When they would leave they would comment to my wife that it was hard to believe he didn't have much longer to live. That this was the best they had seen him in years. I would go up every evening and spend some time with them but I pretty much took care of work and the house because my wife was there all the time. Well the only person who had not made it home yet to see grandpa was my wife's youngest sister. She was married and lived about two hundred miles to the south of us. She was in charge of accounting and they were in the middle of their mid-year or year-end inventory, closing the books, so she couldn't get away until the next weekend. Grandpa was still alive and some people were still showing up to pay their respects so her sister packed her suitcase and headed home after work a week from Friday. She and her oldest son, Joe, arrived around 11:00 PM Friday night, stayed at our house that night. We got up in the morning, had breakfast, and talked for awhile getting updated on what's going on with everyone in the family. She left around 1:00 PM (afternoon) to go to the hospital and didn't return until it was after 5:00 PM Saturday evening. She was just beside herself, what a wonderful time they had that afternoon. Grandpa went way back to when she was just a little sprout and the July 4th's spent at Simonton Lake with Aunt Ruth and Uncle Hersch and the rest of the family. She had a hard time believing that grandpa didn't have much longer to live. We had dinner and then she headed back home, she had work she had to get done before Monday morning due to the inventory the previous week. The next morning, Sunday at 4:00 AM, the phone rang. The hospital called to let us know when they made their bed-checks between 3:00 and 4:00 AM, grandpa had passed away. I didn't realize it then with all the excitement but that was exactly eight hours short of being precisely two weeks right to the hour!!!! When the Holy Spirit had said, "He only has two weeks to live." You talk about answer to prayer - WOW! And it's not over yet!

Its now about three weeks later in the middle of the week, grandpa was buried and everything was pretty well back to normal as best as could be expected. I am in bed sound asleep with a big day scheduled for tomorrow. At around 1:30AM (morning) I bolt straight up in bed, wide awake. Wider awake than I usually was at 12:00 noon on any given day. I was so wide awake I did something that I had never done before. I was so wide awake I reached over and grabbed my cigarettes that were lying on the table beside me and went out into the kitchen, sat down at the counter and lit a cigarette. Our house is an old house and years ago they converted the old back porch into part of the kitchen. They removed the back door completely and cut an opening in the back wall where a window used to be and put a three foot by four and a half foot counter top in the opening. They finished off the back porch which was all windows and moved the locked door out to where the back porch screen door used to be.

We live on a river and this night there was a full moon about 12:00 o'clock high, no wind and the river was like glass with the reflection of the moon light lit up the expensive houses on the other side of the river. You could see the plush green lawns rolling up to the back of the mansions, it was beautiful. I just sat there enjoying the view and into my second cigarette when I realized what time it was and knew I had to get back to sleep because of tomorrow's work load. So I put my cigarette out and went back to the bedroom, put things back, laid down, covered up and went back to sleep. Thirty minutes later the same thing. I bolted straight up in bed, wide awake and again I get my cigarettes and go back out in the kitchen to smoke a cigarette. Same thing, enjoying the view and into my second cigarette realizing what time it is and say to myself. "I've got to get some sleep, this is ridiculous. So I put my cigarette out go back to the bedroom and put everything up and get in bed, roll over and go back to sleep. Thirty minutes later the same thing all over again. Exactly the same, nothing woke me up I just bolted straight up in bed wide awake and took my cigarettes, went back out in the kitchen and was smoking a cigarette, enjoying the view and the Lord gave me a vision. A vision is like I said before, a short video film and sometimes with narrative. This vision started out with a let's say bucket, upside down and the top (bottom) was sticking up into the clouds. It was white on the inside of the bucket and there was just a little tiny speck in the top center of the bucket. I started to look down to get some kind of an idea what in the world I was seeing and this like column got wider as it came down and the color changed from white/white to an off white color. Still confused, I rushed back up to the top to try and figure out what that small speck was. When I got there I realized that it had moved, so I started watching it. It was descending down ever so slowly and it got down far enough it became two dots. Now I'm really confused. It got down farther and it became two lines, one longer or taller than the other one. It got down further and it was two people, a man and a woman. He had his hand around her waist and they were both waving. It got down further and it was Grandma and Grandpa. It got down further and you should have seen the peace that radiated off their faces. It was like a glow of contentment. It got down far enough that I could see that Grandpa was speaking. When they got down far enough I couldn't hear what he was saying but I could read his lips. Do you know what he said? He said, "Thank You, Thank You." The vision went away; I put my cigarette out and went back to bed and slept like a baby through the night, got up the next morning, rested and had a good day at work. Let me tell you what happened! There's a poem titled "Footprints" author Unknown. If you have never heard it or read it, go to a bible book store and ask the sales clerk and they will give you a copy or sell you one for next to nothing. The reason the author is unknown because he knew who wrote that just like I know who is writing this. I, today, believe that is what we will all do is walk back over our lives with the Lord. It was when Grandpa got to the point in his walk with the Lord that he had told my wife he didn't want to live anymore. He turned to the Lord and asked; why didn't You take me then when I was ready to come home? The Lord just plainly told him that he wasn't coming there until grandpa and I prayed the sinner's prayer together that Sunday morning. Grandpa was so beside himself he asked the Lord if he could come down and thank me and the Lord let him. You will never convince me otherwise.

That is the most revealing, beautiful testimony that I can share with you but it doesn't mean that I'm done yet. What the Lord allowed me to see, to be real honest; I didn't think He would allow anyone to see. I always knew in my heart that that was the only way you're going to get there but to me it was only going to be because of His Word and my faith in doing that. He wouldn't allow anyone, the absolute privilege to know by seeing with their own eyes. Praise The Lord!

CHAPTER TEN
MORE TESTIMONIES - WISDOM:

Well if you haven't reached the point of beginning to see things a little differently, let's keep going. It even gets more interesting as we go on. The next situation that developed was I was going to the Saturday morning workshop, a fellowship I enjoy. I had parked my van and turned the engine off, looked both ways for traffic and opened the door to get out. I have one foot sticking out the door of the car and the Lord spoke, He said; "Chuck, what can a blind man see in love that you can't see?" That stopped me cold with one foot sticking out of the van. It was so far out of my thought realm that I repeated it, "What can a blind man see in love that I can't see?" I was really confused; I got out of the van and started to cross the street repeating that in my mind and the Lord gave me another vision. Understand I can see a vision, cross the street, turn again to walk up the staircase to the front door, all at the same time.

The vision started from the back and it was two people walking down a sidewalk together holding hands. The one on the right (inside) was a man about six feet one inch tall, casual but neatly dressed and moderately structured. He was holding onto the hand of a woman who was about four foot one inch tall, overweight, hair stuck out all over the place. She had on a WWII styled dress with a floral design of small daisies that was wrinkled and soiled. She had on men's styled shoes and white socks that were dirty, stretched out and hung loosely around her legs. Then, he let me see them from the front - the man was nice looking, smiling, looking straight ahead,

53

forward, not at anything and he was talking; he was blind. The woman was smiling, she had teeth missing and she almost looked worse from the front than she did from the back. Her face was pock marked and she had a large growth on the side of her neck. After I had seen everything, the vision went away and the Lord spoke again, He said; "Chuck, he loves her for her heart; she lays out his clothes for him in the morning, she fixes all his meals and cleans up afterwards. She washes his clothes and cleans his house, she talks to him, reads books to him, and she goes on walks outside with him. She does everything for him because he can't provide for himself. He loves her for her heart!" He then said; "You would never get to know her heart; you would reject her on sight!" Stopped me right dead in my tracks again, I mean now. I had to say yes, you're right; I know I would. One glance and I would walk on by or turn and go the other way. He taught me something that day, something I won't forget just like all the other testimonies.

Smith Wigglesworth set a standard I have tried to live by and he said it in a way that I like. If you don't know who Smith Wigglesworth was, he lived in London, was born in the 1800's and died, I believe, around 1948, in good health, at the age of around 70. I'm not sure on the exact time but he was a devout man of God. He was known to have raised people off their death beds. He would allow nothing from the outside in, no newspapers or magazines, no radios, nothing. If you came to his house for an interview and had a newspaper folded under your arm and knocked on his door, he would have opened the door but when he saw the newspaper he would have told you to go get rid of that trash then to come back and slam the door shut in your face. He was quoted as having said; "I'm not moved by what I see, I'm not moved by what I feel, I'm moved only by what I believe."

When I read that, I laid the book down and turned up to the Lord and said, "Lord, I want that!" You see, always before the things that I saw created the way that I felt and that is what I came to believe. Whereas now I believe that I know the truth "God's Word" that's what I believe and that is what I want to move me. I would rather try and see what He sees, feel what He feels and think like He thinks. What the Lord taught me in that education process was not to look at the race, gender, weight, height or how you are dressed, but to look into a person's eyes. You can see and hear a person's heart if you look in their eyes. I put that to work fifteen minutes later as I entered the meeting late, the person chairing the meeting was a friend of mine and there was a chair open right beside him so I went there and sat down. John was explaining that earlier the problem he had with God was because God had made him black. When he said that I nudged him in the side and whispered (I thought), "John!" He said that about three times and every time that he would say it I would nudge him in the ribs and say, "John!" I didn't mean to or think anyone could hear me but the third time I did that he turned and whispered, "What?" I said; "You never told me." He said; "Never told you what?" I said; "You never told me you were black!" The whole place cracked up, I obviously had a more powerful whisper voice than I thought. What I said was not said in jest or to create laughter, what I was saying was; who cares, it doesn't matter. It's you they like and I like and it doesn't have anything to do with the color of your skin. The Bible says a lot of thing along that line of thought. It says, "Judge not for as you judge you so shall be judged and as you measure it will be measured back to you."

History lesson, I learned this from collecting coins, currency and stamps at the end of the last 1½ years of sitting in the black box I'm about to tell you about. Do you know where slavery got started and why? It actually got started way back in the beginning of the Bible when Mosses led God's people out of bondage of the Pharaoh in Egypt to the promise land (Israel). Egypt is in North Africa by the way. It then got transferred as a life style of the more prominent people. They would hire maids and servants to care for their personal needs at a wage of a place to live, food and a very moderate salary or tips. The United States was a descendant of England. People fled England in the early 1700's to the new world due to religious persecution and then we rebelled in the Revolutionary war because of taxation without representation. That was the founding of our country. The thirteen original states were all in the North East and South East. The only crops you could grow in the South were basically cotton, tobacco, and peanuts. You couldn't make a living farming those products with the population in those days so they were in need of cheap labor. Africa was the same way, there were not many crops that they could produce other than mine diamonds (white man's gold) and hunt animals. So here are all these people with little or no education and nothing to provide a living for their families with. The powerful confiscated the young Africans; loaded them on boats and shipped them to the United States and they sold them for slave labor to work the fields in the South. The slaves for the most part didn't have any voice, some were fortunate and got treated fairly well but more were mistreated with no respect. They were given living quarters, something to eat and worked in the fields and houses all day. Abraham Lincoln was the one who freed the slaves and caused the Civil war. I have a stamp with His quote on it and I can just hear him saying this in 1860 before the House of Representatives, the Congress and Senate. Quote of Abraham Lincoln; "You, who enjoy freedom and refuse it to another, do not deserve it for yourself." That my friends split this country right in half the North from the South with the Emancipation Proclamation That is also why, I believe, he was assassinated by John Wilkes Booth at the Ford Theatre at the end of his term in office.

History lesson number two is the Kennedy assignation. I believe that Kennedy was assassinated because of the fear of the, "Separation of Church and State". At that time the Catholic Church was the prominent Church in the east and was feared by the other Churches to gain control or authority of the spiritual freedom to worship. The Kennedy's were Catholic and a lot of people feared that he, being as charismatic as he was, would pass legislation or turn the country towards his religious beliefs, that we would become a religious nation. In addition, there were those who did not like his father because he took advantage financially during the depression. He had bought a lot of people out for next to nothing. Do you know that the year that Kennedy was assassinated or shortly after, legislation was passed totally changing the separation of Church and State? Thomas Jefferson in regards to the separation of Church and State said that we would never be a Religious nation, a Baptist, Methodist, Catholic or so on, nation. He was in total agreement with George Washington who said in his farewell speech, which was removed from our history books in 1958; "If you take Christianity and the Christian morals out of our government and out of our education systems, we would fall. They are the two pillars on which we are founded." Another spokesman of the time said; "That there is no way a nation can control the people. The people would have to control themselves so we had to have Christianity and Christian morals taught in our schools for that to happen." Another spokesman of that time said; "That it was the education of the young today that would be the next generation's leaders." It was also changed that we could no longer have prayer in school or display the Ten Commandments or religious documents in the federal buildings or on school properties. That was when the ever so wonderful ACLU was founded. The best definition I've heard of that organization came from an elected city councilman who came seeking my vote this coming election. He referred to the organization as the "Anti-Christ Liberation Union." Personally I like that definition. I do not understand how a handful of Atheists, which is a religion that does not believe in God, can change a nation who's heritage and foundation is Christianity. A belief that is in God, in which is taught in the Churches of America. Enough for my version of history, I thought I would just throw it in. It makes sense to me and it does disturb me. You know Luke 1:37 says; "That nothing is impossible in God." I just finished telling you how He had set me straight up in bed, wide awake, three times. Well I was in the middle of one of my battles and I prayed for guidance that night before I turned in to go to sleep. Three times while I was asleep, the book, chapter, verse number registered in my mind while I slept. One time it was so clear (loud) I almost turned the light on to get the Bible and read it, but I didn't. When I awoke the next morning that was so clear in my mind that I reached over and got the bible, turned to that book and chapter, went down to the verse and read it. It said: "Make him who is stealing from you to stop stealing." I just looked it up, it is (EPH. 4:28). That happened to be what the problem was and the answer or the solution to the problem and I know that I had never read that verse or heard anyone minister on it before. At least it definitely did not register in my mind and I don't forget much anymore if it has meaning to me.

Another time I was out playing golf with two of my best friends Gordy and Dick. Gordy was a good golfer, I wasn't bad back then but in all the time we played golf together, which was about twice a week, I could never beat him net/net. If I would shoot a 79 he would turn in a 77 or a 78. I won a lot of soft drinks off him but I never beat him. We laughed a lot at each other and at ourselves over some of the dumbest things we would do. The three of us were playing on Gordy's home course; we were on a par 5 which to the right of the fairway was a fence, out of bounds, with a corn field on the other side. Gordy teed off first and just crushed the ball. I had a good drive but he was probably fifty yards out in front of me. Dick and I both hit our second shots and I was in a good position that with a good chip or approach shot I could maybe one put and get a birdie (one under par). It was now Gordy's turn to hit his second shot and both of us knew that he had a five wood that he could hit forty yards farther than my three wood which was a longer distance club. If he hit his five wood like he normally did he would be on the green in two and possibly be putting for an eagle, (two under par). So he got out his five wood, addressed the golf ball, and took his back swing just crushing the shot. It went out about a hundred yards arching upwards to get to elevation and it just took a hard bank to the right and sailed out into the corn field. You know he was irritated, so he got another ball out and dropped it down, lined up and took another powerful swing and again just crushed the ball only to end up with the same result, out of bounds again. Now he is livid, so he takes the third golf ball out of his bag, throws it down on the ground. He lines up and without much preparation just creamed this one also and the same thing, a hundred or so yards out, then a hard right and over in the corn field out of bounds. Three golf balls in a row now out of bounds and by now he's beating his club on the ground and blankity blank this and that and I'm trying to contain myself from just rolling on the ground and laughing my heart out, I could barely contain myself. Finally I looked at Gordy and said humorously, come on Gordy; "Let go, let God". Gordy bent over, turned, looked at me and said, Chuck; "God doesn't care about my golf game!" Before I could say anything Dick spoke up and said, Gordy; "God either is or He isn't." I thought about that and I said to myself, that's dumb, why would Dick say that? He knew Gordy believed, knew the Lord and I knew that Dick knows, that he believes and if there is any question about me they have to be blind or crazy. Why would he say that? That's stupid!

It wasn't two weeks later and I'm on the road in my sanctuary (car) and the Lord spoke, He said, Chuck; "I either am or I'm not." I looked down and shook my head in disbelief, "why in the world is He asking me that?" Finally, I looked up as I always did and said; "Lord I know that you are; why are you asking me that?" The Lord spoke again. He said; "If I am then why do they only turn to me when they are in trouble or need something? Why don't they turn, or focus, on me when everything is going fine and they are having fun?" As usual, that is the end of the conversation. I ran into Gordy two nights later and I called him over to the side. I said; Gordy; "I don't ever want to hear you say that again." He said; "Say what?" I said; "That God doesn't care about your golf game!" He looked at me as to why? I told him what the Lord had said to me and I said; "He cares about everything that you do - so don't tell me that again!" I smiled patted him on the shoulder went and sat down. I don't remember that he ever said that to me again.

CHAPTER ELEVEN
ARE YOUR LOVED ONES SAFE:

I was in another spiritual struggle. My oldest son decided to go back to College and play soccer. I wanted to see him succeed but all I could think about was our previous experience. I got home early on a Friday night and I was sitting on the back porch reading. I had the Bible and the Strong's Exhaustive Concordance with me, reading as I was waiting on my wife to come home because we had plans to go out to dinner that night. I was taking a break just sitting there looking up at the clouds, thinking about everything that was going on and the Lord spoke again, He said; "Your son's going to a Christian College. If he finds me there, what does that mean to you?" I thought about it and that was the fruit of my concerns, so I let go. "The battle is the Lords." He had heard my prayers and my concerns and knew my heart. I know the Bible says; Rom. 8:31 "If God is for you, who in the world can be against you." Two weeks later I got a phone call around midnight, it was my son, and he had borrowed a car from a friend and was headed home and had an accident coming home. He said he knew he had the green light and the other car just came through the intersection and crushed the passenger's side of the car that he was driving. There were no witnesses to the accident and the other driver swore he had the green light. The car my son was in was not drivable; it had to be towed away so he wanted me to come out and pick him up.

As I drove out to get him you can imagine all of the negative thoughts going through my mind. I am going to have to pay to replace the car he

61

had borrowed; everyone was going to be upset and on and on. I just shoved the thoughts out of my mind; I refused to think about them. I got there and picked him up and my normal tendency would be to lecture him on borrowing other people's things, but I didn't. I asked him if everything was okay, if he had gotten hurt. We hadn't driven a block yet and he said that everything was okay that he wasn't hurt, then just a few seconds later he said; "Boy am I glad I did what I did last night!" I said; "What's that?" He said they had a guest speaker at church that afternoon and he was so impressed that he drove back for the evening service and went up at alter call and gave his life to the Lord, he said; "You know He really helped me back there, I could have easily gotten hurt or worse." Needless to say - no more negative thoughts. I congratulated him for his choice and said that I had been praying for this for years. The young man's car he had borrowed and his parents didn't even ask about the car. They were concerned that he was okay; they lived in Michigan and had no fault insurance, so the car was of no concern to them.

You know if I would just be patient, supportive and plant the right seeds, the Lord will see that they are watered. What more can you ask for? He gave you his Life, he gave you his Name, the name that is above all names, and he gave you his Word. Do you know the Bible says; "That in the beginning was the Word and the Word was with God and the Word was God. That He was in the beginning with God and all things that were made were made through Him and nothing that was made was made without Him (Jesus)", (John 1:1-3) if you want to read it. The Bible also says in (Prov. 4:20-22), "My Words are life to those who find them and health to all your flesh." And in (Mark 13:31), "That Heaven and Earth will pass away but my words will never pass away." In (Mat. 24:35) the Bibles says, "The word of God is sharper than any double edged sword, dividing to asunder joints and morrow, spirit and soul, thoughts and intents of the heart." He has given it to us to use. It's free; it's a gift from God. All you have to do is receive him and believe in him. I told you several pages ago in my testimony about my wife's grandfather that there is only one God, one heaven, one hell. I don't know of anyone else who has promised you eternal life, a life where there is no sickness, no disease, and no temptation. The only way you're going to get there is through him. *The Lord of Lords! The King of Kings! The one Whose Name is above all names, that one is "Jesus Christ", there is no other.*

I got carried away again. You know people say that Christians are nothing but hypocrites, that we go to Church and say one thing and then come out in the world and do the opposite. Did you know the Bible says we are all sinners and have fallen short of the Glory of God? (Rom. 3:23). All of us, that means preachers, teachers and doers of the word; even the Pope. I mean just look at the way I messed up my life and kept getting in trouble, falling short. He loves me, he has to love you! He forgives me do you not think he will forgive you? You know one person wrote or said: "That more people rob themselves of faith due to their inability to forgive themselves." The Bible says; "Forgive that you may be forgiven" (Luke 6:37). Do you think there might be a reason why? It also says; "Why do you look at the speck that is in your brother's eye and you refuse to look at the plank that is in your own eye" (Mat. 7:3). Have you looked at the man in the mirror lately? Is that someone you would want to have for a friend? Is it someone that you could trust?

I have some extra room so I'll tell you about my experience with smoking. I told you that I used to smoke five packs of cigarettes a day for a long time then I changed brands which were longer cigarettes and more tightly packed so I only smoked about three and a half packs a day of those. At one time I had so much tar built up in my bronchial tubes that I had to take medicine just so I could breath. I used to have coughing attacks so bad that the top of my head would tingle and start to turn numb, then I would lose my vision, and everything would go black. I just couldn't get enough oxygen from coughing so hard. I never did pass out but it was scary if you were driving down the highway sixty five miles per hour and one of those attacks happened.

I was on my way to Church one Sunday morning in the spring of the year and I was smoking with the window slightly cracked. I started to cough and it irritated me. It wasn't one of my bad coughing attacks but that day it just irritated me so bad that I ran the window down and through the cigarette out in disgust. It was one that I had just lit. I then looked up through the top of the front windshield and I said; "Lord, I was just thinking, when I gave my life to you, you said that my body was now your Temple and I *don't think that you would like me smoking in your Temple." In my mind's eye I could just see me walking into the Temple in Jerusalem with a cigarette hanging out of my mouth and I don't think that would be acceptable. I then said; "But I'm going to be real honest with you Sir; I have just as much a problem with my smoking as I had with my drinking, you're going to have to help me, thank You, Lord." I looked back down and drove on to Church and really didn't think much more about it. It was about five months later in the summer time and I was on my way to a city that was about forty miles south of where I was employed. I was in the middle of having communion with the first bite of a fresh doughnut and the first sip of a new fountain drink and I was smoking a cigarette, believe it or not. I had one of my bad coughing attacks where I would lose my eye sight and lean to the right side of the car so if I were to pass out hopefully I would pull the car off the road, hit something and stop. When my coughing stopped and my head began to clear, my sight was coming back I said; "Wow, is it that bad?" We had a conversation. The Lord spoke and He said; "There are strongholds about you that the only thing that will break them is prayer and fasting." He reminded me of the scripture where the Disciples had tried to drive the demons out of man and they couldn't. He saw the Lord coming down the other side of the road so he went and asked the Lord if He could drive the demons out of him. The Lord spoke and the demons came out and asked if they could go into a herd of swine that was over in the barnyard and the Lord said go. They went into the herd and the herd broke down the fence and ran into the lake and drowned themselves. Later the Disciples asked the Lord why they couldn't do that and the Lord said that; "these kind come out only by prayer and fasting" (Mat. 17:21). So I knew it was scripture but I had never fasted one day in my whole life before, I didn't have any idea what it would be like. I did know that there were a lot of different kinds of fasts so I asked; "What kind of a fast?" The Lord said; "Water." Now I'm really concerned, because I knew He fasted for forty days and nights and went up into the mountains after He was baptized, but I had to ask, I said; "How long of a fast?" The Lord said; "Three days." I thought for a minute and I said to myself, I can do anything for three days so I said to the Lord; "I'll do it, do I need to start now?" The Lord said; "No start in the morning." I then had this question*

I had to ask because I knew that this was what it was all about. I had no idea how in the world I was going to do this if the answer was "yes," but I had to ask. I said; "Do I need to quit smoking now?" The Lord said; "No, smoke in moderation and when the fast is over I will take it from you." I said; "I will do it Lord, Thank You." I was obedient and went on my first ever water fast the next morning which was a Thursday. The only person I told was my wife because she got upset that I wouldn't eat any dinner at night. The fast ended on Sunday morning and I was going to a Church that was about forty miles away and I had gotten up late so I rushed to get ready and hurriedly drove over to the Church. I got a parking place right in front of the Church so I parked my car and reached over to get my Bible and there laying beside it was an open pack of cigarettes which in my hurry I had totally forgotten about. I realized that I had been up now for over an hour and I hadn't had a cigarette yet that morning, then I remembered that today was the end of the fast. I laughed and went into the Church and I ran into a lady that I frequently saw at the different services that I went to and I said; "Let me tell you what the Lord just did." I gave testimony to her that the Lord had delivered me from smoking.

After Church was out and I was heading home, just beaming because it now had been at least three hours into the day without smoking, so I asked the Lord; "Lord should I give testimony before the Church about this or should I wait?" The Lord reminded me about the Parable of the Talents, (Mat. 25:14), where He gave an amount of money to three different people and when He returned the first one had invested what the Lord had given Him and had about twice the amount now, the second one had done likewise and he had about twice the amount which he had been given and the Lord was well pleased. He went to the third one and he was so happy to see the Lord return that he said wait just a minute and he went out and dug it up. He had buried it because he was afraid he might lose it or thieves might come and steal it. The Lord was so unhappy that He took what He had given to him and went and gave it to the one who had earned the most. After those scriptures had passed through my mind the Holy Spirit spoke and said; "Chuck if you do not share what the Lord has done that is the same as burying your treasure, you're going to lose it." So I went to a minister in town that I knew and told him that I had a testimony that I had to share with the Church and if he would let me do that? The next Sunday evening we had a testimony service and I told the congregation what the Lord had done. It was gone, when the Lord takes something it is gone. I never craved a cigarette again, it was about five years later I had to drive south about two hundred and fifty miles and you can guess who planted this seed. I thought to myself that, Gwen a friend of mine had quit smoking and he smokes a cigar now and then when we play golf. Just to have something to do as I drove south to Louisville, KY that I would smoke a little cigar or two on the way down. I ended up back smoking again for about a year and half and I really got upset with what I had done so I walked away from them not to look back. What I came to understand was that if you testify on what the Lord has done the enemy cannot come and steal it from you. If you don't he will con you into thinking that that really didn't happen or you can have just one and that wouldn't hurt. About two weeks later I asked the Lord why He had done that for me, delivered me from smoking? He said; "It was your faith that made you well, you knew it was Me, you believed Me and you did what I told you to do."

You can trust me when I tell you that you cannot conceive of the Love, Mercy and the Forgiveness of the Lord. He says in His Word, "Ask Me anything and I'll do it" (Jn. 14:14); "Ask Me anything." The only question is; "Will you receive Him, and will you believe Him?" "All things are possible to him who believes" (Mark 9:23).

CHAPTER TWELVE
MORE TESTIMONIES - VISIONS:

*T*his testimony is one that I like to share. I like to share them all but some of them are so revealing of not only what he wants me to know but of the related scriptures. This testimony I shared with a minister who had just closed the third day teaching on Spiritual Warfare. He had asked that all would pray for him because after each teaching he would come under spiritual attacks and he needed people to stand in the gap, in support and protection for him. After I shared this testimony with him he asked if he could use it, I laughed and said that anything God has given to me he was welcome to, that I really appreciated his teaching that week.

This testimony has me back in my car, my sanctuary and I'm no longer sure what I had been doing. I just know that whatever it was, I was with the Lord. The Lord gave me another vision. This time I was standing in a row of people and there were about eight people on either side of me and I was in the middle. As I looked out to get a picture of what I was seeing there was a column just like the one I was in just in front of me and in front of them was another column of people. It just went on and on and then the column of people turned upwards towards the sky. There, standing in a round, blue sky, opening surrounded by clouds, was the Lord. He had a white robe on; he was looking upwards toward the heavens. His arms were raised stretching upwards toward the heavens and the sleeves of His robe sagged down being much larger at the hands than at the top of the arms. We were literally marching into Him; we went in just above the stomach and just below the rib cage. Once you entered, you were no longer visible; you disappeared. There were hundreds of thousands of us in this column. Once I had an understanding of what I was seeing, I started to go back to where I was at. I noticed that about thirty yards on either side of the column, which was in a tunnel of light; it was pitch (tar) black. It looked like sand from the column over to the darkness. As I was coming back, I saw one person leave the column, walk over to the darkness and stuck his head in. It disappeared, then he pulled his head back out, came back over and joined back into the column. I then saw a person leave the outside of the column, walk into the darkness and he never did come out again. I saw one more person come out of the darkness at an angle and he was rubbing his eyes like he was trying to focus due to the brightness of the light. He then walked over and joined into the outer ranks. I'm now back to where I started and I realize that even if I wanted to go look into the darkness, which I didn't, I knew what the darkness was, I would have to cause a major disturbance. We were marching, for me to get to the outside I would have to say excuse me, pardon me, I'm sorry, I mean I would have to cause a major disturbance and mess everything up. I liked being where I was but I asked the Lord; "Lord I really like where I am but why am I in the middle?" He said; "What you are seeing is the prayers of other people." Just think a moment about what that vision revealed. Not only the power of prayer but the scripture (Mat. 8:13-14) says; "The path to heaven is narrow and so is its gates but the path to destruction is wide and so are its gates." The only way you're going to get to heaven is through Jesus.

It was later on the Lord spoke to me in my car. My car really was and is a haven for me, you would be amazed at how far I can travel and don't remember hardly any of the trips at all. Some days I would take the long way to get to my accounts so I could spend more time with the Lord. This time he said; "Chuck, show me a mountain?" I looked down again and thought why is he asking me to show him a mountain? Everyone knows what a mountain is! I then looked up and answered, I said; "It's something that's too big to walk around and too tall to climb over." That may sound a little sarcastic but if I think about it, it really wasn't a bad answer. He then gave me a vision of four short videos. Trust me I knew all of the details, how many lights were on, who was awake and asleep, what time it was and *where things were kept or hidden, everything. The four short videos identified and were in the following order -*

1) *Indebtedness*
2) *Cigarette addiction*
3) *Alcoholism or addiction*
4) *Drug addiction or narcotics*

After I had seen these and understood exactly what I was seeing, the Lord spoke again, He said; "These are mountains!" I could explain in detail why they are mountains, today; I understand why they are all are mountains. They are all strongholds that will prevent you from doing that which is perfect, good and the will of God. They will all lead you in to sin, sexual immorality, theft, lying, cheating, profanity, anger, hate, gluttony, you name it. They are all spiritual, mental and physical strongholds. They are spiritual because they take you away or keep you away from receiving God and doing His will for you. Indebtedness is physical, mental and spiritual because you spend all your time worrying about how to make more money, working more hours, two jobs etc. Not going to Church and tithing like God says you should, because you don't have the money and you're too tired. Cigarettes are spiritual because, what is God saying for you to hear while you're out smoking your cigarette? Did you know that the Bible says? "To call those things that aren't as though they are and believe in your heart and not doubt with your mind and they will be", (Mark 11:23-24). That, "If you have the faith of a mustard seed you can say to that mountain be removed and cast into the sea and it will go" (Luke 17:6) Did you know that a mustard seed is a very tiny seed and grows a hearty plant that birds come and make nest in its branches.

One of the problems that I used to struggle with was waiting on the Holy Spirit and then keeping in step with the Holy Spirit. These are Biblical; they are Scripture. The Bible says: "We should not squelch the Holy Spirit" (1Ti. 5:19). If the Holy Spirit nudges you and says go do this or that, then you need to do what is being asked of you. You may not understand why, but you will when it's finished. The Holy Spirit in me is a soft spoken voice that rises up from within. He kind of nudges me or pushes me towards doing what he says to do or wants done. Waiting on and keeping in step with the Holy Spirit takes patience, awareness and attention. My number with the Holy Spirit seems to be three, the number three shows up more times when the Holy Spirit is speaking. When the Lord speaks, it is very audible, it is like you and I would be talking to one another. His voice comes from up above and down into me. There is a question I always like to ask people, especially if they don't believe that we are a spirit that lives in a body (house) and live in a spiritual world. By the way spirits do not have any color to their bodies, nor slanted eyes. The question is; "Do you think that every thought that goes through your mind is yours?" Think about it!

CHAPTER THIRTEEN
THE CROSS:

*H*ere is a testimony that will help you see what I was saying about the voice of the Holy Spirit. It was a normal day just like most days and I was getting ready to go to work. I was standing in front of the mirror shaving and the chain to the cross I wear just jumped off the mirror at me. I have no idea how long it had been this way but this day it was like someone took it out of a display case and held it before me. The cross and chain I wore was gold plated and the gold was still in good shape on the cross but it had totally worn off the chain. The cross was gold and the chain was silver. I thought maybe I needed to go and get a new one; but after thinking about it I decided that it was what it stands for and represents, that is what is important. Who's going to know anyway? So I finished shaving and went to work having decided that it was okay as is. About six weeks later it was a Friday and I was finished early with nothing to do. It was about 1:30 or 2:00 in the afternoon and I was only about fifteen minutes from the office and only had about ten minutes of work to do there so I went into a Bible book store and looked around and didn't find anything that really caught my attention. I was back out in my car with still a lot of time to kill. I was trying to think where I hadn't been recently that I could go and spend some time just talking. I was sitting there thinking and the Holy Spirit nudged me and said; "Go buy a cross!" I thought on it a second and said; no I didn't need one there's nothing wrong with the one that I have. So I'm still sitting there trying to think of where I could go and the Holy Spirit nudged me again and said; "Go buy a cross!" Again I thought on it and said; no it's stupid to spend money on something I don't need and besides its way out of my way. I'm still sitting there thinking and the Holy Spirit nudged me the third time and said; "Go buy a cross!" I thought on it a second and said; what the heck, I've got the time and there's nothing else to do so I drove thirty miles out of the way and bought the last cross they had that was identical to the one I had been wearing. I shopped around for awhile in the store to see if they had anything new that interested me. I didn't see anything so I left with the cross. I laid the bag over in the passenger's seat; looked at the time and realized I had spent a lot more time than I had thought. So I took the shortest route I could think of to get back to the warehouse and turn in my orders; I then left to go home for the evening. I was in a hurry because I was now running about twenty minutes late and my wife and I had plans for the evening. I hurried home and rushed in to do what I had to get ready before my wife got home. We went out to dinner and then through the weekend as normal. It's now Monday morning and I open the car door to leave for work and what do I see; that cross was sitting in the bag on the passenger's side of the seat. It irritated me because I knew I didn't need it and besides I'm always praying over my finances and I had spent money on something I didn't need. Stupid! The next thing you know I'm back doing what I enjoy and my job. It's now the next morning and I go out to get in my car and there still sits the bag with the cross in it. I had gotten busy and totally forgot about it. This went on for about six weeks; getting up in the morning, getting in the car and there still sits that bag with the cross in it. I would get busy and always forget about it. I kept getting more and more upset every time I would see it and after about six weeks I was so mad that I took the bag with the cross in it and opened up the back of my station wagon. I had a box back there that had things that I very seldom used but on occasion needed, so I took the box, took everything out of it and put the bag with the cross down on the bottom and then put everything on top of the bag (Cross). That's how upset I had gotten over buying that cross.

It's now about two and a half months later, I had totally forgotten about the cross and it was a Thursday evening which I normally spend at home with my wife. This evening she had something she had to go to and wouldn't be home until around 10:00 PM. Well I don't watch television and I really didn't have any projects started. I didn't feel like just sitting home alone, so I decided I would run over to the club and see what was going on. I went in and the woman who runs the club (Taco) was there so I asked her if anything was going on that evening. She said yes; there's a meeting in the basement that's going to start in about ten minutes. I said; great and headed down stairs. There were four teenagers sitting there and I really wasn't interested in getting involved. I always seem to end up in control and they struggled with things that I have a problem relating to. I heard some people talking in the other room so I stuck my head in the door, it was four women and I asked if they were having a meeting. They said yes but it wasn't the type of meeting I would usually take interest in. What the heck I didn't have anything to do; my son was still causing me concern so I asked if they minded if I sat in. They said; no, I was more than welcome. We were about fifteen minutes into the meeting when the door opened and in came another woman. She took a chair across from me and when I glanced at her as she came around the table she looked beaten, exhausted. When it came her time to talk she apologized for being late but she said she had been down the street standing on the bridge, a bridge I used to fish under when I was a young boy, contemplating SUICIDE. She said that and I couldn't take my eyes off hers or my ears from listening to every word that came out of her mouth. You see, I knew exactly where she was at mentally and emotionally. While she talked, three times the Holy Spirit said; "Give her your cross before you leave tonight!" I mean it was the clearest I have ever heard the Holy Spirit speak. I wasn't sure how I was going to do this but I was going to do it regardless. I didn't know how the others would receive what I was going to do and I didn't even know how Barbara; she was going to receive it. We always close in a circle, holding hands, with the Lord's Prayer but the table was too big for all of us to hold hands together so we moved out to an open area at the end of the table. When the prayer was finished the other women moved over to the corner and were talking, so difficulty number #1 was taken care of. That left Barbara and I standing there alone. I started to remove my cross and speak at the same time. I was going to say I hope you won't be offended but I never got to the word offended and she saw the cross, she exclaimed; "Oh no! I've always wanted one." I handed the cross to her and said; "Barbara, it's just a metal chain with a metal cross on it. There is no power in this; the power is in who and what it represents." I said; "When you go to court tomorrow wear this and when you're walking up the steps to go in, stop, hold this in your hand and ask God to be with you and to give you the words and actions to take. Okay?" She said she would, thanked me again and we left.

I never saw her again for about eight years. I was going to a church south of town at that time and I had gone up to say something to the minister after the service. I finished, turned and was walking up the aisle to leave and here she came running. She threw her arms around me and called me her guarding Angel. I laughed, she really looked good and she told me what had happened. See her problem was that she was married had three children and she was the only one working. Her husband was the alcoholic, had the problem, and she was on welfare because her income wasn't enough to support the family and her husband's habit. He was probably taking her money and cashing in food stamps to buy alcohol. Her three children had left home and swore they would never come back again and her husband was in jail again for public intoxication. Her counselors were insisting that she had to divorce her husband or they were going to take her welfare away and she had to have the welfare plus she didn't want to divorce her husband. She hated his problem but she loved him regardless. What happened; the next day when she went to court she did what I had told her to do, she got upstairs in front of her counselors and the first thing out of their mouths was; "Well, have you filed for divorce yet?" She reared back and said, with authority; "NO! And in the name of Jesus I don't have to!" That was the end of that conversation for always, and she never lost her benefits. She didn't divorce her husband and the issue was never mentioned again. When she got home that afternoon, the neighbor girl, who was eight or nine years old came over with the Bible and wanted to know if she would read something to her. Her three children who left and said they would never come back, all came back. She said she finally did have to divorce her husband; no matter how much she prayed and tried he just couldn't get sober. Do you wonder if the scripture (Luke 1:37) is true? "With God nothing is impossible." Do you know it was over a week later, after that meeting, that I remembered I had that cross back in the back of my station wagon in that box where I had buried it. I went and dug it out, laughed and put it on and you can give God all the Glory! It's like I said "It's all about Jesus". Do you not believe yet that He knows! That He is all knowing!

CHAPTER FOURTEEN
DREAMS AND VISIONS:

It's now around the year 1997 in the summer. I had a friend of mine tell me about a reoccurring dream he kept having. He was having problems with his marriage and his wife would just get totally upset with everything, pack her bags and leave him. Three months later she would be calling up, wanting to talk, patch everything up and come back home. It would be wonderful at first and then about three months later she has packed her bags up and left again. It had been going on this way for over a year, a year and a half. Well he kept having a dream. He was standing on the edge of what looked like a swamp. The water was green with algae, there were alligators, the grass was tall and it was wet and muddy. There was no sunshine, it was heavy with trees, there were snakes, and it just wasn't a place that you wanted to be. He would look over on the other side of this body of water and on the other side the water was blue, people were swimming, there was a large beach with just a few shade trees. People were on the beach playing volleyball and having fun. He wanted so much to get from the side he was on to the other side that he would head out in one direction and start walking thinking he would be able to walk around to the other side. He would walk for days and there just seemed to be no end, no way around, so he would turn and go back to where he had started from and go the other way. Again two days later to find there wasn't any way to get around that way either. He would end up back at the same spot, frustrated, wanting so much to get to the other side. He would finally say; the heck with it, sit down and take his shoes and socks off, roll up his pants and head straight out into the water headed for the other side. He would get about half way across and here would come his wife on a pontoon boat and say; "John! What are you doing down there? Come on get on board, everything will be all right." He said that he would get on the boat and she would take him back to the wrong side, every time.

I laughed with him after he finished telling me his dream but later on the Lord let me see his dream in a different light. The side he was on was hell and the side he wanted to get to was heaven. The pontoon boat with his wife on it was temptation or Satan. Two weeks later the Lord gave me a vision. The vision was the same body of water only I was standing on the beach side. I was standing at the edge of the water looking out and there were my two sons shoulder high in the water headed for the other side. I had my hands cupped over my mouth and I was yelling come back! Come back! I felt a presence behind me, I turned around and it was the Lord in his white robe. I went to lift my hand to say; "why won't You help me?" I never got the words out of my mouth, He like brushed me to the side, walked up to the edge of the water, raised up his arms and looked up into the heavens. It turned bright white in front of him. You couldn't see anything. When the whiteness, like fog, slowly disappeared, there were my two sons standing in front of the Lord, out of the water or on the edge, facing him. The vision went away and I said; praise the Lord, He's heard my prayers and He is going to help me! Two days later I'm with my friend Gordy and I tell him about John's dream, the Lord's interpretation and then the vision. I was just about to say; "Praise God, Gordy! God's going to help me!" Before I got the first word out of my mouth, Gordy said; "Chuck, God's telling you to get out of the way." I immediately responded back; "Gordy, I know He is! I know so much that He is that if I don't get out of the way, one of these days He's going to take me out of the way." That's how much I knew he was right and I had been wrong. Gordy no sooner said what he said and I immediately responded back. I didn't even have to think about it. The problem was - I didn't and he did!

You see every time my sons would go out headed for trouble or in trouble, rather than letting them fall and have a need for God, so He could do what I had been asking Him to do, I would run out, throw money at the problem and bring them home to reason with them. It didn't have as much to do with my not trusting God, as it had to do with where I had been before I turned to God and my feeling of being responsible. You see my parents didn't have a clue as to what my problems were when I was fourteen. They didn't have any idea of or knowledge of what my life was like after I was sixteen. They didn't know until I was 48 years old and went and told them, seeking their forgiveness; where I had been from the age of fourteen to the age of forty five. I didn't want my sons to go to the same place that I had gone to. I know better but no matter how hard I tried, I would give them to God only to grab them right back as soon as I saw danger or the other one would start exaggerating the truth. Today it's not a problem anymore and when I'm finished you will understand why.

CHAPTER FIFTEEN
THE BLACK BOX:

I have tried to prepare you. So hold on, we are about to decelerate for a huge turn in the road ahead. Probably a year went by with no changes on my part and I was just at the front end of another one of my problem areas with my sons. I was at the beginning of a new situation. The company I was working for had been and was continually in a huge growing process. The industry we serviced was nationwide and they wanted fewer suppliers and that their suppliers to be located where their manufacturing facilities were. This meant we had to open up additional outlying branches and to bring on new items to supply if we wanted to be a player in this new market. Over the previous five years we had expanded into the southeast and the far west areas with branches and had increased our product range considerably. We had gone from around a 130 million dollar company to around 325 million dollar annual gross sales. Our last acquisition was huge, we bought out a supplier who was doing around 375 million a year annual gross sales and had five different or additional product lines plus the same products we carried. They were one of our competitors. That put us close to ¼ billion dollars annual sales. We did something the exact opposite of what we had previously done in the past. Instead of letting them operate as normal and put one or two of our people in their corporate offices and slowly change them over to our computers and systems we put their top people in our corporate offices, moved to their computers and adapted their business concepts, which scared me and others to death, so to speak. Number one I didn't like their concepts or agree with them, I always felt that they just bought their business on low pricing, not selling. At least the products I competed against them with, plumbing products. Bottom line it meant now rather than selling a product line I had close to thirty years experience with to thirty accounts. I would have to sell those products plus electrical, hardware & fasteners, building products and flooring & adhesives plus other products to only four accounts. So I would have far less accounts to deal with but I would have over 300,000 new products to become familiar with as to how and where they were used, who we bought them from. I had to know which products were superior products, which ones were competitive products; were there products I could substitute if we were temporarily out? Everything! It was a nightmare of a task; it didn't' have anything to do with selling product or service anymore it was now all about selling your reputation and completely trusting everyone to do their part and be there to back you up if you got in trouble. In other words smile a lot, tell jokes and don't for heaven sakes get into definition or performance conversations. I no longer knew what we had, where it was used or what I could substitute; if I was selling price or product, or who my competition was. It was a nightmare!

I made the decision; God's telling me to get out of the way! I've got a huge problem now with my employer, my job! "I will trust God with my family, which I should have done anyway; and I will concentrate on getting in line with this new responsibility." Wrong decision! I should have just given both situations to God, trusted in Him to see me through and continue to do what I had been doing for the last eleven years. God knew exactly what I was going to do and there was something he wanted to teach me or I had to know. As of today I can't think of any way he could have made me understand this, other than the way he did. I will tell you what it was that I had to understand.

1) To know the Lord and love Him is one thing! That's where I'm at, at this point in the book.
2) To know the Lord, love Him and know you cannot live without Him is another thing! That is what I had to know.

Journal: I'm going to break for a minute before I continue to tell you what happened. I just returned from a two hour lunch with the pastor of the Church I attend now. I just sat down to continue writing this book and the Lord just now gave me a revelation. When I left for our lunch meeting I had just written number two above -- I needed to know: "That I cannot live without him."

If you go back to Chapter 7, I told you about my struggle with the scripture that read, "The fear of the Lord is the beginning of wisdom" (Prov. 9:10), and then how the Holy Spirit defined the word "fear" to me. What I have written in both situations is exactly true and correct but the wisdom of that, the revelation, is: "To know that you cannot live without Him" is what the fear of the Lord is. In other words, I knew the Lord, I loved him but I still did not fear Him. Not the way He meant. Just reason with me a second; let's say that you have emphysema from years of smoking and you are on portable oxygen so that you can breathe. You know that you have to have an air supply or you're going to die. Right! You realize your tank is almost empty so you decide to go and change tanks before you get busy doing something else and run out of oxygen. You go to get a new tank and find out that your wife obviously didn't get this week's delivery yet. You're out! What happens? You are immediately concerned, afraid, trying not to panic, which would only make things worse. You would, or I would, go immediately to the phone and dial 911 and say, "My name is _____, I have emphysema and have to have oxygen and I'm about out. I don't have any refills left. Send an ambulance or something, I have to have oxygen to breathe! Give them my address and phone number and make sure they can help me, tell them to please hurry and try to relax until they get there. Why! Because I know I can't live without it. I get the oxygen on time and I bet you that will never happen again. That's the fear of the Lord!

Anymore I'm like a child (with God) and their mother. If I was a child and I was out with my mother in the living room coloring and she sees that I'm entertaining myself staying busy so she gets up and goes down in the basement to change loads of clothes in the washing machine. I get tired of coloring and look up and see that mother is gone; I just don't say well she will be back in a minute. No! I get up and go and look for her. I go out in the kitchen, no mommy so I go into the bathroom, no mommy. The next thing I'm headed for the bedroom yelling Mommy, Mommy! And the next thing you know I'm running to the back door crying, screaming Mommy! Mommy! She hears me yelling and rushes upstairs to see what the matter is and I say; "There you are-I thought you left me!" She picks me up, hugs me and tells me; it's okay now, mommy didn't leave you, its okay! I just don't wonder too far away any more. Now here is the other part. "The fear of the Lord is the beginning of wisdom." The Beginning! Wisdom and knowledge are two different things. You could call wisdom the revelation of knowledge. What you know but maybe don't really understand, all of a sudden out of nowhere you understand - that is a revelation. It's been revealed. What I just shared with you is the explanation of why when I get out of this black box; I was at a higher level spiritually than when I went in. That's why the things I didn't understand, I now understand; that's why I have on impulse, not knowing in advance, taken spiritual stands when before I would have to be guided to or think them over first. That is why I've been getting revelations rather than visions. He gave me knowledge through all the things I've told about so far but I needed wisdom! I remember years ago when I read the scripture that says, "If you lack wisdom, ask God, for He freely gives wisdom to all that ask." I laid the Bible down and looked up, said: "Lord, I lack wisdom and you said; (quoted the scripture), so I'm asking you for wisdom!" Thank You! I'll tell you, if you do not understand love, tolerance, patience or how absolutely wonderful, powerful, magnificent the Lord is, I hope this book will make you hungry. You do not want to miss the ride or the final destination, believe me. Who knows He may be having me write this book so that I will understand? I quit six months ago trying to figure things out, they always turn out being a part of something HE wants me to understand or to do further down the road. I know every time I think this is it, I find out I'm just at another turn in the road. I don't know if I've written this yet but it would be a good place to say it again. The Lord did not say: "Come let us reason together;" He said; "Come and believe me!"

If you want to have some fun, read (Isaiah 1:10-20) where it is written, Come now, and let us reason together. "I don't want any more of your sacrifices you people of Sodom, Gomorrah because of your sexual immorality, *your sins - Do these things and then come let us reason together for this is what I'll do. If you refuse and rebel, you will be devoured by the sword." They didn't and HE did. If you want to know about sexual promiscuity, freedom read the story about Sodom and Gomorrah, I wonder where the word sodomy came from. There is change and forgiveness. It's only too late, when it's too late and that time is much closer than what we might think. In my opinion there is no time left to tarry in making a decision for Christ and asking for help and walking away from your sins. I'm sixty six now and the seven years of tribulations and the return of the Lord Jesus could be over before I'm seventy three. All the cards are on the table now; it's just a matter of when, so to speak, the betting starts. I hope you know who's got the winning hand! Let's go back now and take a look at how He has taught me. I've told you the situation and what my decision to do was. I also told you the end of the story and the reason was so that you wouldn't read on always thinking how could anyone do that or let themselves get in that place with the walk that he has had and the blessings.*

Well its two years later now, the job is more of a nightmare than I had even thought it would be. I had spent so much time with the Lord that in some ways I had not given my accounts as much attention as I should have. I didn't neglect my accounts, not keep interest in their needs, problems or make sure they had everything they needed. I felt I was good at sales, successful and always had my customer's best interest in mind. I just had a tendency to spend more time getting from place to place, taking the long route rather than spending that time with them. So I had a lot of concerns and an overwhelming job of familiarization with all of the new products. If someone would ask me, do you have this? I would say; I'm sure we do let me go get a sample and some pricing and I'll be right back. Well all the things I used to do and loved to do like spend time with God; they all got lost, buried in the rush, worry and turmoil. I mean all of them. I didn't even go to Church anymore on Sunday or Wednesday evenings. Nothing! Two years later the attack came; I was so far out of fellowship with the Lord that I was out of righteousness with God. He saw me (Satan) way out there in the wheat field, as I called it, out of fellowship, hacking around doing this and that. Once you are the Lords, he has got to go point you out and ask if he can have you, just like the book of Job in the Bible. He did and the Lord said; "You can't kill him but you can torment him." Torment he did; I had never been beaten as much or as bad as I was this time. I was on my knees every night begging God to help me, I mean begging! Not a peep.

I don't know how many weeks I was mentally tormented to the brink of not being able to go any farther. He had me going 10,000 miles an hour mentally from the time I would wake up until I finally collapsed out of exhaustion into semi-sleep. I was sleeping out on the couch because I didn't want my wife to know. I had lost 45lbs and was at the point I couldn't take anymore. This night I again was exhausted, beaten, collapsed onto the couch and passed out. It was Thanksgiving evening, 1998 and I will never forget this experience. He, (Satan) made all the demons leave, unstrapped the chains and took what felt like a 10,000 lb weight off my chest and let me rest finally and sleep in peace through the night. He, (Satan) stood in the bedroom doorway behind the couch while I slept in peace. When I awoke in the morning, the sun was shining, I was rested and it was over. I opened my eyes and felt the relief, the freedom and I said with joy, "Praise the Lord!" thinking He had come and rescued me. Satan leaned over and whispered firmly in my ear and said; "I never knew you!" I bolted up off the couch and said; you never knew me, in total disbelief, shock, I said; "you will know me, I'll go to Church eight days a week if I have too. I'll live in the Church!" Satan said; "No! There's not enough time, it's too late." I lost it; I was totally defeated, broken. I knew that the scriptures said that the Lord had said; "There will be those who will come and say we did this in your name and that in your name and I will say I never knew you." It was so bad that I ran and got a bible and opened it up and guess what I read; every time I would go to a different section I would read exactly what I didn't want to read or see. You see Satan knows the scripture just as well as anyone, believe me. If I had not been as badly beaten and out of righteousness as I was, I would have just turned and said, "Leave me in the name of JESUS." "GO!" That verse is written about the end of times when this life is over and we will all walk with the Lord and look back over our lives. That verse is not for the here and now, it's for the end of times when there will be those who will come and say that they did this and that in His Name and HE will say; I never *knew you* (Mat. 7:23). But I was totally convinced that I had committed the unpardonable sin "blaspheme against the Holy Spirit" (Mark 3:29). I went with my wife that afternoon over to my brother in laws house for Thanksgiving. The whole family on my wife's side was there, her sisters and their husbands from out of town, everyone. I did the best I could to appear happy. I said hi to everyone and talked for a few minutes and then went over in a dark corner and stared blankly at the T.V. set. I think everyone got so busy talking to each other they totally forgot that I was there, which was the best that I could hope for. I would get up, slip in my coat and go outside and smoke a cigarette or two and then come back inside and go set in the corner. I remember when the sun had just gone down and the eastern sky, the clouds were white on top and dark on the bottom. I watched them knowing that any minute they were coming to get me and drag me off to the pits of Hell, like the movie Ghost. I almost ran into the house thinking I might be safe with everyone else there. I'm telling you, in my mind, it was all over. Well we got home that night and I lumbered my way through the days thinking that today would be the day. After about two weeks, I realized that I wasn't going to be drug off to hell, that I had some time left, so I decided I was going to go and see if there wasn't some way I could beg or plead my way back into forgiveness. I went back to Church on Sunday morning, Sunday evening and Wednesday evening which was intercessory prayer night. The Pastor and about eight of us would sit on the floor in a circle and talk about needs or concerns over ourselves, families and others and then break up each going to where they felt the most comfortable and get before God. We would do that for about an hour or longer and then gather and discuss what if anything that we had heard or had seen in the Spirit. Well that was my favorite time because I could be alone and I would pray in the Spirit, hoping no one had the gift of interpretation. I knew what I was praying for; I was pleading with the Lord to restore me to righteousness and reveal to me my salvation.

I started going to a Christian Psychologist once a week to see if maybe he could say something revealing that could help me. I reacquainted myself with my spiritual mentor and we would get together one night a week and go to a meeting. I went to his church with them one Sunday evening and did get something that I could try and hold onto. The Pastor talked about the scripture or included it in what he was ministering on, that says that God will restore you to righteousness, up to seven times. The problem was two things. Number one, I only told two people that I had committed the unpardonable sin. Ask me anything after that and I would just start crying. Number 2, I would not open the Bible. I did not open the Bible from that thanksgiving day of 1998 until August the 6th, 2006 after 12:00 noon. The only two people I ever told that I had committed the unpardonable sin was the Psychologist that I was seeing and soon to be the Psychiatrist I was going to be seeing. I am not going to go much farther with the torment or the insanity I lived in the next four months. I will tell you that as long as I was with the Christian Psychologist or in the Church they couldn't bother me but as soon as I would leave and get in my car; I don't even want to try and define what I went through. It ended the night, it was around midnight and I slid into the parking lot at the Hospital I ran into the hospital, wet my pants and insisted they admit me. The night receptionist said that I would have to come back in the morning that no one was there to admit me. I almost yelled; "You don't understand, I was here just this afternoon and they said to come back if I needed too. Call them!" She took my driver's license and had me wait over by the elevators while she called. I had to have scared her half to death. She called two security guards to watch me while she called upstairs. I don't think that she wanted to be left alone with me if they said I would have to come back in the morning. Finally she called one of the guards over and told him that they had gotten permission from the Psychiatrist I had talked to that afternoon to admit me. They would be down with a stretcher to get me to just have me wait a few minutes longer. I kept watching the door I knew they were coming to get me; it seemed like eternity until they got there. I told them to strap me down, tighten the straps tighter as if they couldn't break the straps or get me free. I know it seemed like it took at least two weeks for the elevator to open, close, go up one floor, open again and the cart to be pushed eighteen feet to the entrance door. Then another week to hear the door buzz open, be pulled in and hear the door finally go click as itself locked behind me. I was safe. I told them to give me something, anything, just knock me out. I didn't want to see, hear or say anything for three days.

Well finally they got me up, told me where the towels, linen and clean robes were. They gave me a razor, toothbrush and paste, and showed me where the shower was. I got settled in and finally I had to talk to the Psychiatrist. He informed me that the first time I had admitted myself and had the choice to stay or leave. This time he admitted me and I wasn't leaving until he said I could. The only thing I told him or would tell him was that I had committed the unpardonable sin. Any other question I would just cry. Two weeks later after he got the medications seemingly balanced where I could at least function without crying every time someone said something, he told me if I wanted to and felt up to it I could leave but he wanted me to get started with some therapy, I told him I was seeing a Christian Psychologist and that was what I was going to continue doing. He consented but insisted that he would control the medications. It ended up I would see him for fifteen minutes every three months to review my status. I had an open line, eight hours a day, if the medications weren't working right. My wife was the only one who knew where I was and could come see me, which she did every evening. I never told her or anyone what was wrong or what happened.

I struggled but went back to work, of course they were concerned but I assured them that everything was okay that the medications were doing great and there weren't any problems or concerns, nothing to worry about. It took everything I had to get out of the house to work by 10:00 AM and then I would have to head home around 3:30PM, I couldn't take any more than that. It took about a year and a half to get the right balance of medications so I could function without times of anxiety and depression. For seven years I sat in what I'm going to call a black box. A box that the entrance door slammed shut and was locked the moment the door clicked shut at the hospital ward. I wouldn't open a Bible, wouldn't go to Church, couldn't be on my feet and work much over six to six and one half hours a day. You couldn't get me to say hardly a word, I quit going to the Christian Psychologist, and I would just sit in my easy chair and stare out or at the front window at home. I finally reached a point that I started to try and figure out how I had committed the unpardonable sin. I would come up with something and think that's what it was only to end up saying. "No, God would have forgiven me for that." When the door to the black box, the steel door slammed shut and the lock, solid brass, a big lock was closed together, locked, it was that night when I finally heard the snap of the lock on the door at the hospital. I finally got a tiny little bubble that I hung onto for dear life, a tiny bubble of hope. I couldn't figure out how I had done what I knew I had done. I held onto that bubble for dear life, knowing the only thing I could do was sit there until I finally died and hoped that that tiny bubble was the truth and everything else was a lie. I sat there like that, sitting in front of the door that had slammed shut; for almost five years. The exit, which I didn't know there even was one, was at the other end of the box. You see no one could get me out of that box, not even God, if He wanted too, because I would not tell anyone. I was afraid too. I was afraid that you would say, "Oh, you have committed the unpardonable sin." I couldn't live and have that confirmed.

Journal - I hope you're finding humor in this because for the last fifteen, twenty minutes I've been crying so much I can barely see the paper I'm writing on and the words are coming so fast I can barely keep up. Thank God I'm going to have to edit this.

Well finally, five years later, I turned and headed for what I found out was the exit. I turned when I made a decision. I made a decision. The decision I made that turned me around was that; I decided even if I was going to spend eternity in hell, I was not going to serve that beast, I hated him for all that he has done, not just me; the whole world. I had made my own stupid decisions but I decided that I was going to get as many people saved as I could. I didn't want anyone to have to go where I was going.

About six to eight months later my oldest son kept calling, wanting us to come to the church they were going to. Finally, my wife said that she would like to go, at least try it. The grandkids were there and that was reason enough for her. Well if she wanted to go to church, I was more than receptive to take her. I wasn't for sure where she was spiritually and I could support anything reassuring her with confidence; that the pastor would minister on. This was I'm going to guess round August of 2005 that we started. We attended there faithfully for a year and a half until the minister upset me so much that I walked out, never to go back again. The Bible says if you go into a house and you're not received, kick the dust off your sandals and move on. So I did. I forgave him for four things that I'm sure of. I wrote them off saying he was just overworked, tired and hadn't had time to think clearly on what he said. The fifth time was the straw that broke this camel's back. I am not going to put up with or listen to that being ministered from the pulpit of a church; I'm just not going to. It's when he said don't you have anything to do with those darn twelve step programs; I was gone. Well let's go back just a notch. It's now Sunday morning, August 6, 2006. The pastor I was just talking about was on the last week of a three week sabbatical. The church had grown so much in the year and a half we had been there, the pastor started doing three services on Sunday morning and one on Saturday evening and they didn't want him to get burnt out. That's why I let him off the hook the four previous times and these were not just little comments that upset me. He literally butchered the 23rd Psalm when he ministered on that one Sunday. I told my wife that day that I wasn't coming back again.

I am a difficult person to minister to and I know it. To minister to me you have to have to meet some pretty tall requirements, I am better today than I used to be. The church has to almost be non-denominational with few church traditions or routines like stand up, sit down formats and dull, boring hymns song out of the songbook in the back of the pews... It has to be strong, strong in praise and worship music. I want twenty minutes of praise and worship music if not the whole service. I want uplifting music, people on their feet, hands in the air, singing, four or more musical instruments in the band. If you want to dance in the aisles, have at it. The minister has to be spirit filled and preach out of the Word of God Bible. I don't care how many books you've written, I want to know what God says. No time length on the services, (I'm giving in that area). There are Alter calls at the end of service, if nothing else just to open up the Alter to anyone who wants to come up and spend time before God. You have to be full gospel, what I mean is both the old and the new testaments. I do not want to hear that doesn't apply to today, that's old covenant. I want to know every word that's in His Book. My God does not lie or show partiality. The Jewish people are still and always will be God's chosen people and Israel was and still is the Promised Land and when the Lord returns that's where He's coming back to. Does that mean they have rights or privileges that we don't? No, Jesus shed His Blood, died at Calvary Hill for the atonement of the sins for the whole world; both the Jew and the Greek. In other words anyone who will receive Him and believe Him will be saved.

Back to the black box, well it's the last week of the Pastor's sabbatical and the Associate Pastor is ministering and he shared his testimony with the congregation this morning. He told how when he first started in the ministry both he and his wife were Missionaries and they lived in Florida and were six months from going back out on another assignment. His brother was also a missionary and he was working in Africa on assignment. Since they didn't have anything to do for six months, they decided to go over to Africa and help his brother. They were all together in his brother's jeep outside of the village and they were stopped by a tribal native with a rifle. The Pastor got out of the jeep to tell the bandit that they were missionaries and he was welcome to help himself and take whatever he wanted just to let them go on and finish their work. The tribal person got upset because the minister was looking straight into his eyes. He told him to stop staring at him. Well neither one could understand what the other one was saying, so nothing changed. They just kept saying the same things back and forth. Finally the tribal person got so mad because he wouldn't stop staring at him that he made him turn around and shot him in the back. He held the rifle right against his back and pulled the trigger. The minister heard the rifle go off, felt the impact, and waited for the warm blood to start running down his back. Nothing happened! Twice he was shot in the back at point blank range. He heard the rifle fire; felt the impact and nothing happened! His wife was so upset she got out of the jeep and was screaming at him. He held the rifle to her head, pulled the trigger, the gun went off. She felt the impact and nothing happened. This tribal person was so beside himself that he looked for a way out. He ran to the edge of the dirt road and looked down to see how steep the hill was that he was standing besides. The minister was now so infuriated at what he had attempted to do to his wife that he flew at the tribal person, caught him in the midsection and they tumbled down the hill. The minister got on top of the tribal man, took his belt off, wrapped it around his neck and pulled as tight as he could. He kept it that way until the man went limp. He thought he had finished him off, killed him. So he got off, put his belt back on, picked up the rifle and started to pull himself back up the hill. He said he got half way and heard rustling behind him. He turned and he had not killed the tribal man, he was running off into the bushes to get away. Well they got back into the village and they went to the constable's office to give him the rifle, they didn't have any use for it, they were missionaries. They told the constable what had happened and said; evidently the man had blanks in his rifle and didn't know it. The constable took the rifle and pulled the banana clip out to look at it and in it was live ammunition. What a testimony!

We always have lunch with our best friends after Church. They go to a different Church but we get out at about the same time. I got there early or my wife had to go straight to work from Church, one or the other, I don't remember for sure. I know it was just the three of us there at that time and I told them about the great testimony I had heard that morning at Church; then said that I couldn't figure it out, that I was depressed, down in the dumps. I hear a great testimony, I'm on all kinds of medications, for depression and anxiety; it just doesn't make sense! It's now about 12:30 going on 1:00pm and I'm home sitting in my easy chair in the living room with my feet propped up, which puts my head in a position where my chin is almost touching my chest. My wife comes in to kiss me goodbye because she has to go back to work. I tell her not to work too hard and I'll try to have supper ready when she gets home. God does the Impossible!

I'm just sitting there staring at my lap and the Holy Spirit told me why I was depressed. He said; "That might have been you up there giving your testimony at one time and look at you now!" That broke me! You see the faith I used to have said if I could go back in time to that exact spot I wouldn't be a bit surprised to find three round flat pieces of lead laying there on the ground where they had been shot. Not surprised at all if God didn't put His hand between that rifle and the backs or head of His servants. Well I'm now just sitting there busted again, you might just as well taken that bubble I was holding onto so tightly and threw it out of sight into a lake. I'm just sitting there and this comes in threw my mind three times this way like a ticker tape being fed in one ear and going out the other side! "Knock and the door will be opened unto you." "Ask and you shall receive." "Seek and you will find." Three times that way and I knew it was wrong, the scripture reads;

"Ask and you shall receive, seek and you will find, knock and the door will be opened unto you. For all who ask receive, and all who seek will find, and all who knock the door will be opened unto" (Mat. 7:6). I knew it was wrong but I didn't care, I was broken again. Then the Holy Spirit said, "verbalize it; speak it out loud." I didn't even consider or think about praying. Chin on my chest and eyes closed, I opened my mouth and this is what came out: "Father, this is Chuck; I stand at your door and I'm knocking! (Pause - in my mind's eye HE said it would be and time enough has passed, the door is open and I'm there in His presence now). I said; "Lord, Lord I know I don't deserve this, I really know I don't deserve it, but Lord I'm going to ask you to please restore me to righteousness and reveal to me my salvation." I stopped; I've got tears rolling down my checks by now. I then said; "Lord, if I have gone too far, committed the unpardonable sin, lost my salvation!" I then paused! I then said, " I don't want to live anymore!" I then stopped! I just sat there hoping to just disappear, vanish, dissolve, and go away. I had just let go of that bubble I had held onto for seven years! Seven years! I just laid it out on the table, all or none, and by the way I'm now crying again I don't know if you can imagine what I had just done or not. I'm actually sitting here crying like a baby, I can't help it. If you knew God the way I did and had just came to the end of seven years without Him, you would understand my emotion. I'm sorry, I just sat there, empty, broken with nothing more to say. You see the Bible says that what comes out of your mouth is the overflow of your heart (Luke 6:45). I had just laid my heart on the table, at His mercy. I sat there and the words started to come slowly, one two at a time. They were all scrambled up, not in the order they were written but I got enough of them that I knew it was scripture but I didn't have a clue, I couldn't piece it together and the word dismayed came. I knew that was in the scripture I was trying to piece together, I was positive of it.

So I opened my eyes, reached over (two weeks ago, for some reason I had brought these out and had left them leaning up against my easy chair - coincidence right) and got the Strong's Exhaustive Concordance and looked up the word "dismayed". It's only interpreted about sixteen times in the whole Bible. I quickly scanned down the books, chapters and versus it was interpreted in. I came to Isaiah and I always liked that book. It was Isaiah

41:10. I read the few words in that line of scripture where it's used and it was the verse I was trying to piece together. I quickly reached over, grabbed my Bible, and opened to Isaiah 41:10 and read. It says, "Do not fear for I am with you. Do not be dismayed for I am thy God. I will strengthen you, yes I will help you. I will uphold you with my right Hand of Righteousness." I jumped off the chair, I was almost breathless. He just told me He was going to uphold me (restore me) to righteousness! I grabbed the phone, called my oldest sister and for the first time told her what had happened, where I had been and what just took place. What God had just done! How He had done what I knew not even God could do. You see if He hadn't scrambled it up, I would have thought it was just me wanting to hear what I wanted. There is absolutely no way that I can take the perfect answer, scramble it, feed it into my mind one, two words at a time and throw in a word that I'll know that will be in the scripture. It's impossible!

I don't remember how many people I called and told but I've just been reborn again in my heart. I've been given life again! It's now three days later (I know this is going to sound stupid but you have to remember I was out of fellowship for two years, just spent seven years in an all but hopeless black box with no light and I am in no shape to logically consider things or think them through. If I had been I would have never been in that black box in the first place. Well its three days later and I'm thinking and I said; "Lord! I asked that you reveal to me my salvation and You didn't do that." Again I was sitting home in my easy chair with my legs propped up, chin down in my chest and again the words started to come one, then two words at a time, enough that I again knew it was scripture but they again were all scrambled up and I couldn't put it together. This time the word was "henceforth". Again I reached over grabbed the Strong's Exhaustive Concordance, looked up the word henceforth and it too was only interpreted about sixteen times. I went down through the verses and came to John 14:7 and that was the verse. Well that wasn't the answer but it was written in red which meant it was the Lord speaking and He knew I would read the rest of what's written in red and figure it out. I don't know if there is a direct answer to that question in the bible? He had to use a verse He knew I liked in order to get me to the right spot in a way that I knew it had to be Him, not me. That chapter is when the disciples are asking Jesus to show them the Father and Jesus says; "If you have known Me you would have know my Father also and henceforth you not only know Him you see Him", Phillip is still questions the Lord so He continues to explain so that Phillip will understand. When you get down to about verse 17 in the Spirit Filled King James Version of the Bible, in black script letters it is written, "The answered prayer." Can you believe that? It goes on and it's close to the time of the crucifixion and Jesus says; "And I will go to the Father and He will send another (Holy Spirit) who will live in you and abide in you forever. The world does not know Him and cannot see Him but you will know Him because He will be in you." I read that and I said, just a minute! He said He would restore me to righteousness, now He just said He was going to give me the Holy Spirit and it was forever! If I had committed the unpardonable sin He would not restore me to righteousness nor would He give me back the Holy Spirit, the sin is unpardonable. He couldn't and He wouldn't because the sin is unpardonable and He said it was forever so that means the Holy Spirit is still in me. Wow. I started praying in the Spirit knowing He had to be in me. I laughed, called my sister again and told her what He just now had done. She, like everyone said; "praise the Lord" confirming my testimony. I'm telling everyone I can think of who knows me and is used to listening to my testimonies. I'm even calling people who I'm not sure are believers.

It's now three days later, I'm again in my easy chair with my feet propped up, chin down in my chest and the thought went through my mind; "Should I be testifying about this so soon or should I wait and get a little better renewed or established in my relationship?" This time He gave me the scripture just like its written but I didn't have a clue where it was in the Bible. I had to look it up in the concordance. It's Revelations 12:11 "And they overcame him (Satan) by the blood of the lamb (Jesus) and the word of their testimony." It's still not over, it's now four days later and I'm coming into the house from outside. I've just gotten to the living room about four feet from my chair and I'm about two minutes into going back through this week, week and a half, thinking about what He said and he stopped me right where I was, dead in my tracks. I mean stopped me cold, frozen in place. I have never heard the Lord speak this loud or in this tone of voice and I really don't care if I ever *do again! It was so loud I was surprised the neighbors weren't at my front door to make sure everything was okay. He said with a loud, angered voice, "Do you not believe My Word?" "Do you not believe what I say?" I said (immediately), "Father, forgive me; I cast that down in the Name of Jesus! I have not, nor will I ever question or think on that again." I'm not really positive it was all me, or if it was the other one, who was laying the questions in there and I was then thinking on them. It doesn't matter now because it's not coming back again. The issue is settled, finished and things are back to normal again. I am close to being totally off all the medications and that's been kind of a comical experience. Go tell a Psychiatrist that the Lord has just set you free and you want off all the medications and see how he or his nurse reacts. I do have to apologize because I'm glad they were there and concerned about my welfare. They did everything they could to try and help me with my spiritual issues. They are trained to identify mental problems. I've since quit wanting to share my experience with them. I've more or less just taken a stand that says, "I told you that the problem was spiritual when I came in and I said that I had committed the unpardonable sin and I'm now telling you that I know I did not commit the unpardonable sin and the solution was spiritual." So, let's stick with helping me come down off these medications with the correct elements and dosages.*

CHAPTER SIXTEEN
TESTIMONIES CHANGE

*F*or the next weeks I've been sharing my testimonies with just about everyone who knows me. I've had some very enlightening responses and over the last six months there was only one person who did not receive my testimony and I don't go to that Church any more. Like the Lord said! "If you go into a house and you're not received, kick the dust off your sandals and move on" so I did. I called the Pastor of the church I had gone to frequently years before. It had been almost thirteen years since I had been there but I do and have always considered both the Pastor, his wife as friends and he or they are ones who can minister to me. Like almost everyone I've shared that testimony with, when I got to the end you could hear the joy, smile in their voice when they would say Praise the Lord! This Pastor again shared something with me that he had previously shared and it's something you may want to hold on to. He said! "Chuck if you think you might have committed the unpardonable sin, you haven't. If you have committed the unpardonable sin you will know that you have because you have to make the decision to do it. Knowing that's what you're doing, you can't do it by accident. I will say only one more thing; you have just read the most descriptive version of my testimony than anyone has. The reason why is because only as of two days ago did I completely understand why I sat in that Black Box for seven years. Before I knew I was right and I felt I really understood why but I didn't until two days ago have the wisdom of "knowing that you cannot live without Jesus," in regards to His Word; is "The fear of the Lord." I knew that was what was different but I never even remotely considered one with the other. The two people who got me the most was the Christian Psychologist I had gone to for four to six months on the front end of this problem? It was about three weeks after I was out or free that I called him and asked to make another appointment with him, that I had something I wanted to tell him. IF someone takes the time, regardless if you pay them or not for their service, I feel that they should know what happened and that you appreciate their being there for you. Well we set the appointment for later the same week or the first of the next week, I'm not sure which. I was on time and we sat in his office and he listened to me talk, it was an hour and thirty minutes. The meetings are only scheduled for an hour at a time and usually between the beginning and the end there is about ten lost minutes. When I finished, I realized the time, I apologized reached and got my checkbook, pen out with everything open on his desk to write the check. This was like a spontaneous reaction, while I reached to my back pocket for the checkbook I was starting to apologize. My apology and leaning over the edge of his desk to write the check concluded at about the same time. I said for heaven's sakes let me pay you; how much do I owe you? He sat back in his chair with the most astonished look on his face, said "owe me!", "owe me!" "You don't owe me anything." No! You have really helped me. "You don't owe me anything." I'll tell you when you share the Lord and give God the glory and He's received that way you just get a warm felling all over. It is one of the most positive, powerful experiences you can have.

The other person was a friend of mine also. It's now the end of November, 2006 and I'm at a major show for manufacturers, dealers and suppliers to the industry I serve. I'm at our booth and turn around and we see each other about the same time, smile and raise our hands to great each other. He says "Chuck" surprised to see me because it has been at least thirteen years since we have seen each other. Howard is Amish and though I didn't sell him much and he didn't build that many units, I loved to go call on him. Howard was like I said Amish, which are people of very strong, strict faith and he would enjoy listening to my testimonies. Well if you will listen to me talk, hang on because you're in for a ride. If you call me and you don't have much time tell me right away that you only have a minute and there's something you need to know or whatever, otherwise fix a tall drink, get in your comfortable chair, lean back; relax a minute and then call. Because if you let me get started hang on it's almost impossible to get me to shut up. Once I start talking about the Lord it's all over. Well we stood and got reacquainted somewhat with where we are now and so forth and I said - Howard! Let me tell what just happened not long ago, my last testimony. I tell Howard what happened and how the Lord got me free and he had the most serious look on his face. HE said; "Chuck! There are people at the Church that really need to hear this. Would you be willing to come and talk to the Church?" I kind of stood there, startled. I said; "Yes!" "Yes that wouldn't be a problem at all. Here let me get one of my business cards and if you can get permission for me to come and talk, call, and I'll be there." We talked awhile longer and he had to leave and I had to get back to work. I was still in shock. Just to think that he wanted me, a city person, to come to his Church and talk was almost unbelievable. I knew he wouldn't call, because there is no way that an outsider is going to be allowed by the elders of the Church, to come in and speak. Not possible! It's just the fact that he was not only sincere about it, but that he even considered letting or asking me to. If you do not know the Amish people and their traditions then you can't understand what I'm saying. Myself! I have a lot of respect for them. Their down to earth people, they are loving and respectful, hard working, and forgiving people. They are a community and no frills. They are very strong in both their traditions and beliefs. I just fill honored to have been asked to speak before the Church.

CHAPTER SEVENTEEN
TRIP TO OREGON

I've already told you about The Black Box. Let's take a look at how things not only immediately changed just getting out of that box, but have continued to change. It sometimes seems there aren't enough hours in the day to keep up. Let's go have some more fun. I hope you're having fun; I am because there is nothing better than sharing the Lord and what He has done.

It's now the first week in Sept. 2006 and on rather short notice I have to fly out to Pendleton, Oregon on business. The longest leg of this trip is flying from Detroit, MI to Seattle, WA. My booking agent has me seated in the center seat rather than in the aisle as usual. I'm sure it was due to the length of time between reservations and departure. When I got to my area the gentleman that had the aisle seat was already seated so he had to get up for me to get in, so I couldn't help but look at him and when you're standing there watching somebody undo their seat belt, stand up and move out in front of you, you can hardly help but have an impression of that person. I remember he struck me as a business man; someone who might even own his own business. He was casual, but very neatly dressed, well groomed. He looked to be within a year of my age, just about to retire or just retired. I didn't think anything about it or really care about it; that is just the image that was left in my mind. We were airborne and up to a level that we are no longer in a steep climb but still gaining altitude. My sister had given me a book written by Kenneth Copeland who is an Evangelist out of Fort Worth, TX. He has a large, good ministry and I believe does television broadcasts.

The book was titled "Righteousness". So I took it out of my briefcase and began to read. I just devoured that book even though it was only about fifty pages long; I read it in fifteen to twenty minutes. Kenneth Copeland had put on paper what I had stood on and believed in for years and had yet to hear a pastor minister on it. He just wrapped it all up in a neat little package. I think I read that book eight times while I was gone that week.

When I had finished, I put the book back in my briefcase, glanced at the gentlemen seated beside me and sat back in the seat to relax. The person on my right was sleeping I think and the gentleman on my left was just looking at the back of the seat in front of him, in thought. So I turned and spoke to him, I said; "Boy, what a powerful book I just read!" He turned and said; "Oh! What was that?" I said that it was written by Kenneth Copeland, not knowing if he knew who Kenneth Copeland was I described his ministry. I then said that the book was titled, Righteousness. I said that and he turned to look back at the back of the seat in front of him he said; "Oh!" So I turned back to look straight at the seat in front also. I'm sitting there and the Holy Spirit said; "He's agnostic." I didn't think anything about it; I just went back to thinking about what I had read. It was about a half hour or so later they came down the aisle with the brown cart they use to serve soft drinks and snacks. When the stewardess asked me if I would like something to drink, I asked if it would be okay to have two diet Pepsi's. I still have a problem, a compulsive behavior problem. It was when she handed me the two diet Pepsis I had requested, she had to reach out right in front of the man seated beside me and I chuckled, and said; "You have to forgive me; I have this compulsive behavior problem. If one's good, I seem to have to have a hundred of them." We chuckled at that and that got us to talking. He asked me if you had all the money you needed, where you would want to go that you haven't been. Where would you like to live? Or if you could do anything you wanted to, what would you do? I thought on it a short moment and answered him back then we just sat there talking about those type of things for awhile.

I have absolutely no idea how I got the door open, I never do. But it was an hour or so later and I'm just sitting there sharing my testimonies with him. The things God did or said, the visions, whatever. I know it was my faith, my beliefs because that's the only thing that gets me going that way. Like I said, you can't shut me up when I start talking about the Lord. They announced over the PA system that we needed to get our seat backs up straight and buckled in, that we would be landing soon. I realized I had been sitting there running my mouth all this time and he never got a word in edgewise. I apologized, shook my head and said; "I'm sorry; it's just that I get talking about Him and I can't shut up." He said; "No! No! You are the first person who has ever been able to...I can't think of the word I want." Finally he finished speaking, "I was the first person who ever made God real, believable." I laughed and said; "You have to understand, it's not me that speaks; it's the Spirit that's in me that speaks." He said; "I know." If he's agnostic and knows about the Holy Spirit that meant he had to have been in the Church at one time and got turned off and turned away. So I said, "Let me ask you a question?" He said; "What's that?" I said; "Do you think that every thought that goes through your head is yours?" He's a thinker; I knew he was and he was intelligent. He turned and looked back at the seat in front of him, so I did likewise. We were now coming in for the landing and he turned, looked at me, probably four minutes had gone by, and said; "No!" I turned and had a huge smile on my face, nodded my head in agreement and turned back as we were about to land. I'm waiting to touchdown and the Holy Spirit said; "You just saved a soul." I said; "I didn't pray the prayer of salvation with him." The Holy Spirit said; "No, but you revealed me in a way that he will search for the God you defined and he will find me just like you did." I thought, WOW! That's great! If I stay out of the way and let Him do the work, everything turns out just wonderful.

This same week, I'm now in Pendleton, Oregon. I fly from Seattle, WA down to the far southeast side of Washington at Walla Walla and rent a car to drive forty miles to Pendleton. It's the second day and I wake up and have to use the restroom right away, I drink way too much diet Pepsi. I went to sit up in bed to get out and my back just screamed; the pain was unbearable. I've had back problems since late June and had been taking Darvocet for them to help relieve the pain. When I got out of that box I threw the bottle of medicine off to the side, prayed over my back and went on with no problems. Here it is four or five weeks later and I can't get out of bed. I tried four times to set up only to have to lie back down due to the pain and I have to use the restroom. The fifth time I just forced my way through the pain and got set upright in bed. Glad that was behind me, I swung my legs over the edge of the bed to stand up and the same thing all over again. I've got to use the restroom; so the fifth time I forced myself up onto my feet out of bed. I was on my feet and everything seemed okay. I used the facilities and returned to the bedroom. I was walking back and I thought; I must have just turned the wrong way too fast or something, I'll just go lay on my side for five or ten minutes and it will be okay. So I did just that. I walked over to the edge of the bed and just flopped down on my side laying there resting. My eyes were closed and I really wasn't thinking about anything. I never even gave this a thought; I never even considered doing it or anything. I took my right hand and pressed my thumb down onto my side. I then stretched my four fingers around my back where they laid over the area that had been the worse. I said; "Satan! Do you understand that you have your hands on God? Is that really what you want to do? I think not; so I'm going to tell you that you have ten minutes to get your hands off and leave. I want you and the likes of you to leave - leave in the name of Jesus. Go! Get out now!" I then spoke to my body, I said; "Body, get in line with the Word of God - the Word of God says (Pet. 2:24) by the stripes of Jesus you are healed. It didn't say you may be or you could be healed; it said you are healed. So; you're healed, start acting like it." I then said; "Flesh, shut your mouth; I don't want to listen to you anymore. There's not a darn thing wrong with you so shut up." I just laid there on my side for about eight minutes not thinking about anything, just relaxing. I was rested and wanted to get to work so I let go of my side, sat up, stood up and wiggled around a bit then went into the bathroom and got cleaned up and left for work.

Not really thinking about anything still. I get in the car and the other one said; "you committed blasphemy; you called yourself God." I said; "I did not call myself God. I said you had your hands on God." Cor. 6:19. "When I gave my life to the Lord, my body became His Temple and He lives in this Temple, the Holy Spirit. So when you put your hands on me, you're putting your hands on God so shut up and get out of here." Guess what? No more pain, no more conversation, it's gone, over and it did not return. Just take a guess where all of that came from? I never thought on one of those things I said they just came out of my mouth. Not one thought! I'm telling you He is unbelievable and Luke 1:37 covers it all, "Absolutely nothing is impossible in God."

CHAPTER EIGHTEEN
TAKING STANDS AND REVELATIONS:

It's now November, 2006 and for the last three months you can't shut me up. If you called me wanting to sell me something you would end up listening to me telling testimonies on the things God has taught me, shown me or done for me. I've only been stopped once and all the other times I end up apologizing for running my mouth so long. I can't help it; I don't even try not to anymore, I just open my mouth, find away in and start talking. I don't even know how I got in most of the times. That is what it was like when I shared my testimony with my Amish friend at the show and he wanted me to come and tell his church.

It's now mid December, a weekday evening, my wife is working her second job and I'm home paying bills, writing checks. We are ridiculously in debt. I'm 66 and have been drawing my social security checks since the first of January, 2006. I'm working part time in customer service, sales for a company out of California. My wife is still (thirty five years seniority) working a full time job and sixty three years old. She also works twenty hours a week on a part time retail store job and sells Avon on the side. We both have a problem which I'm not upset over, she likes to take advantage of the sales at the clothing, kitchenware, small appliances retail store where she works. She gets an additional twenty five percent discount and loves to buy things for the family, grandkids and friends. She is a workaholic and has a great heart for others, very giving. I have the largest problem. Number one I'm in that black box for seven years and the company I was working for filed bankruptcy five years earlier. I couldn't find a job due to my age and my income level. I even tried getting a job bagging groceries at the supermarket and couldn't get hired. Unemployment ran out so we ended up spending over eighty thousand dollars just trying to keep up and make the ends meet. Plus with nothing to do I got into collecting coins and currency which I am now in the process of trying to sell. By the time I got this part time job and social security benefits, we were headed for trouble with the house financed up to the hilt and everything else. You still have to live. The collecting I didn't have to do, but I did have to keep my sanity. After all, I'm on all kinds of medication due to this black box episode. Really I can't ask for more, I love the job I have. I have known the people for years and sold their products for sixteen years. I get to travel, expenses paid and I get paid mileage for area driving. We're making ends meet; not getting ahead; but, I'm not complaining; it could be worse. All and all, I'm elated to have my salvation and relationship with the Lord.

I'm paying my bills, like I started to say, which is a bi-weekly experience for me. I've written about seven checks and have about three more left to write. I sat back to take a break for a moment, catch up on my soft drink that's been setting there with the ice melting. I don't really have anything on my mind. I don't like our situation but like I said it's currently manageable, nothing I'm going crazy over, worrying about, just sitting there. The next thing you know I open my mouth and say, "Debts, you're paid. House, the mortgage is zero! Cars you've been paid in full - zero balance. Credit cards you're all paid - zero! Halleluiah! Go, be cast in the sea! I'll look on you no more! GO! GO NOW! In the name of Jesus! Leave!" I looked up at the ceiling and said; "Lord, you said; to call those things that aren't as though they are and believe in your heart and not doubt with your mind and they will be." You also said; "If I had the faith of a mustard seed, I could say to that mountain go and be cast into the sea and it would go." I just called my debts paid and in my heart I believe and I do not doubt with my mind so they are paid. So I told them to go and be cast into the sea and my mustard seed of faith says that's done, so thank you Lord! I looked back down, picked up my pen and finished paying the other three bills. Ask me today how I'm doing financially. I'll tell you fine, everything's been paid off...gone. I don't *have much in savings but we're in good shape and I have my collection that I'm probably going to sell. How about you? Two months later you come back and call me a liar. You're debts aren't paid off! As a matter of fact what I saw, you are close to being in trouble! I would say, "You don't understand I just took care of those in December and all the records haven't been updated yet. They're paid! I'll tell you this much, I don't think about them anymore. As a matter of fact, I have had a tendency to forget to pay them. Two weeks later, at the new Church, I started tithing ten percent or very close to it for the first time in my life and have been ever since. I never considered doing that before. I know the scriptures; but those thoughts never went through my mind, not once. I just opened my mouth and that's what came out.*

Now it's about a week later, still in December. It is, I believe, a Tuesday evening. It had to be a Tuesday or Wednesday evening because my wife had to be home. Monday, Thursday and Friday evenings she works. I was sitting in my living room chair, reading or doing something and I remember my wife kissing me good bye. It was around 7:00 or 7:30 PM. She said she would be home around 10:30. I had told her to have fun and I would be up and see her when she got home. I think she had card club or some gathering to go to. I went back to doing whatever it was that I was doing. It was about 15-20 minutes later that I set back in the easy chair to relax a minute and take a break. I was either reading a book, paying bills or something and I believe I had just finished. I remember that the T.V. had been left on and I don't watch hardly any television. Normally I would just reach over, get the remote and shut it off, but this night I got the remote and scanned over the six or seven network channels that are in that channel area. We have satellite hookup and got it about two years ago when I was still in that black box. There is a potential of 999 channels on satellite television. There wasn't anything I was interested in that was on. I knew there wouldn't be; I was probably just curious what was on. I was just about to shut the TV off and the thought went through my mind. I wonder where the Christian channels are. I used to have ministries that I enjoyed watching. Since I was in that black box, I had lost interest and wouldn't watch them anymore. So when we switched to satellite, I never had looked to see where they were at. I remembered when they installed the converters they had left an index (channel) guide card with

111

each converter and I had one in the little wicker basket that sits on the end table besides me. I looked and it was gone. Well now I know that I would for sure just shut the TV off and said, "I'll run across one later and find them then." Not this time; I got up went around looking for one. It was around fifteen or twenty minutes later that I had found one and returned to my chair. I looked over the index card, found the channels range (300's) they were on, took one at random and keyed in the channel numbers that took me directly to that channel. Benny Hinn was on, so now you have my interest. Benny Hinn is an evangelist who is Jewish and converted to Christianity when he was a young man. I have a couple of his earlier books and would always listen when he was on T.V.

You find me a Jewish person who is converted to Christianity, received Jesus Christ for who He is - The Messiah. Their prophets had prophesized His coming and that He had come, while the rest of them are still waiting for Him to come the first time. You have someone you won't hold back, someone who is on fire. You're going to find me there possibly in the front row. Well I'm listening and I find out it is the annual or semi-annual fund raising campaign they have to raise money to support the LE SEA Broadcasting Ministry. They televise Christian Broadcasts via satellite TV into Europe and the middle east/west countries. He told how in 2007, China was going to allow the Christian Broadcast to be received or televised into China. Now you really have my attention; that is a huge breakthrough. I've read books on how Christians were persecuted in China. Then he told how when he would go home a year or two ago, back to Israel, how if he would even say the name Jesus Christ people would back off and raise their hands as if to block it out. It was like he would have said, "I'm Satan and I'm going to get you." He said that this year, 2007, Israel was going to allow the Christian broadcast to be televised in Israel! I almost came out of my chair. When he said that, a revelation hit me just like you would have taken a two-by-four and smacked me upside the head. What hit me was: The only thing left in the book of Revelations, the end of times, that I couldn't come up with was how in the world the Lord is going to get the Temple rebuilt in Jerusalem. The temple has to be rebuilt before Jesus Christ returns. If I haven't been misled, sitting almost two feet on the outside of the old Temple grounds, the wall; is one of the largest Moslem Masque anywhere. I know that the time of the return of the Lord is near, real near and that the Jewish people have everything prepared to go into the new temple including the Ark of the Covenant, I've been told. But to rebuild the temple on the grounds where it once stood you're calling for Holy war. I don't care if the Masque comes down by accident, anyway; even if it's not rebuilt. To rebuild the temple where it used to be; in my mind is Holy war. Now since that Masque had been established in place that is now Muslim Holy ground. The revelation was that the Bible says when you give your heart to Jesus Christ your body is now His Temple. Was John seeing the physical, structural building or did he see his people turn around and receive Jesus Christ for who He is. Is he talking about the building or the people, His chosen people? Because if they turn like Benny Hinn did and receives Jesus as Lord, their promised Messiah, His Temple has been rebuilt. May be or may not be, but at least I can now see a way for that to get accomplished. For two months I would not claim that as a revelation of God and only told a handful of people about it. Today five months later I claim it as a revelation of God. There are way too many coincidental or accidental situations that got me on the right channel at the right time with the right person speaking and saying the exact thing in a way that I get a revelation. Number one I don't believe in coincidences or accidents or things happen by chance and number two since the black box this is exactly how things have been happening. Very little talking anymore; everything now is revelation knowledge. Like I said revelations are a little more difficult to discern than visions and talking to the Lord. You have to ask yourself if it's just you or is it Him showing you something.

CHAPTER NINETEEN
A TIME TO THINK:

I had quit writing my book two weeks ago and have been doing nothing but journaling since the beginning of April, 2007. I have never kept a journal in my entire life but things have been happening so fast spiritually that I won't be able to keep track of them if I don't journal. It has been like a spiritual downpour ever since I got that revelation back in December that the End of Times could begin at any time. I haven't even told you how He got me to start writing this book which I started eighteen years ago. To give you an idea about what I'm trying to say, two weeks ago I wrote the last chapter to this book two chapters early. It was like I had to finish the book now and then the next day I quit writing and start to journal. April the 2nd I had the Holy Spirit all over me and by April the 3rd it was so heavy that I called everyone I knew to see if they were seeing or hearing anything spiritually. I told them that I felt like I was a bedbug that was sitting on the top of a sheet that was covering a sleeping giant and any minute now this sheet was going to come back and he was going to throw out his legs and stand up and he was big and he was ugly. The first Tuesday of every month we have a club night with friends, eat dinner and then the women like to play penny poker, which I really am not into but I enjoy it for the conversations and the fact that we are all friends. After desert I usually quit playing and go rest for awhile until they finish playing about one hour later. Tuesday evening was April the 3rd and I'm lying on the couch resting and I have this vision of the Lord speaking to the World. He spoke first to the World, then to the United States

115

and lastly to Israel. Well it's now time for us to leave and the vision had just ended so when I got up the morning of the 4th I make a journal entry of the Lord speaking to the World the previous evening. What bothered me was that when I made that journal entry I closed speaking to each section with the words "Sayeth the Lord". I don't think that way; I don't speak that way; so why did I write that way. I immediately went to the Lord and asked Him; "Is this You Lord or is this me? I have to know either Yes it was you or No it was me. I will stay before You until I am sure of Your answer." I apologized to the Lord but explained that I am just not used to revelations of the Holy Spirit yet, that I'm used to visions and talking with Him. The last four days I have been remorseful; grieving, knowing there are those who will not turn and receive Him, believe Him, those who are deceived and still go to Church; if it is Him speaking. I'm now out in the living room again and have been in peace meditating over everything still not positive that it was Him that wrote the page about the end of times. I do believe for sure that everything up to then was Him and what I have written in my journal is other than; "The time is now, that He is finished!" Here again we now have another question; "Why?" Was it the Holy Spirit who has led me to see in His Word and given me the revelation of those things or is it just my interpretation and had come across them coincidentally. I'm not saying that everything is what I've seen; I'm saying that it now can make sense to me. I mean, if His answer is yes, I can tell you why to everything going back to when I was born. Why I drank for thirty-one years, why I smoked five packs of cigarettes a day, why I sat in a black box for seven years and why I have spent most of my life, it seems, in demonic hell. If the answer is "No it is a warning" that the time is near then I can still answer all the questions; but if the answer is just "No" I now have more loose ends than I had before I started.

The reason I am now writing again is because I'm at peace - does it really matter if it was Him or if it was me? Isn't it something we all need to take a closer look at and the sooner we do the better? There are a lot of things you will never convince me are not true. Everything up to and including the last chapter I have seen and experienced. Yes, He has tried me and knows my heart, (the black box for seven years) and yes, I do know His voice and have seen His ways, (The whole book). The other thing I am positive of is that there is only one God and He has provided the way that we can all come to Him. That there is only one of two places you're going when you die. It is going to be up there with Him (Heaven) or down there with him (Hell) and there is only one way you're going to get up there with Him and that is in; an through Him. You will either receive Him and believe Him; or you're not going there. He is God, Jehovah, the I Am, the God of Israel and His Name, the Name that is above all Names is Jesus Christ (Jesuaha Hamasheia). So if you die tonight or sixty years from now does it matter who's been talking or when He's coming back?

I don't know if you know this or not, but one of the things I shared with the Pastor of the Church I'm attending was the revelation I got about drugs. I had looked up in the Strong's Exhaustive Concordance the words, drunken and drunkenness and they were interpreted probably 1,000 times from the Hebrew and Greek Scrolls. I know with the problem with drugs in today's world, they had to be mentioned or interpreted at least as many times also. I looked the words drugs, narcotics, so forth up and not one word. I could not believe it. I rushed to the last book in the Bible, Revelations, John's writing of God's vision regarding the end of times, and not one mention. I was totally confused with drugs being more devastating than alcohol and not one word mentioned in the whole bible. The only words I had a question on, or wasn't comfortable or positive I knew what they meant were the words; sorcery, sorcerers, and sorceries. I looked them up in the Concordance and what I told the Pastor was they were interpreted only seven times in the New Testament. Three times they were interpreted; they came from the Greek word Pharmakon. There are three words; meaning the same only plural etc., Pharisaios, Pharmakon, and Pharmakos. The other word you may have used as interpretation would be Drug i.e. spell giving potion or druggist (pharmacist) or poisoner. I looked up every word you might have chose to use in the Concordance and I found that the word was interpreted once in Galatians as Witchcraft and the other three times were in the book of Revelations, all three times in the very last book in the Bible.

Well I had quoted this from memory so when I got home I got the Concordance out to make sure that I was correct because it had been about twelve years ago that I had come across that. I found that the words sorcery, sorcerer, sorcerers and sorceries were interpreted only fourteen times in the whole Bible, six times in the Old Testament and eight times in the New Testament. Four times in the New Testament it was a different Greek word that was interpreted and it meant deception, magicians, etc. They were all in the book of Acts. The other four times came from the words Pharmokon, etc and guess where they were? Rev. 9:21, Rev.18:23, Rev.21:8 and Rev.22:15 - five versus from the end of the Bible. Now I'm more excited and interested than ever before. I mean the Bible was translated into English back in the 15th Century. Why would they use the word drug as definition back then? Witchcraft and Sorcery were a lot more prevalent then. Anyhow, I got the Bible and read around the word sorcerers and sorceries inserting drug or drugs etc. Here I'll show you the scriptures.

Rev.22:12 (red)   "And behold, I am coming quickly, and MY reward is with Me, to give to everyone according to his work."

Rev.22:13 (red)   "I am the Alpha and Omega, the Beginning and the End, the First and The Last"

Rev.22:14 (blk.)   blessed are those who do His commandments that they may have the tree of life, and may enter through the gates into the city.

Rev.22:15 (blk.)   But outside are dogs and sorcerers (drugs, deceivers) and sexual Immoral and murderers and idolaters, and whoever loves and practices a lie.

Rev.22:16 (red)   "I, Jesus, have sent my angel to testify to you these things in the Churches, I am the Root and the Offspring of David, the Bright and Morning Star"

Rev.22:17 (blk.)   And the Spirit and the bride say, "Come!" And let him who hears Say, "Come!" And let him who thirsts come. Whoever desires let him take the water of life freely.

Rev.22:18 (blk.)   For I testify to everyone who hears the words of the prophesy of this book. If anyone adds to these things, God will add to him the plagues that are written in this book.

Rev.22:19 (blk.)   And if anyone takes away from the words of the book of this prophesy, God shall take away his part from the Book of Life, from the holy city and from the things which are written in this book.

Rev.22:20 (blk.)   He who testifies to these things says (red) "Surely I am coming quickly." (blk.) Amen, Even so, come, Lord Jesus!

Rev.22:21 (blk.)   The grace of our Lord Jesus Christ be with you all, Amen.

I wonder how the Lord feels about alcohol and drugs, sexual immorality and so forth. If you really want to get blown away, read these versus in Revelations. Chapters 9, 18 and 21.

Rev. 9:21 (blk.)   and they did not repent of their murders or their sorceries (drugs, deception), or their sexual immorality or their thefts.

Rev.18:22 (blk.)   And he cried mightily, with a loud voice saying Babylon is fallen, is fallen, and has become a habitation of demons a prison for every foul spirit, and a cage for every unclean and hated bird.

Rev.18:23 (blk.)   And the light of the lamp shall not shine in you anymore. And the voice of the bridegroom and bride shall not be heard in you anymore. For your merchants were the great men of the earth, for by your sorcery (drugs, deception), all the nations were deceived. Who is Babylon today in this world? When this book was written, Babylon was the power of the world if I'm not mistaken.

Rev.21:8 (blk.)   But the cowardly, unbelieving, abominable, murderers, sexually immoral, sorcerers (drugs, deceivers), idolaters, and all liars shall have their part in the lake which burns with fire and brimstone, which is the second death.

Reason with me one second please. John also writes in the scrolls about "giant locusts." Until the 1960's, there was nothing you could envision as to what John was writing about or seeing. Viet Nam was the first time I recall helicopters as being a main instrument of warfare or in existence. Maybe they were before. I don't remember them when I was a teenager or in the Korean war. The helicopter is the only thing that I could envision as possibly being a "giant locust." I'm not saying that is for sure what John was seeing I'm saying that finally there is something that could be called a giant locust. In 89AD or whenever John was given this vision what possibly could you write to define a helicopter if that's what he saw? How would you define drugs back then? I've already told you about the temple being rebuilt in Jerusalem, that it could be the Jewish people receiving Jesus Christ as Lord!

CHAPTER TWENTY
WHY CHRISTIANITY

I came back from breakfast with our best friends after Church and today our friend's sister joined us. She goes to a different Church but we get out at about the same time. Her brother, who goes to a different church yet, had given her some literature on his church's beliefs. We have a lot of different concepts floating around about religion (which is a word I absolutely hate). I am a Christian, believer; I do not have a religion or religious beliefs. I, my spirit, body, heart and soul is the Church, a part of Gods Church. According to scripture He "Jesus" is the head and we the Church are the body. I'm a Christian, born again; Spirit filled and speaks in other tongues, which is a gift that is freely given by God. I go to a building on Sunday morning and other times to praise Him and worship Him. I go to spend dedicated time with Him, communion. Hopefully there will be someone who's called to minister the Word of God (Bible) so that I can get a deeper understanding or wisdom of God. If we spend the whole morning singing, praising and worshiping the Lord, that's fine. Bottom line, it's all about God, Jesus - not Chuck and not Church traditions. I guess I got carried away with that, sorry. I guess bottom line is I don't care how many books you've written, that's for free time education. I want to know what God says. To me there two questions a person need to deal with:

1) God either is or He isn't!

2) *The Holy Bible is from the first word in Genesis to the last word in Revelations, hand written by the Holy Spirit (God's word), or none of it is. It either is or it isn't!*

Why? Because look how long it took Him to get me to understand why He said, "The fear of the Lord is the beginning of wisdom." If I didn't believe the Bible was what I said it was, look at what I would have missed out on. Either I am the dumbest person who has ever read God's word or you're going to end up just like I did. With a whole lot of loose ends and things you didn't like or understand. I would have just shoved them off to the side, skipped over them or just threw them out. Besides, how could anyone have the wisdom to write or the foresight to identify the world to be exactly as written over centuries ago? Look at where the best I had to offer took me. You don't think He is and that He is coming back again, maybe sooner that you think. Then where has this thing called "love" been hidden? Why all the strife, greed, sin, sexual immorality, promiscuity, hate, envy, sickness, disease, wars, violent storms, earthquakes, volcanic upheavals, tidal waves, drugs, alcohol, smoking - do I need to go any farther. I think love, joy, peace; respect is a pretty ingenious idea. It sure sounds a lot better than what we have now.

I may be wrong but I think we have been seduced, misguided or spiritually tempted into a lot of lies:

1) *They want me to believe that my ancestry goes back to an ape!*
2) *That there is no God!*
3) *Satan, demons - you have to be crazy if you believe that!*
4) *Man only uses 17% of his brain, just think what we could do if we could Use 25%!*

Bertrand Russell, a philosopher would have probably said; in regards to Man evolved from an ape! This strikes me as curious! If man evolved from an ape; then why are there still apes in the jungles? Did some of them have the foresight to see into the future and decided that they didn't want to get caught up in two or three hour traffic delays during rush hour in the big cities? That they would rather hang around the jungles and eat bananas and have a harem? Why isn't there half ape, half humans running around today or recorded in history? Why don't you see apes with human babies living in the jungles? If we had evolved from something then the old would be gone and the new (us) would be here; wouldn't it?

In regards to man only uses 17% of his brain then; if that is true, how fifteen minutes after a car screamed out front of you and you had to slam on your brakes to keep from hitting it, you recompose yourself and look back out the front window to see what this idiot did and he is almost three blocks down the road out of sight. You hear the sirens screaming and the next thing the police are everywhere and you're being asked questions about the car that you almost hit. You can't answer hardly anything other than it was a sedan, black and looked fairly new. The license plate, sure it had one but you only got a brief glance at it and couldn't remember anything. Six months later they call you in to the police station and ask if you would be willing to go under hypnosis to see if you could recall more information about that vehicle and you consent. How is it you can tell them the license plate number that you barley remember seeing. Where did that come from? When people have near death experiences, they almost always say there was a tunnel of light and their whole life just flashed by them as they went in. How does that happen? Where is all this information and why can't you retrieve it. Are you so busy processing all the new information that you never learned how to retrieve it, or is this a spiritual environment that we are dealing with? What if the 17% is the work area of your brain where all the programs of interpretation take place, the work area where you think and compare information? Can you imagine how busy that area would be interpreting all of your senses, feelings and processing short term memory? What if the other 83% is a storage area and that process is spiritual. How much activity would you see in there? Then the Spirit can get to it; they can get to it through hypnosis or lie detectors but you just can't jump in there and grab what you need when you need it. I don't know, but my God does not make junk.

These three lines I wrote on the side of a coffee cup over seventeen years ago, I threw it away, and three days later couldn't come up with one word *but seventeen years later struggling with my speech at the GB#31 I came up with all three lines.*

1) You can't have what you have unless it comes from Him, Who is true!

2) You can't keep what you have unless you give it away!

3) You can't give what you don't have!

How in the world did I come up with that? I had set the cup in front of my sponsor; he read it; and turned, smiled and said "that's good." After the meeting, I threw the coffee cup away certain I wouldn't forget it and three days later I'm with my spiritual mentor and I wanted to tell him what He wrote on that cup and I couldn't come up with the first word of any of the lines. I tried for two days and couldn't come up with one word. Seventeen years later I'm trying to prepare a talk that I have to give in three weeks and I struggle something terrible getting something on paper that's any good at all. Four times I wrote only to read what I had written and compared it to the format, only to rip it up and throw it away. Two weeks later after my trial run in front of my peers, knowing I wasn't ready, fell flat on my face. That night I was thinking about a scripture that I came across by accident and it showed up in three of the four papers I had written. I was thinking about that scripture and the Lord gave me a vision. Then I'm thinking about the vision, and I get another scripture. We go home and I sleep on it and the next day I get up write a nine page presentation in half the time I had written the previous four. I'm reading over what I had written trying to put it to memory and every time I read it I get a different, deeper understanding about what I have put on paper. After about twelve attempts with the same results, I give up. I'm just sitting there playing around with some thoughts that I enjoy thinking about - spirit, soul, heart, eternity and things of that nature and guess what? Here comes those three lines I had written seventeen years ago and I then included them in my presentation, amazing!

Here, I'll give you some things to think about:

1) God doesn't make junk! You have exactly what you have to have and the exact format, programmed and the exact capacity which is required.

2) Words are spiritual. If you watch me while I'm talking to you, you see my lips move and hear what I say don't you. Do you see anything go from my mouth over to your ear? Read John 1:1-2

3) Thoughts, thinking are a spiritual transaction or exercise you can put all the activity or sensing devices on a person and you will not get a reading on what is spiritually being processed. No matter how hard you try.

4) We are a spirit that lives in a body and has a heart and a soul (Kenneth Hagen).

5) This may be correct or not but it's the way I visualize myself today:

Spirit = Encompasses the entire inside of your flesh - it is the workhorse, it moves you.

Soul = your whole mind or 100% of your brain.

Heart = The essence of who you are, what you believe, your feelings, your will.

Will = What you do. And last is righteousness which is to me more easily interpreted as right standing.

The Bible says:

1) "What comes out of your mouth (Words) is the overflow of your heart" Mat. 12:34

2) Life and death are in the power of the tongue" Pro.18:21

3) "The sword of the spirit (Word of God) is sharper than any double edged sword dividing to asunder joints and morrow, thoughts and intents of the heart." Heb. 4:12

4) "My Words are life to those who find them; and they are health to all your Flesh." Pro. 4:20-22

5) "Set a guard over my mouth; put a watch over the door of my lips" Pam 142:3

6) "I did not come to judge the world, the words that I speak will judge you in the end." John 12:47
7) "Heaven and earth will pass away but my words will never pass away." Mat. 24:35
8) "In the beginning was the Word and the Word was with God and the Word was God. That He (Jesus) was in the beginning with God and all things that were made were made through Him. And nothing that was made that was made was made without Him." John 1:1-3

The Father, Son and Holy Spirit.

Jesus   =   *The Heart, Soul of God - the Body of God, in the flesh!*
God   =   *The Heart, Soul - the essence of all - the Word!*
Holy Spirit = *Spirit of God - The workhorse, action, the fulfillment of the Word!*

God is deity, all encompassing, everything and Jesus Christ is God in the flesh, the heart and the soul of God. Then the Holy Spirit! All one like us, but yet separate.

Omnipotent = *Almighty, having unlimited authority and influence.*
Omnipotence = *Force of unlimited power.*
Omnipresent = *Present in all places at all times.*
Omnificent   = *Unlimited in creative power.*

Read John 14:6-31. It's in red, the Lord speaking; it identifies all three aspects of the God head and remembers we are made in God's image. There are three parts to God, God the father, God the son and God the Holy Spirit. God is all one (Jesus Christ) yet separately, omnipresent and all the above. There are three parts to us - Heart, Spirit, and Soul - but we can only be in one place at one time and are under the authority and control of the above, not equal to. We create by separating and assembling or putting things together. God speaks them into existence. That is why there is power in your tongue, you have to be careful what you say or speak. Words have authority and power. I gave you the scriptures about the spoken words and their authority.

Your brain is the most protected part of your being. It is housed by an outer shell (skull) and all your primary senses are attached directly to and near your brain. You have eyes, ears, mouth, nose, skin and nerve ends throughout your body. It's riding in like a cushion air ride trailer. There is a thick jelling or fluid that separates the brain from the skull. Your heart, soul, the mind of your spirit man is in your brain and around your brain. The 17% of your brain that shows activity is the programs of interpretation of your senses. It's the work table of your mind. That's where the interpretation of what you see, hear, taste, feel, and smell is laid and then processed, the processing of that information (thinking and comparing information) is spiritual. It's compared to stored information and if there are any changes then your heart gets the new information and either is updated or rejected. The end result everything gets put into a storage room which is the 83% of your unused brain. That area you cannot get into or just reach in and pull it out. If you could you would spend the whole day just trying to fry one egg for breakfast at my age. That's why you have the programs of interpretation in the seventeen percent area of your brain. They're being added to and updated all the time so that you can think or reason and have feelings, a heart. Remember God is all seeing and all knowing. You can't get in that 83% by choice but he already knows what's there. That is why you have to FORGIVE others their sins and then ask to be FORGIVEN your sins. Otherwise they just sit there like a neon sign flashing in the dark. Sins are deadly. If you are unwilling to forgive it holds you in bondage and creates all kinds of sin, hate, anger, fear, etc. and you cannot be forgiven if you do not forgive others. Chuck Swindal closed his ministry one day asking, "Just what is it that you won't let go of? What is it that you think you can do a better job with than what God can?" And or heaven sakes don't forget you in this process. One person wrote that most people rob themselves of faith due to their inability to forgive themselves. If you don't forgive yourself, you're not any better off than when you started the process. And if Gods willing to forgive you and you're not, where does that put you? Kind of above Him!

Is that where you really want to be? The only one I know that put himself there got cast out of Heaven.

The battlefield in spiritual warfare is the worktable of your mind. That's where the battles are fought. That is what Satan wants control of is your mind. If he can get control of your mind, he's got you. You will lash out in hate and anger, rob, steal, kill, drug, drink or whatever. Those are just some of the strongholds he loves to get you into. Praise God there is a way out and there is forgiveness. There is NOTHING that you have done that God cannot or will not forgive you of. There is only one sin that is unpardonable and that is blasphemy against the Holy Spirit. In my opinion, you really have to know the Lord and you have to make a decision and tell Him you do not want Him anymore; to leave. This is a decision not an accidental occurrence in the time of panic or anxiety.

Demons are (to me anyway - the way I see them), negative thoughts. If you don't think about what you're thinking about, they get processed, accepted just like all the rest. Once you give one a place in your mind the next one comes and the next one is worse than the first one. Before you know it, they have you concerned, then worried and all of a sudden you find yourself full of concern, worry, fear, anxiety and depression. If the thought puts itself above God, outside of God, if it leaves a taste, image of concern, doubt or worry, cast it down in the name of Jesus and do not give it root in your mind. Make it leave, speak the opposite of what it is saying in your mind. If it says you can't do that then say I can do that. Just make sure it lines up with God's Word. You have absolute authority as to who can get in your space and stay and who can't. If you have received Jesus as Lord, He gave you a lot of authority over spiritual things. You have His Word, He's given you His Name and they have to leave in His name. They cannot stay. At first you may have to convince them, because they're used to having their way with you. You need to show that you not only know what you're talking about, but you believe it also. I'm not going to stand here and tell you that everything I have written in the last several pages is exactly the way it is. No way! Most of it I know makes sense in regards to scripture. You would have a hard time convincing me I'm wrong about the 83% of your brain or spiritual warfare. Obviously you can never convince me I'm related to an ape any more than you can about what I've written regarding God/Jesus Christ and my testimonies. I won't budge on those issues or the way I see the Trinity in relationship to us. Like I said, it's my way that I can visualize things and it makes acceptable sense to me. I also do not believe in accidents, coincidences, etc. Nothing happens in my God's World by mistake and the reason for the bad times is to bring you closer to Him. God will not let you suffer beyond what you can bare. I do not know why some people are taken when they are taken or in the way they go. I do know that we are a work in process and the process is not going to end until we get up there. And then again this just may be the beginning?

Well I hope I've given you something that's reasonable, something to consider thinking about. I hope I haven't come across as insisting or demanding. My objective is to give you another way you might want to consider this life, another way to look at it and hopefully with God, Jesus Christ. There's only one thing on my heart, from the first word I wrote to this word. It is that you will consider and give the Lord your heart, a chance. That maybe I could give you another way to look at it or a reason to reconsider your walk through life. "He will never leave you or forsake you." I do not want anyone to go where I have been. To get to where you only have four hours to live and hope He will tell you, like He did me. I'm alive, living and a Christian today only because He loved me and my parents taking me to Church when I was not even able to walk yet and keeping me there until I was eight years old. A seed was planted that there is a God and that there is a life after this one, a heaven, a hell and that the minister told about this God reading out of the Holy Bible. It was the continual prayers of my mother and my oldest sister, Nancy, over our family. It certainly isn't because of my previous life or what I deserved. You see it's never too late, until that door closes, just don't wait and take a chance. You never know when this life is going to end for you or for all of us; if the end of ages is going to be 2014 or tomorrow, if you are going to get run over by a semi running a stoplight on the way home from work or wherever? You will never know when that event may take place. You may have just finished reading this book and decide you need to go somewhere to get the kids or to the grocery store or back to work, whatever. Don't take a chance; make a decision for Jesus now before it is too late. He died for you; is that not enough that you will try to live for Him? Speak this with your mouth:

> Jesus I'm sorry for what I've done. I do believe now that you are God's only Son, that you are Lord over all heaven and all the earth. That you died at Calvary and were crucified that I might live in righteousness, in God's grace and spend eternity with you in heaven. Jesus, please help me, take this crusty old heart of mine (who you are, what you believed and the way you feel about things) and throw it away. Give me a new heart of flesh (love, compassion for life, faith) and come and live in me. Be my Lord, my Savior. I give my life to you now! I believe that you are the Son of God, were crucified (put to death, nailed to a cross) and on the third day God raised you from the grave, the dead and you ascended up into the heavens. You're alive; You are Lord over all Heaven and the Earth.
>
> Jesus, I let go; I forgive those who have trespassed against me (everyone, call them out by name). I forgive them; give them all the blessings you had in store for me.
>
> Now I ask you to forgive my trespasses (sins) that I have done. (If you can write them down on paper, ask forgiveness and then burn the paper or bury it at a gravesite of a loved one you had sinned against).
>
> Come into my heart, live in me. I give it to you. Now! Thank you Lord! Thank you for your Word (promises) and I thank you for hearing my prayer. Amen

Welcome brother, sister - welcome to the Church (God's Family) you have just assured yourself a seat on the bus, knowing you don't deserve it - none of us do. We're all sinners saved by God's Grace, the shed blood of Jesus Christ. If you die tonight or fall over getting up or out from where you are and die in the next minute - you are saved - saved from eternity in hell and guaranteed eternity in Heaven with Him, He is now Lord over your life. When you said Amen you closed the door on the old and now things are new.

Call someone you know that understands (believes) or write and tell me or a Christian Minister you have seen on television. Tell someone, because then the enemy cannot try and steal your beliefs from you or stands less chance of being successful in doing that. If you let him con you, he can make this life miserable but he cannot take your salvation. You are the only one who can throw that away, it's sealed, and your name has been written in the Lamb's (Jesus) Book of Life. If you have decided to think about if first before you pray that prayer, consider this thought:

You can spend the rest of your life believing whatever it may be that you believe and die then find out that this prayer was the truth, the only way; there is a heaven and a hell. What have you lost?

On the other hand . . .

You can do what I said, pray that prayer, believe, read the Bible and try to change your way of doing, thinking and die and find there is no God, no Jesus Christ, no heaven, no hell. What have you lost?

Number one you will have had a better life during your time here, less worry or fear, to walk in peace, love, joy and care more about others than yourself. I'm not saying everything is going to be a cake walk from now on. You have an enemy that will try desperately to keep you in sin and steel your faith. He will do whatever he can to make your life miserable but you have the victory because he can't win. He's defeated and he knows it, all you have to do is take a stand in the name of Jesus and he or they will have to leave. They can't stay.

The Bible says that Jesus was the light that came into the world (good, hope, direction, life) and Satan when he was cast out of heaven was the darkness. They were allowed to walk the face of the earth in darkness; I believe long before man was created. Why do you think that most crimes of violence happen at night rather that during the day? The sins of passion, drunkenness, drugs, sexual immorality etc. happen more often in the night hours than during the daylight hours. Did you know that darkness cannot live in light? When light comes, darkness has to leave, it cannot stay. Darkness does not push the sun down at evening. It doesn't follow right behind the sun in the sky; it can only come when the sun has fully sunk below the horizon. Just go into a room at night and turn the light on, what happens to the darkness? Jesus was the light and Satan was the darkness. Jesus gave you His Name, His Word, His Blood, how can Satan stay? Use it; do it; it works; it has to work. I proved it to you in my testimony. The scripture says, Rom.10:9; "If you confess the Lord Jesus Christ with your mouth and believe in your heart that God raised Him from the dead, you will be saved."

Just remember one thing; it is only the shed "blood", life, death and resurrection of Jesus Christ that you have salvation. It is God's Grace, your faith and the shed blood of Jesus Christ on Calvary Hill a little over 2,000 years ago. It is not by works, should anyone boast; Eph.2:9.

I want to thank for your patience in bearing through my writing which I know is not the best in the world. English was not my major in high school so I am sure that you have probably ran across spelling errors and punctuation errors and I ask that you do not let them distract you from what the Lord is saying. But I do have a good heart; I love you and care about you and I'll look forward to being with you in that Promised Land.

CHAPTER TWENTY-ONE
JOURNAL SUMMARY:

*T*his book was started on March 8th, 2007 and was finished on April 15th, 2007. It was written in long hand and then entered into the computer, edited and it was finished in May of 2007. So the book was written long hand and then entered into the computer for spell check and punctuation in less than three months. Starting around the end of March I stopped writing and started journaling things were coming so fast. IF you could see my notes you would understand; I am the only one who could possibly decipher them and I'm not positive I can all of them. It has to do with the end of times and the return of the Lord, Jesus Christ. To tell you what has happened I would have to write another book which I might. This book has accomplished what the Lord had intended it to accomplish. My whole goal and my heart are to make God real, believable; I can't live without him and I don't want anyone to not have the opportunity to know Him. I don't want anyone to go where I seem to have spent most of my life, especially for eternity. Trust me; you do not want to go there. If you think this life is hell, you haven't even tasted the real thing and you do not understand the words, torment, suffering, a living mental torment and hell. I hope this book gives you something to consider.

It is now Nov. 10th, 2007 and things have reached a point that I decided to change this Chapter and put it here at the end of the book. I have tried and told this to four people who are Ministers and I have written a group, (3) letters and mailed them to an Evangelist whom I respect and a Prophet whom I respect. I have gotten some good attention in some cases and then I *have been cut off right at the start in others. I had one Pastor say; "Chuck, the rapture is going to occur before the seven years of tribulations and we are going to be out of here, period, and end of conversation." The problem I have is exactly what I told the Lord. I, very humbly, said; "Why me Lord? Why not, Benny Hinn, Pat Robertson, Kenneth Copeland, Lou Engle, etc; I don't have a voice, known; who am I to tell? The Lord just smiled and said; "tell those who will understand." It's kind of like He was saying; "I've been trying for forty years and nobody will listen to Me!" You see I didn't come from a common school of Theology; I have not been to a Bible College or served an internship under a Pastor. As a matter of fact I haven't even read the whole Bible from cover to cover. Do I know the "Word;" am I called to be a Preacher, Evangelist or a Teacher? NO; from a technical standpoint but YES; I do and I can do all of the above. To rationalize, why me; I think has to do with my whole life. Number one; I have been down there and do know the turf; so to speak. Number two; I can relate and communicate to those who are still down there, but may not realize it yet. Number three; I understand; "Grace, Mercy, Forgiveness, Love, Joy, and Peace in the Lord." Number four; I understand and do now have, the "Fear of the Lord," which is; "the beginning of wisdom." Number five; I know what it is to be born again; Spirit filled. Number six; He has been my teacher. I walk in miracles; visions, now revelations of the Holy Spirit and I know the voice of the Lord; Holy Spirit and have seen their ways. I said that I have seen their ways not that I understand God. No (creation) of God was meant to understand Him or to know what He knows. It was meant that we receive Him and believe Him. No man (creation) has or exists; that can contain Him. God is not only infinite, out that way with no end; He is finite also, which is the other way with no end. Einstein in understanding the Atom and splitting it found that it was a trinity consisting of Electrons, Protons and Neutrons and I am equally sure if you were to break them down individually you would find the same thing; three or a Trinity. Bottom line when the Lord left to prepare for His return He left a note on the door and the Holy Spirit read it to me. It said; "I have tried you and I know your heart;" "you know My voice and have seen My ways." The only way the Holy Spirit could have made it more concrete is if He would have said; "Signed the Lord." From here on are the three letters*

I wrote and the illustrations the Lord gave me and included are some of the visions and pictures He drew. I will leave it up to your discretion if you think this is of God, man or Satin. Before I start to include these, the other day on a radio ministry program I listened as the minister said that there was now one in North Korea who claims that he is the "Christ" and there is also one in London who claims that he is the "Christ." He said that the Jehovah Witnesses and the Masonic Lodge were listening to the one from London. I also heard that there is one in South America who has a large following and claims that he is the Christ. The Lord says, regarding the "End of Times;" that there will be those who will come saying that; "I am Him," not to believe them; Luke 21:8. When the Lord returns He will appear in the sky; just as it is written and He will step down in Israel not London or South Dakota in the U.S. or anywhere else. The other thing is the "Rapture," and when it will occur. Nobody knows, or will they know. He said; "To have your lantern full and be ready, not to be caught sleeping." I feel very comfortable that I am going to be here to the very end and I am not going to be surprised to find out that the "Rapture;" is post "Tribulations." If it was me trying to make a choice I think about right now I would be on my knees surrendering my life to Him; asking Him to be Lord over it and would start preparing myself by getting into His Word; going to Church under the assumption that it is going to be a post "Tribulation;" "Rapture" and that He is coming back and soon. You definitely want to be going the right way and as prepared as possible even if He doesn't return for another 1,000 years. Like I said; you can go get in your car right now and get ran over by a runaway semi and die within the next half hour. If that happened it doesn't matter when; all that matters is where. No decision for Christ is a decision. If for some reason you would wonder if I am Him, I'll put it this way; Sundays I'm in Church; Monday noon I am in an intercessory prayer group with the Pastor; Tuesday evenings I'm at another Church on my feet; hands in the air; singing, dancing and praising Him. I find myself quite frequently praying that He will have Mercy on my soul. I love you and may God Bless You and those around you.

It is written in Ish: 55:8 "For My thoughts are not your thoughts, Nor are your ways My ways." Says the Lord! "For as the heavens are higher than the earth, So are My ways higher than your ways, And My thoughts than your thoughts." So just receive Him and believe Him, don't try to intellectualize or understand God. All you need is to believe, having faith, knowing He is within; that He is a God of His Word. It's worth more than all of the Gold or Silver on the earth. It's eternal - forever!

SECTION TWO
REVELATIONS OF THE HOLY SPIRIT
&
PROPHETIC VISIONS

Date: 10/17/2007
To: Whom it may concern...
From: Charles Mc Cuen

Subject: Revelations of God, the significance of "7" and the End of Times:

I have been trying for two months to write this, being one of two letters that the Holy Spirit has put on my heart to write. The other letter is to a prophet and his call for revival in the youth. I fasted for forty days and was at Nashville, TN on 7/7/07 which was a day of perfection in the year of perfection. I had a spiritual experience that gave me insight as to why I have been given these revelations of late. I have been blessed that the Lord took me out of one Church, Dec. of 2006, and put me in the Church which I now attend. Pastor Lee has listened, not being critical and has asked questions leading me to scriptures which have given me insight. He has given me by far more time than anyone should deserve. I am sure that is why the Lord has taken me there.

I am going to ask that you take a moment and pray that the Holy Spirit will give you understanding and direction in what I am going to write. The Lord has given me visions and definitely given me a voice. As of Aug. 6, 2006 I moved into another realm of God which is revelations of the Holy Spirit. Your secretary suggested I be specific and in respect I totally agree, knowing your busy schedule. I definitely need your council it's about the United States and how or where we are in this picture. It's about the Church (people) and Religion and what we need to be doing, what we are not doing. I need to know who can help me, who can guide me in the right direction. It's also about the election of 2008, pending legislation and the voice of the Church. If we don't unite and become a voice we are going to lose it. I am sure you will ask the question, why me? I did. Blessed but totally humbled as never before I said, "Lord! Why me? Why not Pat Robertson, Kenneth Copeland, Benny Hinn, Lou Engle, I don't have a voice (known), who am I to tell?" The Lord just smiled and said "Tell those who will understand."

This revelation started, just covered with the footprints of the Holy Spirit, in mid December of 2006 with the revelation of the Temple being rebuilt in Jerusalem and the revelations still keep coming. The wisdom in all of this is that the Lord said, "No one knows the hour or the day in which He will return, not even the angels in heaven, only the Father knows". You know and I know that the question isn't the hour or the day that the Lord will return. The question is where will you go and spend eternity if you die today. What people don't understand is that no decision for Christ is a decision. What I am going to share with you I do not believe is for the World to be told or the United States because I know there are those whose minds are closed and would only say who do they think they are, or no its going to happen this way, or wouldn't believe it at all and then there would be those that would say "Wow, I've got five more years before I have to do anything, I can just keep on having a party. The statement is that we all know that the End of Times is imminent and on the horizon, it could begin at any time, if it already hasn't begun. This is the revelation and at the end I will explain in brief summary how this was revealed to me.

After sharing this with four different people in the Clergy and to answer all their questions the Holy Spirit put it this way. The 7 years of Tribulations started at midnight on 4/3/07. Gods time clock is digital and has three dials on it. At .01seconds on 1/1/07 the first dial stopped with the number "7" on it. At midnight on 4/3/07 the second dial stopped with the number "7" on it and an hour glass that had 7 years of sand in it was turned over and the sand has been slowly sifting into the now empty bottom container. When the last grain of sand falls through that tiny hole, that hole will now appear in the sky and standing in it will be our Lord and Savior "Jesus Christ" the third dial will have stopped with the number "7" on it. It now reads 777 the end of the sixth day and the beginning of the millennium or 1,000 years of Heaven on Earth. I dug a book out of my library "Armageddon" written my Grant Jefferies (Prophet) in the late 1980's. He had followed Jubilee years. Which I believe the Bible says that following 7 days of 7 years, which is 49 years, the next year, is a year of Jubilee and all debts are forgiven the 50th yr. He had, which I've come to understand is a common interpretation of Theology, the creation of Adam at 4,000BC and a year was 360 days or 12 months of

30 days each. He had the 7 years of Tribulations starting at the year 1993 and the end to the Sixth Day, the 120th Jubilee cycle being the year 2,000AD and the beginning of the 7th Day. The Holy Spirit asked me. "How do they know that God created Adam exactly at the point of 4,000BC?" If they are off 14 years 4 months and 3 days then Grant Jeffries had come up with the revelation just the wrong starting point. Besides is that even relevant or is it the understanding of the Number "7" that is relevant?

The revelation of Daniels prophecy of 70 weeks, it is now June the 30th and I am putting together some reading material to take with me on my trip down to Nashville on Friday July the 6th. I had made copies of everything the Lord had taken me to during the last six months and at the last minute I decided to make copies of Mat., Mark and Luke when the Lord speaks about the signs of the end of times. I had put them in plastic sleeves to protect them and I was just glancing over them to make sure I had gotten all the verses when it jumped out at me that there was one line in this sea of red words that was black so I went and read it. The interpretation that I was left with was that it was saying "you really have to understand this". I thought why did they interrupt the Lord to say that? So I went to the bottom of the page where you have verse definitions and it said to read Dan. Ch.9, the Prophecy of 70 weeks and Dan. Ch.11:31 and Dan. Ch.12, the Prophecy of the End of Times. So I got my Bible and read from Dan. Ch. 9 Prophecy of the 70 weeks all the way through Ch.12 the Prophecy of the End of Times plus the next 10 to12 versus where he speaks of the 1290 days and the 1335 days and a light goes off. I went back to the Prophecy of the 70 weeks and it is broken down into sixty-two weeks, seven weeks and one week. It never says any more about the seven weeks and the Holy Spirit said "The seven weeks are the seven years of Tribulations!" So this Prophecy the weeks are now turned into years and it takes place during the seven years of tribulations. The sixty-two weeks, (years), the streets are paved in Jerusalem and the Temple is rebuilt. The one week, (year), Israel makes a one year covenant and half way through the covenant it is broken and the Temple comes down, Jerusalem falls and the abomination of desolation takes seat in the Holy Temple. In order for the streets to be paved and the Temple to be rebuilt Israel had to be a State and they had been without a country until after WWII they were re-instated. I got the Encyclopedia out and looked up Israel. On Nov.28, 1947 the United Nations under the direction of the United States declared Israel a State. It was May 14, 1948 that Israel had written a Constitution and established a Government. If you add sixty-two years to that window you come up with Nov.28, 2009 to May 14, 2010. If the seven years of tribulations started on 4/3/2007 and a covenant is signed between Israel and I believe Islam to either worship or rebuild the Temple on 4/3/2010 you are in that window and precisely three years into Tribulations. Then half way through it is prophesied the covenant will be broken and the Temple will come down and Jerusalem will fall. You will be precisely three and one half years into Tribulations, the battle of Armageddon or what will become WWIII a nuclear holocaust. You have to understand; I have never studied Biblical Prophecy or read Daniels Prophecy of 70 weeks before. I have never thought about or studied the number 7. Plus I haven't even told you who I am and have only told you some of the, what I call Footprints of the Holy Spirit. Why did I run copies of the End of Times in Mat., Mark and Luke and why did that one black line of scripture create such a level of curiosity. How did the two incidents (revelations) fit perfectly together in the windows of opportunity? How in the world did I come up with the illustration of the number "7" which I have included? I later found in the back of the Spirit Filled King James version of the Holy Bible where you had written in the section of Answers to Spiritual Difficult Questions. What is the mark of the beast? In summary you wrote that the mark of the beast was 666 where as the number of man is 6 and Satan takes over the Head of a State or a man. You then said that 7 was the number of God, meaning perfection or completion.

I don't know if I could adequately define in detail all the footprints, where the Holy Spirit has taken me, how and what He has revealed to me. This is just the tip of this iceberg. You have to understand what happened and how He revealed this to me and part of the reason why. Part of the reason why is because I do not have a common convention of theology, my mind is not fixed. To me the Word of God is the Living Word and the final authority on all issues and if I do not understand and need to know, He will teach me. The revelation started in mid December with the building of the Temple and that the seven years of tribulations could start at any time. Then all the things *that happened from Jan. through Apr.1, 2007 and on April the 2nd and 3rd the Holy Spirit was all over me, I called everyone I knew who would listen to see if they were seeing or hearing anything. I felt like I was a bedbug that was sitting on the top of a sheet that was covering a sleeping giant and any minute this sheet was going to come back, this giant was going to stand up and he was big and he was ugly. At 10:00 pm on Apr. 3rd I had a vision of the Lord speaking to the world. The next day I journal that vision and was bothered by what I had written and the implications so I turned to the Lord and asked, Lord was that you? Or was that me? I have to know Lord, I apologize, Lord I'm just not used to revelations, I'm used to visions and talking to you. I said that I would stay before Him seeking the answer "Yes", it was Him or "No", it was me. For seven days I stayed before the Lord and the last three days I went on a water fast and told the Lord that if I awoke Thursday and had not heard the word "No" then the answer had to be what I had heard every night which was "Yes". Thursday morning I was awoken around 3:30am and it was different this time; I went up through an opening in the bottom of the clouds and was immediately in the presence of the Lord and I fell to my knees before Him. He laid His hand on my shoulder and said "rise and look into My eyes". I arose and looked into His face of total composure, peace and He had a slight smile at the edge of His lips. He said, clearer than ever before "Yes" and the vision went away. It was not intended that I ask any other questions, which I would have. I fell back to sleep in peace and around 5:30am I was awoken again this time by the Holy Spirit. He said three times "The thousand years ended on Wednesday," "The thousand years ended on Wednesday." I again went back to sleep in peace and when I awoke and got out of bed Thursday morning I immediately went out and got my journal to see what had happened on a Wednesday that was significant. The only thing that was significant is it was Wednesday Apr. 4th that I had made the journal entry of speaking to the World on the previous evening Apr. the 3rd. I now go on a spiritual journey with the Holy Spirit that had my whole house concerned, it took from Apr. the 12th to July the 3rd to where the Holy Spirit got me to where I put on paper the revelation of why the number "7" is Gods number, why 4/3 is the perfect combination of two equaling one "7" and how God looks on sexual immorality. I have* included this which I believe that you will also find it, what has been said is extra ordinary.

If I was not convinced that this is of God and the critical importance regarding our nation, the Church (people) in America I would not place this request of seeking your council. It's about the election of 2008, if this prophesy of the Holy Spirit or revelation is of God then who ever sits in the Oval Office after 2008 is going to usher us through the Tribulation period or up to when we fall and the whole world will mourn. I'm not going to talk about that now; I've already taken up more of your time than I wanted to. Thank you very much for listening to me and I will look forward to hearing from you hopefully soon. It is not about me, you or any one; it's all about Jesus, what He wants. He wants out of the boxes we have put Him in and out on the streets. I do know that He does not want that one soul should perish, not one. It took the Lord twenty one years of which seven of those years I sat in a Black Box convinced by Satan that I had committed the unpardonable sin, to get me to the place where I now have the fear of the Lord, which according to scripture is "the beginning of wisdom." That's why when the Lord freed me from that bondage on August the 6th, 2006 a Sunday at 1:00pm I moved into another realm spiritually which is revelations of the Holy Spirit. "The fear of the Lord is the beginning of wisdom" is a scripture that I really didn't like. I didn't want a God that I had to fear I wanted a God that I could love. How stupid of me, if you only knew how I have treated the things that I love over the years you would understand. The fear of the Lord is knowing that you cannot live without Jesus. There is no life without Jesus!

It is now 9:00pm Friday the 19th and I had finished editing this letter this morning and to my surprise I have been really down in the dumps all day. I was debating whether to mail this or not. I drove over to Shipshewana and talked to an Amish friend of mine who I have shared these revelations with. I said; Howard it's like I have this pot of gold I'm trying to share and nobody will take it. Nobody wants to know or will believe me. Later I was sitting in my favorite meditation spot, easy chair, debating if you would even read this long of a letter, which I have done everything to shorten and this revelation just came. I said that the Lords time clock was digital and had three dials on it and at the end it will read 777. I also said that it takes two (creations) to make one "7". If you add seven years to the date 4/3/2007 you have the date of 4/3/2014. If two equals one "7" then 14 divided by two equals "7"+"7" and 4/3 being the perfect combination of two equaling one "7" then the date (clock) does read as He said 777. So on midnight 4/3/2007 you have "777" and on 4/3/2014 you again have "777". The Beginning and the End, God the Father, God the Son and God the Holy Spirit, the 7 years of Tribulations. Thank you again for your patience and listening to me, I'll look forward to hearing from you.

To date 1/20/2008 I have not heard any response to this letter which I sent registered mail and it was signed for on 11/07/2007. I also mailed myself, registered mail, a copy of the material in a sealed envelope and put it in my safe for Copy right protection. The information your reading needs, which only I know what the Lord said and how it all came into being or together, the revelations.

Thank you and may God Bless You!

Chuck Mc Cuen

THE DEFINITION OF THE
ILLUSTRATIONS OF THE NUMBER "7"

I had a pastor ask me why dice? I told him that a dice has six sides, also numbered, just like man/woman or creation has six sides. Our head (6) and our feet (1) equals "7" or our front side (2), male organ, and our back side (5) equal "7" and our left side (4) and our right side (3) equal "7". Besides there is nothing wrong with dice, it's how they are used; there are many good, fun family entertainment games that use dice as a method of moving your token or piece. An example would be Monopoly or Yatzee.

1) The total of any two sides of a dice equal "7"

2) The top number of the dice is the number on your head.

3) God created man out of the soil and according to your writing a (6). So the high numbers (6) and (5) represents the heads, top, of male adults. The number (4) represents the head, top of a male child still in the age of innocence.

4) God took one rib out of Adams body while he slept and made woman to be a companion to Adam. So the low numbers (1) and (2) represent the heads, top, of the female adults. The number (3) represents the head, top of a female child still in the age of innocence.

5) The dice in this illustration are facing each other so that the numbers on the front of each dice represent their gender, male or female organs. Example, the (6) male has a (2), male organ, on the front of it and is facing the number (1) female which has a number (5), female organ,

on the front of it. Having sex the (2), male organ can penetrate or go into the (5) female organ. The number 2 is smaller than the number 5.

6) As I pointed out the sum of any two sides of a dice equal "7". The number (6) male is married to the number (1) female and the number (5) male is married to the number (2) female. Their married because the total of both heads equal one or the number "7". Having sex, in your mind just picture the (6) dice on the inside of the (1) dice. The total on the top (head), the left side, the right side and the bottom (feet) equal "7". On the back side of the (1) female is two (2's) and on the front side is two (5's) which say they are both creations of God, alike but opposite, and the sum of the two sides equal the number "7". Two opposites together can create another just like themselves.

7) In this illustration there are two families a (6) married to a number (1) and a number (5) married to a number (2). Each family had two children, the first family had a son (4) first and then a daughter (3) which are illustrated on the left side of the picture. The second family also had two children. They had a daughter (3) first and then a son (4) and they are illustrated on the right side of the picture. The two family's children are facing each other and on the front of them is the number which represents their organs, male or female. They have yet to reach the age of puberty or pass the age of innocence. They don't have sexual desires or drives yet or have yet to mature that way. Look at the total of the number "7" that is on their head standing side by side and across from one another. They are still in the age of innocence and under Gods protection. Woe to the person who harms one hair on their heads. That Is why 4/3 is the perfect combination of two making one, creation, or the number "7".

8) If you want to see why and how God looks on sexual immorality just move the number (6) with the number (2) or the (5) with the number (1) in sex. Envision one on the inside of the other, you can't get the number "7" any way you try or any side that you add

together. That's how He sees wife swapping, adultery or sex out of wedlock. If you want to see pedophiles just envision a (6), (5), (1) or a (2) sexually or inside of a (4) or a (3) plus look at the barrier "7" that you are crossing. If you want to see homosexuals just do the same thing with a (6) and a (6) or a (1) and a (1) or 6&5 or 1&2. You have the same problem, you are outside of God.

I don't know about you but I found this illustration, revelation of the Holy Spirit, well the only word I can come up with or has been spoken is extra ordinary at the least. I am interested in hearing your comments.

"ILLUSTRATION OF THE NUMBER "SEVEN"

DEFINITIONS

1) SATAN   = "8"   HE PUT HIMSELF ABOVE GOD AND GOT CAST OUT OF HEAVEN.
2) GOD   = "7"   THE NUMBER OF COMPLETION OR PERFECTION.
3) JESUS CHRIST = "4"   GOD THE SON. (THE BODY, HEART AND SOUL OF GOD).
4) HOLY SPIRIT   = "3"   GOD THE HOLY SPIRIT, (THE SPIRIT OF GOD).
5) MAN   = "6"   WE ARE GOD'S CHILDREN, MADE IN HIS IMAGE.
6) WOMAN   = "1"   MADE FROM ONE RIB OF ADAMS BODY WHILE HE SLEPT.
7) MALE-CHILD   = "4"   MALE CHILD STILL IN THE AGE OF INNOCENSE.
8) FEM. –CHILD   = "3"   FEMALE CHILD STILL IN THE AGE OF INNOCENSE.

THE HIGH NUMBERS ARE MALE NUMBERS AND THE LOW NUMBERS ARE FEMALE NUMBERS

"7"

"GOD THE FATHER"

LEFT HAND
GOD the "HOLY SPIRIT"

RIGHT HAND
GOD the SON "JESUS CHRIST"

"3"   **"4"**

"HOLY SPIRIT"   "GOD"   "JESUS CHRIST

HEAD = TOP NUMBER / BODIES FNT. = INSIDE NUMBERS / BODIES BCK. = OUTSIDE NUMBERS

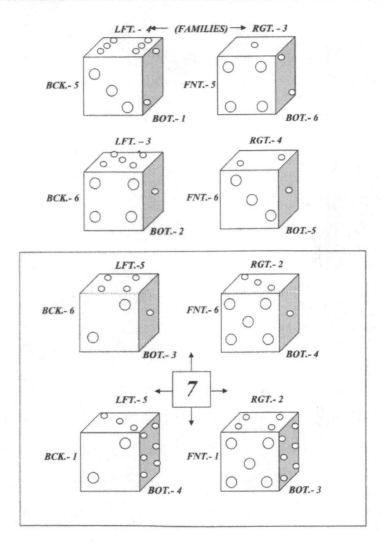

Date: 10/25/07 Thurs.
To: Whom it may concern.

I had originally written this to Pastor Lee and have changed my mind and decided to include it. I had Pastor Lee look over the material I was sending to you for any suggestions and this revelation and illustration, well I just had to send it along.

I awoke early this morning around 1:30 and decided to not get up so I rolled over and slept until around 5:00am, got dressed and went out to my meditation room (recliner). I started playing around with my palm pilot to get more familiar with the features and I got curious about Daniels prophesy of 70 weeks and the temple being rebuilt. I found it on my palm pilot and was shocked because all it said was that the wall would be built. I thought I must have a different version of the scripture in the Spirit Filled K.J. Bible I use so I went and got it. It was the same reading, so I went to the prophecy of the End of Times in Ch.12 and read it and it doesn't say anything specifically using the word Temple. I went back and read the 70 week prophesy again and I could see how I might of come up to that conclusion but I have spoken that and written that with boldness and confidence ever since the Holy Spirit had taken me to those scriptures back in late June. That whole interpretation had to have come from the Holy Spirit. Still questioning somewhat in my mind I went back and read the End of Times prophecy up to where Daniel talks about the 1290 days and the 1335 days trying to figure out what the light was that had gone on in my mind when I first read that.

I played around trying to cram the 1290 or 1335 days into a 3 ½ year bucket and they don't fit if you use a calendar of 360 or 365 days per year so I added the two together 1290 plus 1335 equals 2,625 days. This is the picture it took the Holy Spirit about one hour to get me to see. If His Words are alive and all scripture is written under the inspiration of the Holy Spirit then Daniels prophesies as they were interpreted using a 360 day year were correct for the interpretation of when they were applied in the old testament. The same prophesy (70 weeks) applied to the end of times would be based on a 365 day year. Look at what the Holy Spirit got me to see and the number "7" again.

1290 days and 1335 days equal   2,625 days
  7" years times 365 days equals 2,555 days

Difference   70   The prophecy of 70 weeks or 7.0 yrs. of Trib.
                                     And the time the Temple stands, see Attach...

"7" years times 365 days equals 2,555 days
"7" years times 360 days equals 2.520 days
Difference   35   Is ½ of 70 weeks or 3.5 yrs. mid. Tribulation

The 1290 days is from the beginning of the 7 years of Tribulations until the Temple falls.

The 1335 days is from the time the Temple is built until the end of Tribulations.
That means that the Temple would only stand for guess what. 70 days.

1) Dan. Ch.12:11 reads "And from the time that the daily sacrifice is taken away, and the abomination of desolation is set up (mid trib. When the Temple falls), there shall be one thousand two hundred and ninety days.

2) Dan. Ch. 12:1 reads "Blessed is he who waits, and comes to the one thousand three hundred and thirty five days.

Why? Because the Lord is saying "blessed are those who make it through the Battle of Armageddon, the "7" years of Tribulations." Pastor the two prophecies are tied together. The prophecy of the 70 weeks, alone was interpreted correctly using Old Testament time of 360 day cycles. The End of Times prophesy, the Lord just put the two prophesies together and used the time of today or 365 day cycles. He does know the "Beginning and the End", like it is written. This is what I mean when I talk about the footprints of the Holy Spirit. Just look at the logic, how much simpler could He have told us. Look at the number "7" that is woven all the way through these prophesies. .

In summary it will take 12 ½ days for the Temple and Jerusalem to fall because 3 ½ years of 365 days equals 1,277.5 days and the scripture says it will be on the 1,290th day that the abomination of desolation is set up, which is mid tribulation, verse #11. The reason the 70 week prophesy was broken up into 7wks., 62wks., and 1wk. is because the only way you can use two different calendars of time and say the same thing is to say it like it was written in (Dan. 9:27), "Then he shall confirm a covenant with many for one week; But in the middle of the week - He shall bring an end to sacrifice and offering. And on the wing of abominations shall be one who makes desolate, even until the consummation, which is determined, is poured out on the desolate"

I think the light that went off when I read those two dates of 1290days and 1335 days was that 1290 days is close to 3 ½ yrs and Dan. 12:11 talks about the daily sacrifice (temple) is taken away and the abomination of desolation is set up and I remembered that in Dan. 9:27 it talks about He shall bring an end to sacrifice and offering (temple) and on the wing of abominations shall be one who makes desolate. This is written about the middle of the one week or year or and also the middle of the 7 years. I'm almost sure that is what made me go back to the prophecy of 70 weeks. It had to have been the Holy Spirit that planted that seed or question. I am now sure that it had to have been the Holy Spirit that gave me the whole interpretation, all of them. There are too many "7"'s, way to many footprints or what some call coincidences, which I don't believe in. Pastor if you sit back and look at this whole picture from the middle of Dec., 2006 until now Oct. 25, 2007 if this is not of God do you realize how many questions "Why", that I am left holding on to. If it is God then I can tell you why I drank for 31 years, died (reborn), smoked five packs of cigarettes a day, lived in demonic hell most of my life and set in a Black Box without but a bubble of hope for "7" years. Just ask me anything and I'll tell you why. If it's not of God I don't know anything. I guess regardless, its all "Grace", I certainly know it's not works - should anyone boast.

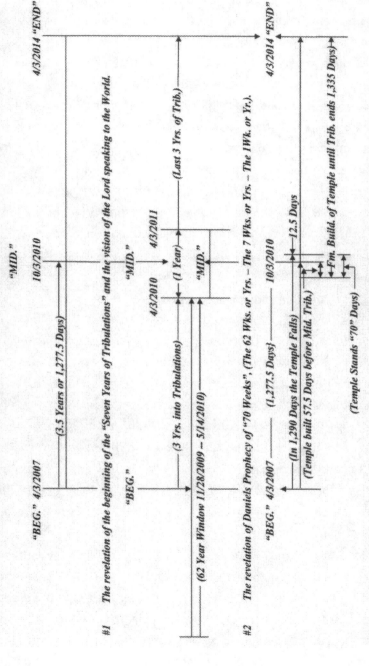

156

Israel was reinstated Israel was reinstated as a Country by the United Nations on 11/28/1947, they wrote a Constitution and established a Government on 05/14/1948. When you add 62 years to those dates you come up with a window that would be from 11/28/2009 to 05/14/2010.

#1 The revelation of the beginning of the "Seven Years of Tribulations" and the vision of the Lord speaking to the World.

#2 The revelation of Daniels Prophecy of "70 Weeks", (The 62 Wks. or Yrs. – The 7 Wks. or Yrs. – The 1Wk. or Yr.).

#3 Daniels Prophecy of The End of Times, Chapter 12: 11-12, when he talks about the 1,290 Days and 1335 Days.

Date: 11/01/2007
To: Whom it may concern:
From: Chuck Mc Cuen

Subject: Prophetic Visions;

This letter is much longer than I had anticipated but I am asking to be a voice at your gatherings; if you will please bear with me I believe you will understand. I had just gotten out of the hospital and heard about your call to Nashville on 7/7/07 and the forty day fast. Knowing nothing about either yourself or your call to Nashville; I still made the commitment to be there because of what all the Holy Spirit had taken me through in revealing the significance of the number "7" and knowing that fasting before the Lord will move mountains. I'm not going to take up your time now by telling you what the Lord has revealed to me but it has been an absolute Spiritual downpour ever since 8/6/2006 and on 7/7/2007 I was about just in the middle of this rain. I want to tell you what I experienced in Nashville. I came down from northern Indiana on bus with another Church and we arrived in Nashville around 6:00 PM Friday evening. You will find this rather exciting, our bus driver, who I am not sure was saved; the last four digits of his cell phone number were 7707. Before we got done with him I do feel comfortable that he is going to search for what we had. The rumor when we came into town was that the anticipated attendance had risen from 100,000 up to 250,000 so we changed our schedule for drop offs in the morning to go first to the stadium. I was there at the gates at least 1½ hours before you were scheduled to open and very close to the front of the line at the gate. The person I roomed with had health problems so we got good seats under the overhang of the box offices on the west side and we were in the shade around 11:00 AM. What the Lord has revealed to me has to do with the End of Times and what He has called me to do. From here on I am going to try briefly to explain what I experienced in Nashville.

It had to be now around 10:30 AM and the band was playing and the infield in front of the bandstand was packed with the youth who were on *their feet jumping up and down, swaying, weaving back and forth, rejoicing to the rhythm of the music. If that sight does not get you into the Spirit then I don't know what will. I found myself either on my feet or sitting with my whole body moving to the rhythm, sounds, watching the youth on the infield. The Lord gave me a vision; I saw the face of the Lord "Jesus;" totally covering the whole infield. You could no longer see the youth they were all under his head; face. I didn't find out until later that there is a scripture verse that says that the Lord is the Head and the Church, people; are the body. It was shortly after that vision that I found myself walking with the Holy Spirit and the Holy Spirit turned to me and said, Chuck; "Have you given your heart to Jesus?" That kind of startled me and I thought, searched my heart for resentments, un-forgiveness or any black spots and I didn't find anything, so I turned back to the Holy Spirit and said; "Yes, yes, yes I'm sure that I have, that I haven't overlooked anything." So I went back to absorbing everything that was going on. It was twenty or thirty minutes later and I found myself again walking with the Holy Spirit and He turned to me again and said; Chuck, "Have you given your whole heart; to Jesus?"*

I didn't handle this as well as what I'm sure Peter did when he walked with the Lord and the Lord turned to him and asked, Peter; "Do you love Me?" I mean I searched and I searched, I went back as far as I could remember to make absolutely sure that I wasn't harboring anything that I needed to make amends for and seek forgiveness of. I must have spent 15 or 20 minutes searching and finally I turned to the Holy Spirit; stuttering and said again; "Yes, yes, yes I'm sure I have, I know I have, and I can't find anything so yes I've given my whole heart to Jesus." Again I found myself back into the festivities of the day and another band was playing now so I'm again on fire watching the youth in the infield. It's now again 15 to 20 minutes have gone by and I find myself again walking with the Holy Spirit. The Holy Spirit turned; now for the third time and asked, Chuck; "Have you, truly; given your whole heart to Jesus?" That broke me; I'm sitting there in my seat crying; what have I missed, there has to be something. In my mind's eye I took a scalpel and severed my brain right down the middle and laid it flat open like a sacrificial lamb. I'm sure this vision came from a poster that I had seen in a doctor's office at one time; there, in my mind's eye was ½ on one side and the other ½ on the other side were like coiled springs of flesh with tiny fingers of blood weaving itself in and around everywhere; my brain. About two thirds the ways down in the middle, half on one side and the other half on the other side was a red pool; pear shaped, of blood or my heart. I picked up sections of flesh and looked under and over everything looking for dark spots. I even took and stirred the blood to see if anything showed up and I couldn't see or find anything. I'm crying and I go to the Lord and I said, Lord; "I can't find anything, there has to be something, just show it to me and I will take care of it. I give you permission Lord; just tear it out by the roots and throw it away I speak against whatever it is. Lord this is not a 98% deal; You either take all of me or none of me; I won't settle for anything less." I don't have any idea how long I sat there but a peace came over me so I felt that the Lord had resolved the problem; that it was gone. I tried to put the two halves of my brain back together and I couldn't get them to stay; they just would fall back open about ½ inch. I tried and tried to get them back together and I couldn't so I finally gave up for the time being and got back into what was going on. I did not know that we were going to have a wedding ceremony and get married to the Lord. If you remember there was a call to go down to the infield and I went. It was spoken off the platform that our hearts were being sewn together with the Lords and again in my mind's eye I saw the two halves of my brain held together and it was a golden needle shaped like a hook that was on a Pirates arm, in the movies. I watched as the two halves were stitched back together and then spoken off the platform it was sealed with the fire of the Holy Spirit and I saw, with my mind's eye; like back in Ancient Days, you would put hot wax on the seal of a letter and just before it dried you would press your signature ring into the wax; sealing the letter. I saw the Holy Spirit do that on that stitched seam of my brain.

It took several weeks for the revelation of what that exercise in faith was all about? The Lord was not questioning my servitude or cleanliness; He was letting me know that what it is that He has called for me to do is for an appointed time which is yet in the future. I am convinced if the Rapture occurs even at Post-Trib., I will not go. I am going to be left behind, not for long, but there is someone that I am going to bring with me. If you were to listen to the two prophetic tapes that I have from the Prophetic Ministry which is at the Church I rode down to Nashville with; you would understand. The Lord; I'm sure was telling me that in order to stand and do what it is that I'm to do I have got to be one string; one instrument playing one song and that song is "JESUS". It's not about you; it's not about me, and it's not about anyone but Him; "JESUS". It took the Lord twenty years to get me to the place that I now am. The best way I can define it to you is that it is written in Gal. 2:20 and I can tell you when and how that happened. August the 6th, Sunday at 1:00PM the Lord did what I would have told you not even God could get me out of this one. I sat; all kinds of medicine, for seven years in what is titled in the book that I am sending to the publishers next week; "The Black Box." Little he; believe it or not had me totally convinced that I had committed the unpardonable sin. On Aug, 6th God did the impossible; He freed me from bondage and not only freed me but put me at a level spiritually that I have never been at before. The title to my book is "Don't BE Late For The Wedding;" I went from miracles, visions and talking with the Lord; Holy Spirit to revelations of the Holy Spirit. Why; because when He let me out of that Black Box I now had something that I didn't have prior to going into that box. He revealed it to me in March of this year when I started writing my book, which He had me do, and I got to the chapter which is titled; the "Black Box." This is a scripture that I didn't like; that I didn't understand, the verse that says that; "The fear of the Lord is the beginning of wisdom." I now have the fear of the Lord and that is why He had me sit in that box for seven years. The fear of the Lord is to know that you cannot live without Jesus. That there is no life without Jesus; there's no air to breathe, no grass to mow or trees to clean up after in the fall. There is absolutely nothing without Jesus and I do not let Him get very far out of my sight any more.

I have had two other visions that pertain to your calling and I will tell you these with fewer words. One of the visions I was standing on the front porch of an old farm house and on the end of the porch was an old butter urn. So I went over and took the handle and moved it around and was surprised to find out that there was something in the urn. So I stood there and stirred the urn for several minutes and then began to lose interest and started to look around to see what else was in this vision of the Lord's. When I slowed down stirring the Lord spoke and said; "Keep stirring!" So I put both hands on the handle and stood there and stirred; stirred and stirred. I finally got curious as to what was going on because I had never seen a butter urn before other than in pictures, so I quit stirring and I bent over and looked down through that tiny opening in the top; into the inside. I was shocked; there were Pastors, Preachers, Priests, Ministers and the Church in there. I immediately looked up to the Lord and said; "Lord, I don't understand?" The Lord spoke and He said, Chuck; "The Church in America is asleep; there are people in the Church who don't even have a lantern and there are people in the Church whose lantern is only one third full." Well as I was thinking on what the Lord had just said the vision went away. I'm sitting there pondering over what the Lord had said and I heard a voice calling out from the Heavens; "Who will speak for Me?" "Who will speak for Me?" "Who will speak for Me?" I raised my hand and said; "I will speak for you Lord, You know I will; use me." The Lord was not questioning if I would speak for Him; what the Lord was showing me was that we in our minds have Him hidden in our hearts and locked up in boxes with ribbons on them. The boxes have titles; Methodist, 1st Baptist, Pentecostal, Catholic, etc. The Lord wants the Church to be woken up; the people filled up, (lanterns) and then to take Him with them out on the streets, into the market places, the barrooms, drug dens, to work or wherever you go. Take Him down into the ghettoes. If the Church in America does not take off its religious adornment; as He called it, when He spoke to the World in another vision that I had; unite, and become a voice in America, we are going to lose it. The ACLU (Anti-Christ Liberation Union) and pending legislation is going to end up taking the Churches First Amendment Right to the Freedom of Speech away. You will no longer be able to preach Sodom & Gomorrah in the Church, that homosexuality is sin, it is already proposed under the hate laws, which Canada passed over a year and a half ago.

The last vision I had and this is in late July or early August this year after 7/7/07. This vision when the first Angel speaks and says; "The date 8/16/2008;" then the second Angels speaks and says; "The place, Washington DC.;" the third Angel rolls down a short scroll and reads a number; "Five Million." I saw the streets in Washington D.C. were overflowing across the small sections of grass, the sidewalks and people were standing on the stair steps up to the apartment houses. Pennsylvania Blvd was packed with humanity; the Washington monument and the Lincoln Memorial lawns were packed with humanity; they were on the steps of the Federal buildings. It was a sea of humanity and the police had barricades set up on all the arteries coming into the city; busses and cars were pulled off the side of the roads and people were getting out walking down into the city. There were loud speakers that had been put up all around Washington. There were helicopters flying around Washington keeping an eye out for any planes that might try and come into the area. The Air Force was on alert status to take out any forbidden incoming flights. It was now later in the evening and I heard a voice crying out from the platform over the loud speakers; "Jesus," and then I heard 5 million voices cry out, repeating; "Jesus" and it just keep going back and forth, back and forth, "Jesus;" "Jesus," and the band picked up on the rhythm and started playing. We just stood there; arms in the air, faces turned to the Heavens crying out the Name "Jesus;" "Jesus." I saw the clouds part and there sitting on His throne in the Heavens was Jesus and He was surrounded by Angels and I say Him stretch out His arm and point down and He said; "These are My people;" "These are MY people." I saw ABC, CBS and NBC television cameras all over the area and I saw people all over the United States and the World watching their television sets as this was going on. The next morning; in the headlines on the front page of all the Newspapers, it reads; Five Million Cry out for Jesus in Washington, DC on 8/18/2008.

I had a Christian Psychologist, a friend of mine; when I told him about that vision say; let's ask for Ten Million. The Seven Years of Tribulations started on 4/3/2007 at midnight; I can prove to you that this was of God. On 4/2 and 4/3 I had the Holy Spirit all over me; I called everyone who I knew would listen and could possibly have heard or had seen something. I mean it had to be something big; I called the Pastor of the Church the Lord put me into as of Jan 7, 2007 and I told him the same thing that I had told everyone. I said that I felt like I was a bedbug that was sitting on the top of a sheet that was covering a sleeping giant and any minute this giant was going to pull back the sheet; throw out his legs and stand up and he was big; he was ugly. That night; Tuesday 4/3 we have a family group that gets together the *first Tuesday of every month; we have dinner and then the women like to play penny poker. I don't really enjoy that so I usually back out after desert around 9:30 and go in and lie down on the couch and listen to the conversations. This night it was around 10:30 PM and I had a vision; it was the Lord and He was speaking to the World. He spoke first to all lands, the World; Europe, Asia, Africa, etc. then He spoke to the United States; last He speaks to Israel. Well about the time the vision was over my wife said that they were finishing up and we were going to head for home. I get up early the next day and things had been happening so fast spiritually that I quit writing my book and had started journaling; which I have never done before; so I make the journal entry of the Lord speaking to the World. It was the way that I had worded what the Lord had said that bothered me. After journaling speaking to each section I wrote the words - Sayeth the Lord! I don't talk that way; I don't think that way and I don't write that way. I immediately went to the Lord and I said Lord; "Is that You or is that me?" I said Lord; "I have to know, either "Yes" it was You or "No" it was me, one way or the other. I told Him that I had a problem, that I was not used to revelations of the Holy Spirit, that I was used to visions and talking to Him. What I had written sounded an awful lot like I think but was it the Holy Spirit that got me to hear and read those scriptures so that I would understand when He spoke? The only thing I can tell you is that the Holy Spirit always leaves what I call footprints, others call those things coincidences which I don't believe exist. You cannot believe what I have gone through this last year. I told the Lord that I would stay before Him seeking the answer yes or no. For seven days of which the last three I went on a water fast I stayed before the Lord and every night I would find Him and every night the answer was "Yes". Hopefully you will find interest; I would love to have someone in the Prophetic line to counsel with. I'll just put it this way; there is no way or no one, not even time could convince me different than what I know. Benny Hinn says that you will never hear the voice of the Lord that He is up there on His Throne in Heaven. I didn't think that I would ever disagree with anything that Benny Hinn would say but I will tell you that on that issue he is wrong. The voice of the Lord is a very clear voice that comes from up/down into you. It would be like you and I having a conversation over a cup of coffee. The Holy Spirit has more of a* tendency to get you to see things, say things, hear things, read things. He like nudges you to do something or He will get you to go out of your way and buy something that you really don't need; only to find out three months later it is the exact thing that you had to have. The Holy Spirit does have a voice, but in me, it is a soft voice and it rises up from within you. I sometimes have to turn my head and strain to hear His voice.

I like usual have talked to much; I apologize, the reason that I am writing you this letter is because once the Lord convinced me of the things that He has shown me I went very humbly to Him and said; "Why me Lord? Why not Benny Hinn, Pat Robertson, Kenneth Copeland or you, I don't have a voice, known; who am I to tell?" The Lord just smiled and said; "Tell those who will understand." Today I understand why He was smiling when He said that; it's like a joke that the Pastor told the other month in Church. The punch line was that the Lords answer to the black man's prayer was; "I've been trying to get in there for twenty years and nobody will listen to Me either." I'm beginning to think that He was telling me; "I've been trying to tell them for forty years and no one will listen to me; you try it for awhile." I do have a voice and my heart is for those who are lost and the Lord is calling me to help wake up the Church in America. We are a Christian Nation; George Washington's farewell speech, which was taken out of the History books, in the schools, 1958 said that; "If you take Christianity and the Christian morals out of our Government and out of our Educational Institutions we will fall. They are the two pillars on which we were founded." Thomas Jefferson in reference to the Separation of Church and State said; "We would never become a Religious Government." That is why they fled England at the turn of the Century in the late 1600's was due to religious persecution I believe under Henry the 8th. The voice that is crying out "Jesus" off the platform in Washington DC on 8/16/2008 is my voice, I know it is. I am offering and asking if you will let me be that voice. I'll hitchhike if I don't have the money; time isn't a problem I'm sixty six years old now and will be sixty seven by then. If you need or could use me at any of the other scheduled events just let me know; I'll be there. I am not Hell fire and Brimstone and the World is coming to an End now. I'm love, hope and have a true compassion for alcoholics, drug addicts, prostitutes, homosexuals those who are lost and don't have.

You see I have had a very successful life in the business, accomplishment arena but from one swallow of vodka at the age of fourteen; thirty one years later was in excess of over ½ gallon of vodka every day and I smoked five packs of cigarettes every day for years and years. It's now been twenty one years since the Lord gave me new life; (reborn) and have not had a drink of alcohol and it's been at least ten years since He took cigarettes away from me. My book is to reveal a side of God that people either don't know or I know they don't talk about. I'm the only one that I know that runs around saying; "Well the Lord said this -------, or gave me this vision -------." I do want to help build a fire in the youth, they are the only way that we can salvage souls for His Kingdom and He does not want that one soul should perish; not one. I don't care how rough they may appear on the edges; He is love and if they will only turn to Him; He will be there with open arms. In closing there is nothing to fear except fear itself. Let me be a voice for the Lord, let me plant some seeds of hope and God. He wants a personal; daily, walking relationship with everyone. I believe that He is always talking; calling, it just that people don't know how to discern the voices and then there are those who have all the answers and won't listen. Then the most unfortunate of all are those who are traveling so fast they can't take the time to ask or the time to listen. I am sending this out and will look forward to hearing back from you; please, even if it is only to say that right now there is no room; which hopefully there will be. I already have the soundtrack of the song that I heard in that vision. It is Ron Connolly and the Hosanna praise and worship team who are singing at an auditorium in New Orleans. I even have a tape of that outing and when they play that song you just can't stay seated. I've used the cassette tape version many times during spiritual war or the battles I used to have to attend with. Will 8/16/2008 be a reality; I don't know. I only know that He says in His Word; "Can you believe? All things are possible to him who believes!"

May God be with you and your vision!

Chuck Mc Cuen

THE SIGNIFICANCE OF NUMBERS IN THE BIBLE:

I have already gone to great lengths to explain the significance of the number seven that runs through the Bible. Just in the Book of Revelations you have the 7 Churches, the 7 Candles, the 7 Angels, the 7 Seals and the 7 Bowls of Wrath that are poured out in the 7 Years of Tribulations. It starts out in Genesis with the creation of the week being 7 days long. That God works and creates for six days and on the 7th day He rests and man has used 7 days as being a standard of measurement in time since the beginning of time.

Well it is 3:30 AM on a Friday morning and I can't sleep; as a matter of fact I am up, dressed, turned the thermostat up and sitting out in the living room in my easy chair. Last night the Holy Spirit started nudging me again to start reading the Bible. I told you earlier that I have never read the whole Bible cover to cover; well, I told you that so that you would understand that what I have written is not from my studies of the related subjects which I have spoken on. That was not something that I was boasting on, or to be quite frank, that I am pleased with myself for not having done yet. So I read a little in the New Testament last night and this morning I took the Bible out to the front room with me and decide to read some more until I get tired and then, more than likely, just dose off back to sleep again. I decided to start with the New Testament in the 1st Book, Mathew and just begin to read the whole New Testament all the way from Mathew through Revelations. I read Mathew Chapter 1:1-17; which is titled "The Genealogy of Jesus Christ", what I call the "Begot's" and have never really gotten anything out of that section when reading it before. Today I get another revelation and that is why I am writing again.

I told you about the young man that my spiritual mentor and I talked with and how he said that if we could prove to him that Jesus was from the linage of King David that he would believe us. That it was Clint, my spiritual mentor that had done that for the young man and that he converted his beliefs over to Christianity as a result of that. Well verse Mat. 1:1 says; "The book of the genealogy of Jesus Christ, the Son of David, the Son of Abraham:" and so forth. It concludes in verses 16 and 17 which written is; 16) And Jacob begot Joseph the husband of Mary, of whom was born Jesus who is called Christ. 17) So all the generations from Abraham to David are fourteen generations, from David until the captivity in Babylon are fourteen generations, and from the captivity in Babylon until the Christ are fourteen generations. At the bottom of the Scriptures it is written in definition of Mat. 1:1-17; that Matthews purpose in recording the genealogy was twofold: 1) to demonstrate continuity between the Israel of the O.T. and Jesus; 2) to demonstrate Jesus royal lineage (Son of David) and His link with the founder of the Jewish race (Son of Abraham). I wanted you to see the significance of those first seventeen verses and that footnote at the bottom in respect to what Clint had shared with the young man that evening in regards to the heritage or lineage of Jesus Christ to King David and Abraham.

The revelation that I got was in the number fourteen. I had never seen the consistency of verse seventeen which again said; 17) So all the generations from Abraham to David are fourteen generations, from David until the captivity in Babylon are fourteen generations, and from the captivity in Babylon until the Christ are fourteen generations. I do not know if the number fourteen shows up with significance in the Old Testament or again in the New Testament, or not, but just the significance of that number in verse seventeen of Matthew Chapter One in regards to the date that the Lord told me that the Seven Years of Tribulations began, on midnight EST of 4/3/2007, is overwhelming. We are in the time of completion of Man's separation from God and Satan's reign on the Earth. When the Lord spoke to the World that evening in the vision that I told you of, He closed saying that; "I Am now going to prepare for My return" and He slammed the door shut when He left. I, in the Spirit, heard it slam shut! *According to the Book of Revelations and I believe that as I am now sitting here writing this page and sense He slammed the door shut on 4/3, midnight EST, 2007 that there is a war going on in the Heavens. The Lord is not just sitting up there on His throne, bidding His time while these 7 years pass; He is cleaning House, so to speak. When His house, soon to be ours also, is clean, then the 7 Years of Tribulations will be over and He will return to clean this mess up here on the Earth. This will not take that long to do, but I believe that Satan, his demons or fallen angels will be spewed out of Gods mouth and the Millennium, or 1.000 years of Heaven on Earth will begin.*

The significance of the number 14 in regards to the End of Ages is this; theology has the Creation of Adam (Man) being 4,000 BC and that the Holy Spirit said: How do they know it was precisely 4,000 BC? What if it was 3,986, four months and three days when God created Adam? Regardless of either, when the year 2,000 rolled over we entered the last cycle of fourteen. The final cycle or completion of mans time on the Earth. The Seven Years of Tribulations did start at midnight on 4/3/2007 and Christ will return and appear in the sky on 4/3/2014. As I stated in the earlier Articles that on 4/3/2007 you had "777", with the third seven being the hour glass that had seven years of sand in it was turned over and on 4/3/2014 you again had the number "777" by dividing the number fourteen by 2 (Male/Female) you have 77 and the fourth month, the third day being the third 7. You also have the completion of the final fourteen year cycle or the perfection Gods, (Man and Time), when you reach the year 2014.

Every time I ask the Lord; am I still going the right way? This happens! I asked Him that question again a little over one week ago and you would not believe what all has happened, spiritually, sense then. Just like I told my Publisher; I am no longer going to say "This is the end, the final chapter to my book". When you get to the page that says "Section Three" then it is finished. I am laughing, but I just stuck these two pages here in the middle because I have closed this book, only Heaven knows, how many times by now.

Just reason with me one more time! I was just thinking again on; why did they have Roman guards set watch over the tomb of Jesus Christ? If you were a Disciple or a follower of Christ would you steal His body from the tomb and hide it; then go out and put your life on the line confessing that He was Lord and had risen up from the grave into the Heavens, knowing it was a lie? Then why would the Pharisees or their followers steal the body; they want to be able to prove that He was a lie; didn't they? If what I have written in this book is not from God; then you tell me where it came from and why? What I have written certainly isn't something that Satan would want you to know and why would I put myself up for ridicule if I didn't believe in what I've written?

"GOD THE "TRINITY"

I still have to go back to John 1:1-3 where it is written, "In the beginning was the Word and the Word was with God and the Word was God." That, "He was in the beginning with God. All things were made through Him, and without Him nothing was made that was made." He and Him is Jesus Christ. Then in John 14:6-14 Jesus makes it even clearer to Disciples. Jesus said to him, "I am the way, the truth and the life. No one comes to the Father except through Me. If you had known Me, you would have known my Father also; and from now on you know Him and have seen Him." Phillip said to Him, "Lord show us the Father and it will be sufficient for us." Jesus said to him, "Have I been with you so long, and yet you have not known me, Phillip? He who has seen Me has seen the Father; so how can you say show us the Father?" Do you not believe that I am in the Father and the Father in Me? The words that I speak to you I do not speak on My own authority; but the Father who dwells in Me does the works. "Believe Me that I am in the Father and the Father in Me, or else believe Me for the sake of the works themselves." To me Jesus Christ is the body of God. He is the heart and the soul of God. He is the only face of God that you will ever see. God is Spirit and words are spiritual. God is the heart or Jesus Christ is the heart of God. What comes out of your mouth is the overflow of your heart. God was the Word and the Holy Spirit was the deliverer and it all came out of the heart of Jesus Christ.

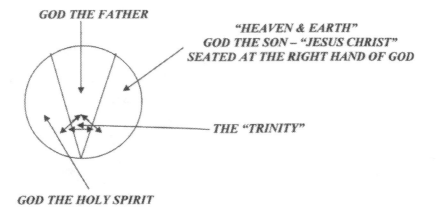

GOD THE FATHER

"HEAVEN & EARTH"
GOD THE SON – "JESUS CHRIST"
SEATED AT THE RIGHT HAND OF GOD

THE "TRINITY"

GOD THE HOLY SPIRIT

Man in "Three" Parts:

Kenneth Hagen wrote that "Man is a spirit that lives in a body and has a heart and a soul. These are my beliefs. Your spirit, heart and soul will live for eternity either in Heaven or in Hell. The Bible says that we will get a new body when we get to Heaven. It is your spirit man that moves your body. Your soul is the storage center for everything you have ever done, ever said, ever read, everything you have seen, felt or everywhere you have ever been. You have spiritual ears and spiritual eyes that can hear the voice of the Holy Spirit, Jesus Christ and see visions of which all of the above are inside. I can see a vision from the Lord and be driving down the road at the same time. Your heart is, I picture it, the absolute center of your soul and it encompasses the whole inside of your skull. I picture it as a deep sea diver's helmet that twists onto his diving suit. Your heart is who you are, it's your will (what you do), it's your emotions, your feelings and what you believe. Here is a picture of a person who has given his heart to the Lord and a picture of a person who has not given their heart to Jesus

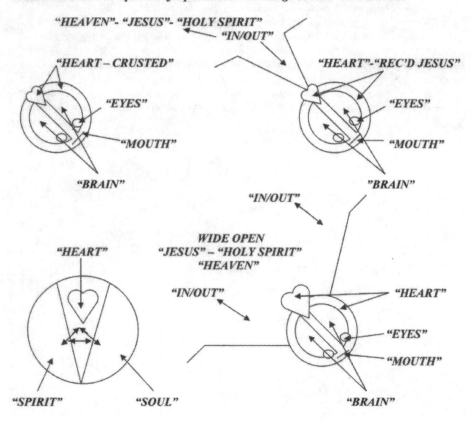

"GOD THE "INFINITE"

Genesis 1: 1-23   In the beginning "God" created the "heavens" and the "earth" (2) The earth was without form, and "void"; and darkness was on the face of the deep. And the Spirit of God was hovering over the face of the waters. (3) "Then God said, "Let there be light"; and there was light. (4) And God saw the light; that it was good; and God divided the light from the darkness. (5) God called the light Day, and the darkness He called Night. So the evening and the morning were the first day. (6) Then God said, "Let there be a firmament in the midst of the waters, and let it divide the waters from the waters." (7)   Thus God made the firmament, and divided the waters which were under the firmament from the waters which were above the firmament; and it was so. (8) And God called the firmament Heaven. So the evening and the morning were the second day. (9) Then God said, "Let the waters under the heavens be gathered together into one place, and let the dry land appear"; and it was so. (10) And God called the dry land Earth, and the gathering together of the waters He called Seas. And God saw that it was good. (11) The God said, "Let the earth bring forth grass, the herb that yields seed, and the fruit tree that yields fruit according to its kind, whose seed is in itself, on the earth"; and it was so. (12) And the earth brought forth grass, the herb that yields seed according to its kind, and the tree that yields fruit, whose seed is in itself according to its kind. And God saw that it was good. (13) So the evening and the morning were the third day. (14) Then God said, "Let there be lights in the firmament of the heavens to divide the day from the night; and let them be for signs and seasons, and for days and years; (15) "and let them be for light in the firmament of the heavens to give light on the earth"; and it was so. (16) Then God made two great lights; the greater light to rule the day, and the lesser light to rule the night. He made the stars also. (17) God set them in the firmament of the heavens to give light on the earth, (18) and to rule over the day and over the night, and to divide the light from the night, and to divide the light from the darkness. And God saw that it was good. (19) So the evening and the morning were the fourth day. (20) Then God said, "Let the waters abound with an abundance of living creatures, and let birds fly above the earth across the face of the firmament of the heavens; (21) So God created great sea creatures and every living thing that moves, with which the waters abounded, according to their kind, and every winged bird according to its kind. And God saw that it was good. (22) And God blessed them, saying, "Be fruitful and multiply, and fill the waters in the seas, and let the birds multiply on the earth" (23) So the evening and the morning were the fifth day.

"ILLUSTRATION"

  God is "Omnipotent", Almighty, having unlimited authority and influence. "Omnipotence", Force of unlimited power. "Omnipresent", Present in all places at all times. "Omnificent", Unlimited in creative power.

  In Russia in the early 1990's they had dug a pit straight down into the earth in Siberia. I'm sure they were trying to find away to dispose of nuclear waste. They were down approximately twenty miles deep, further that man had ever gone, and they couldn't get anyone to go back down to continue digging in that hole. The screams of torment were so severe that they couldn't tolerate it, they were afraid. I read this myself and it got shut up so fast that you never heard anymore about it, to my knowledge, anywhere. The minister of the Church I was attending said; that six scientists from around the World had sought visa and permission from Russia to go in and study those sounds and they were denied access. To my knowledge no one has ever gone back, it either has been filled in or is boarded up and fenced off.

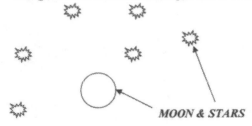

MOON & STARS

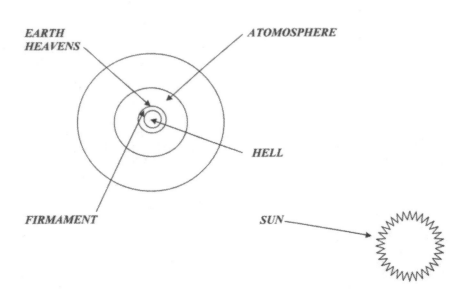

EARTH
HEAVENS

ATOMOSPHERE

HELL

FIRMAMENT

SUN

"GOD IN THE "FINITE"

1) *"NEUTRONS" Are neutral going one way and separate the "ELECTRONS" from the "PROTRONS". "NEUTRONS" represent men and women, children of God or creation.*
2) *"PROTRONS" Are a negative field in the center, going the wrong way, (Satan) or the center of the earth. The pull of gravity is from the center of the earth so is Satan, he is tempting and tempts you to go the wrong way, against God.*
3) *"ELECTRONS" Are a positive field on the outside, going the right way, (Jesus Christ) and the Angels which are in Heaven. He unlike Satan will not force Himself on you but promises that if you will receive Him and believe Him, forgive and ask for forgiveness. He is faithful and will do all He said that He would do in His "Word". If you open your heart to Him, you will spend eternity in heaven when you die.*

Satan is a deceiver, he is a tempting influence trying to get you to do wrong, against God (Jesus Christ). He doesn't have horns on his head and wear a red cape, he is spirit, and he comes in beautiful, handsome bodies and his best works are in drugs, alcohol, gambling, cigarettes, greed, lust, hate, envy, sloth etc...

"ILLUSTRATION" - "ATOM"

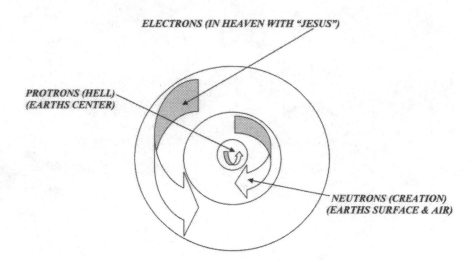

ELECTRONS (IN HEAVEN WITH "JESUS")

PROTRONS (HELL) (EARTHS CENTER)

NEUTRONS (CREATION) (EARTHS SURFACE & AIR)

GOD'S TIME TABLES

The other week I was explaining more to my Pastor about Genesis and how that God created and perfected in six days and then on the seventh day He rests. In respect to the significance of the number "Seven" to God, it also says in the Scriptures (Bible) that we are to "keep the Sabbath Holy," the seventh day of the week. The Pastor asked me, questionably; "Is Sunday the first day of the week or is it the last day of the week?" This is what the Holy Spirit revealed to me and it makes more sense than either the Greek, Jew or common Theology has defined it. The Lord says that the Sabbath is to be Holy, that it is a day that we set aside every week to "Worship God". Wednesday evening is a common day in which we have mid-week services and sits on top of day 3 & 4 or "7". So a week in all reality looks like this illustrated below. If the Lord is going to reveal something to you, regarding time, do you not think that He would use your time zone, your calendar, your definition of a week or do you think that He would use the Greenwich Meridian Time Zone and the Israel calendar of 12 months of 28 days each and every four years they add another month? He would make it a mystery that you would have to figure out.

ONE DAY TO GOD IS 1,000 YEARS TO MAN - "GENESES"

← GOD CREATED AND PERFECTED →						←RESTED→
DAY	DAY	DAY	DAY	DAY	DAY	DAY
1	*2*	*3*	*4*	*5*	*6*	*7*

SUNDAY IS THE END OF ONE WORK WEEK AND THE BEGINNING OF THE NEXT WORK WEEK.

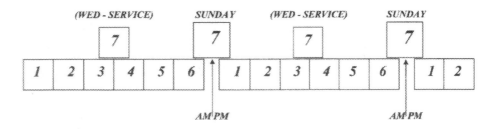

THE "GREAT SEAL" U.S.DOLLAR

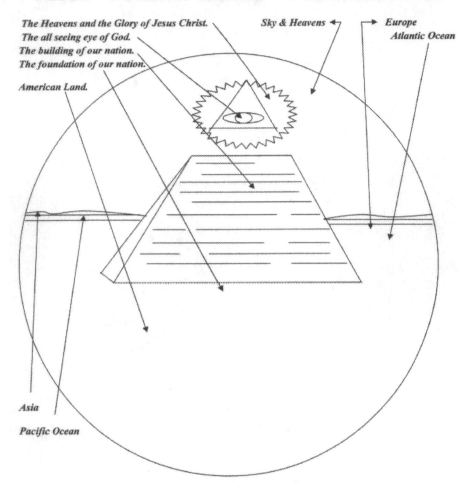

The Heavens and the Glory of Jesus Christ.
The all seeing eye of God.
The building of our nation.
The foundation of our nation.

American Land.

Sky & Heavens

Europe
Atlantic Ocean

Asia

Pacific Ocean

This is on the back left side of a One Dollar bill.

GREAT SEAL - SOMETHING TO THINK ABOUT:

I have included the Great Seal that is on the back of the one dollar bill. They have even made movies about how this is a secret to a buried treasure back when our country was founded and the Holy Spirit showed me that early one morning just last week. It is a good lead into the Christian foundation of our country and I have included the web site where you can get access to some very good information on the subject about our Christian Heritage.

One of our Founding Fathers, George Washington, said in his farewell speech to the Nation, as he was about to finish his administration as President; "If we take Christianity and the Christian Morals that are taught in the Bible out of our Government and out of our Educational Systems, we will fall. They are the two pillars on which we are founded." That was taken out of our History books and our Educational Institutions in 1958. Another Founding Father said that; "There is no Nation large enough to control the people if the people cannot control themselves; and the only way that the people can control themselves is to be taught Christianity and the Christian Morals that are taught in the Bible." Another great spokesman for our Nation said; "that, it is the Education of this generation, that will become tomorrow's leaders." Winston Churchill was quoted as having said after WWII; "If we fail to learn from History, then it is bound to repeat itself." John F. Kennedy said; "Ask not, what your country can do for you; ask what you can do for your country" and Martin Luther King said; "I had a dream!"

Those were very wise quotes and it is unfortunate that we did not take them seriously. If you want to know about the Christian Foundation of our Country, the US, I suggest that you go to www.wallbuilders.com. David Barton is an Historian and studied early American History for I'm sure it's been over thirty years by now. He has a lot of videos and books that you can order for a very reasonable expense and they are well worth your investment if you want to know about what are country was built on and why. If you want to know what has happened since we took George Washington's Farewell Address out of the History books in 1958 and then in 1962 we took prayer out of the schools and rewrote the definition of "Separation of Church and State." Just look at how education levels have just plummeted downhill and how divorces and common law marriages have sky rocketed. How homosexuality has been on a rapid, continual increase and how murder, rape and crimes of passion have sky rocketed and our prisons are overflowing with drug and alcohol problems.

I said those things because of what the Lord said when I had the vision of speaking to the World on Apr. 3, 2007. I know there are those who will say; "I'm a Catholic, Lutheran or whatever denomination and go to Church fairly regularly" or "I gave my life to the Lord when I was seventeen years old. I know that I haven't been in Church for many years but I'm okay." Or "We're blessed; we are Americans, just look at what our country has done for others. Were saved, we are okay, there is nothing to worry about." I know that the Bible says that there is only one sin that is unpardonable and that is "Blasphemy against the Holy Spirit," Mat. 12:31, but it does not say that "Once saved, always saved." It also says that; "My people perish; die, due to lack of knowledge, Hos. 4:6. That's lack of knowledge in God's Word, the Bible. He also says that; "You would be better off to have never heard the Word, than to have heard it and believed it, then turn away from it again," 2Pet. 2:21. It also says that; "My Words are life to those who find them and health to all your flesh," Pro. 4:20-22. He also says that; "Heaven and Earth will pass away but my Words will never pass away," Mark 13:31. Then in John 1:1-5 it says; 1) "In the beginning was the Word and the Word was with God and the Word was God." 2) "He was in the beginning with God." 3) "All things were made through Him, and without Him nothing was made that was made." 4) "In Him was life, and the life was the light of men." 5) "And the light shines in darkness, and the darkness did not comprehend it." When He or I spoke to the World that evening of July 3, 2007 the United States was called Babylon and that we were going to fall. He spoke harshly against our Government for turning its back on its own people and looking always at World Politics and World Economy. The burden of taxation is on the poor or the middle class people in America and not on the wealthy. It was spoken harshly against the ACLU; they were referred to as the Anti Christ Liberation Union. It was also spoken to the Church in America and the ministers were told to take off their religious apparel and to start preaching the day of the Lord. You see we not only have locked God up in boxes called "Religion", we also have locked His Word up in a box called; "Theology". His Word is alive, it's not done, said, over with. His Word was written for the Beginning and today just like it was written for the times in which it was written. He says; "Heaven and Earth will pass away, but My Words will never pass away," Mark 13:31. He also says; "My Word is sharper than a two edged sword; dividing to asunder joints and morrow, spirit and soul; and is a discerner of the thoughts and intents of the heart," Heb. 4:12. Yes you don't want to take scripture out of context, you don't' turn love into hate etc. but get it on the inside, speak it out of your mouth and stand on it. If He said it is; then it is.

That is part of the reason I struggled with the Lord asking if that was Him or if that was me speaking. I know it is a lot the way I feel about things but then again was it the Holy Spirit that got me to read those scriptures, see those things I've seen and hear the things I've heard? The Lord has since shown me many things that I feel a lot more comfortable that it had to have been Him speaking that night. He gave me a vision back in July of 2007. I was standing on the front porch of an old farm house and there was a butter urn over on the end of the porch so I went over and took the handle and moved it around. There was something in the urn so I stood there stirring for awhile and then began to look around to see what else was in this vision and the Lord spoke, He said; "Keep stirring." So I put both hands on the handle and I stood there stirring and stirring. I finally got curious; I have never seen a butter urn before, so I stopped stirring and looked down through that small opening at the top of the urn and inside there were Preachers, Priests, Ministers, Pastors and the Church (people). I immediately looked up and said; "Lord I don't understand?" The Lord spoke and said; "Chuck; The Church in America is asleep, there are people in the Church, (buildings), who don't even have a lantern. There are people in the Church whose lanterns are only 1/3 full. There are those who don't even preach the Word anymore and don't talk to one another outside of their own beliefs." The vision obviously left and I was thinking on what the Lord had said and I heard a voice crying out from the Heavens; "Who will speak for Me", "Who will speak for Me", "Who will speak for Me?" I raised my hand and said; "I will speak for you Lord, you know that I will, use me Lord." My friends He was not questioning if I would speak for Him. He drew me a diagram on paper that showed several boxes on the bottom wrapped with a ribbon, a bow on top and He labeled each box with a different denominational name. Then He drew about eight circles above the boxes, representing people and two of the circles had an "x" in them representing that they went to Church on Sunday and He drew a line from them to one of the boxes. In the middle of the line He wrote "One day a week, Sunday, one hour and $5.00 in the offering plate". He then wrote "do you see a problem with this picture?" The problem that He got me to understand is that some of us go to Church exactly that way and when we leave the Church we leave Him back there in that box with the ribbon on it and go back out into the world, fill our ice chest up with beer, and party. He wants out of the boxes that we have put Him in, He wants out in the market place, in the bar rooms, the work place, in our homes, in the ghetto's and out on the streets where the lost and hopeless are. If you Love the Lord then let's go give Him away. You don't have to beat people up with the Word just be hope where there is no hope, be peace where there is turmoil, be laughter and Joy where there is depression and be concern where there is sorrow. Just plant seeds that there is a God and He is a God that you would want to have in your life, He is Love and Hope. He will see that the seeds get watered, if someone thanks you or wants what you have then you can tell them where you got it, then you can tell them about the Lord. If the Church in America does not pull together and become a voice then we are going to lose it. There is pending legislation, as I am writing this book, to strike out against the Churches preaching Sodom and Gomorrah, that homosexuality is a sin and that you will not inherit the Kingdom of God if you partake and insist on it. It was proposed under the hate laws and Canada, I was told, passed that law into effect over a year ago. Read 1 Cor. 6:9-10 "Do you not know that the unrighteous will not inherit the kingdom of God? Do not be deceived. Neither fornicators, nor idolaters, nor adulterers, nor "homosexuals," nor sodomites, nor thieves, nor covetous, nor drunkards, nor revilers, nor extortioners will inherit the kingdom of God."

The reason that we are Babylon is because the people of Babylon were of one tongue, one mind and they were going to build a tower that would go up into the Heavens. So the Lord made them fall, He babbled their tongues and disbursed them from the city. Babylon was the power of the day back then. Who is that power today? When the signs of the end of times began to show up, with increasing magnitude was after WWI, which was followed by prosperity, the attempt to abolish alcohol and the rise of bootleg whiskey, gangsters, the flappers and the Charleston dance; the women cut their hair short and lowered their skirt line and neck lines. We had the move of woman suffrage, their right to vote. Then the great stock market crash in the late 1920's followed by the Great Depression. Did God do that due to our disobedience? Just look at the boom of technology since the turn of the 1900's up to today. It was WWII, the attack on Pearl Harbor by Japan that brought us out of the Great Depression, then the German slaughter of the Jews, and our involvement militarily in Europe. Einstein begged the Government not to use his discovery of the Atom for weapons of war and we didn't listen to him. We are the only country that has ever used an atomic weapon in warfare when we dropped two bombs on Japan. One on Aug. 6th, 1945 on the Island of Hiroshima and then on the Island of Nagasaki on Aug. 9th, 1945. That sound shook the Heavens and that the US, (Babylon), had just built the tower that went into the heavens. Look at what happened in America after WWII, the baby boom, woman now in the factories the work force, it now takes two people working in a family just to survive and nobody is home with the children. We never had taxes until after World War I. Taxes were imposed to pay off the War debt that we had incurred with the promise that they would be done away with after the debt was paid off; and look at what we have today. Our Nations focus was turned to across the oceans on World Economy, World Politics, then we go to war in Korea which is still going on; we go to war in Viet Nam and then in Iraq, now back in Iraq again. We take George Washington's farewell speech out of the History books in 1958 and then prayer out of the public schools in 1962 and rewrote the Separation of Church and State. What we did was we took God out of both our educational systems and our Government. We, as a country, turned our backs onto God. Did you know that Senators and Congressmen used to stand up and quote scripture in argument as to their being opposed to; or in favor of proposed legislation? I wonder if that still happens today. And then we had a President that claimed having oral sex with another is not sex; or adultery. Mat. 5:28 said; "But I say to you that whoever looks at a woman to lust for her has already committed adultery with her in his heart."

I just returned from our Monday intercessory prayer group and I removed the next comment that I had made. I was about to throw mud and He spoke this out of my mouth not twenty minutes ago. It's Mat. 7:3; "Why do you look at the speck that is in your brother's eye, and you refuse to look at the plank that is in your own eye?" It also says in Mat. 7:1; "Do not judge, for as you judge you so shall be judged and as you measure it will be measured back unto you." That is known as the law of reciprocity; you reap what you have sown. It is also written that "Christ did not come to abolish the Law or the Prophets; He came to fulfill them." It is also written that; "He came that we might have life, and have it more abundantly." This time when He returns it was written in my journal that; "I am now going to prepare for My return, and this time I am not coming back to heal the sick and give sight to the blind. I am coming back with vengeance; said the Lord." The scripture in Revelations says that when He appears in the sky He has eyes of fire and His feet are clad in fine brass. Rev. 2:18.

Now back to why we are Babylon. We are the first ones to go to the moon, then to walk on the moon. Not much later we go to Mars and take pictures and bring back samples of the rocks, etc. I heard the other day that we have plans to put atomic, laser ray guns in space to orbit around the Earth and that Russia is really up in arms against it. Just set the coordinates, then push a button and "poof" there goes a city. The advancement of technology is at such a rapid increase that if you buy a computer today in two years it is outdated and slow. The drop in education levels of the students graduating today compared to back in the 1950's, the rise in common law marriages, divorces, the abortions, homosexuality, the rise of unwed teenage pregnancies, the increase in usage of drugs (sorcery) and alcohol, the rise in crime, violent crimes of passion and murder; that our prisons are overflowing with drug and alcohol problems. The changes in weather patterns; the amount and severity of tropical storms, volcanic upheavals, tidal waves, tornado's, and the fires in the mountains and on the west coast. We don't get the annual rainfall that we used to get and our fresh water tables are down. Is that because we have been mowing down the rain forests in South America in twenty mile wide strips, year after year? I just heard on the radio two weeks ago that the United States and Russia are pooling their resources and going the Moon and to Mars in search of what, (Water)? What has happened to all of the woodland, forests that used to be in Northern America and the rich eight to ten inches of black topsoil? On a windy day in the late spring, after the crops are planted; it looks like a horizontal, modern art painting in brown; when you drive pass the farmlands. Why did the whales and porpoises beach themselves; committing suicide a few years back? Did they know that it is coming to an end; or was it because of all the nuclear waste and garbage that we have been burying in the oceans, because we have yet to figure out a way to dispose of it? Or have we driven them nuts with our experimentations and use of sonar waves to manipulate our submarines through the hidden depths of the oceans? If we have not built a tower that goes into the heavens and if this does not qualify for the "Signs of the End of Times", my friends, then I don't know what will and I certainly would not want to be here if it doesn't. Do I need to explain further? The good news is that He is coming back; please tell our brothers and sisters, the Jews, Israel and that it may be soon. The best news is that it is not too late; you have not gone too far, that salvation and life eternal is still an open invitation if you will receive Him into your heart and believe Him, repent and turn from your wicked ways, and then you too; will inherit eternal life, salvation.

The Lord has blessed me with many visions of which I have only shared a few with you but I want to tell you of this one before I finish. This vision was of giant people who had long necks with small heads on them and their heads were sticking up above the clouds. Their faces, eyes, were staring forward and they had a look of arrogance and pride on their faces as they looked at the missiles traveling off into space and the satellites orbiting around the earth. What they didn't see was that their giant feet, their shoes were crushing down houses and stepping on the people down below injuring and killing them. I don't know; I'll leave it up to you to decide if this is of God, Satan (demonic) or Man. Maybe just a wild imagination, maybe I missed my calling and should have written science fiction novels for the movies. The only thing that I will say in my defense, in His defense, is that He is just like He said that He was, unreasonable or above our ability to reason. After all that the Holy Spirit has taken me through in the last fifteen months I'm inclined to think that the Rapture will be Post-Trib. The Bible does say that Christians will be persecuted in the End Times and I think if we were to be told the truth about the financial status of our Nation you will find out that we are not only deep in debt but broke. There is no money in the Social Security fund, there is nothing but IOU's in there. There is no gold or silver in reserve to back up our currency. True or not, I just heard the other day that we are borrowing money from Japan. They just keep printing and minting currency under the pretense that it is to replace worn out money. If you are still here after the Mid Tribulation period it is going to be a difficult time for many. Our country and the people are so deeply in debt and money is going to be all but worthless. I can see it being like the Great Depression and possibly under martial law by another power near the End, and the return of the Lord. I'm not going doom and gloom on you; if you know the Lord there is nothing to fear except fear itself. I just think that it is later than you may realize and my two concerns are that number one; you give the Lord a chance. He loves you; after all He died for you. Luke 1:37 says; "With God, nothing shall be impossible." The Lord also says in John 14:13-14; "And whatever you ask in my name, that I will do, that the Father may be glorified in the Son. If you ask anything in my name, I will do it." Number two; I'm concerned that no one is talking and I'm afraid of our ability to deal with these Tribulations if *we don't wake up to the reality that we could possibly be here up to the end. Like I've said several times already it doesn't really matter when He is coming back; what matters is are you ready, do you have a lantern and is it full of oil and the wick trimmed, or will you be caught sleeping? He says in His Word, Mat. 24:40; "there will be two standing in the field, one will go and the other will stay", that was written in regards to End Times and the Rapture. I just don't want anyone to be late for the Wedding, caught off guard and haven't made any preparations. I just want that you see the possibilities of what could be sitting out there in front of us and possibly not that far into the future, over the horizon. Some questions you may want to console with your minister on. Most of these cannot be answered and some of them they may have an opinion on but really don't know the answer to. Just consider the questions below, I can't tell you the answers, but I have already expressed my opinion on some of them.*

1) *Once saved! Always saved?*
2) *Will the rapture of the Church (people) be, Pre-Trib., Mid -Trib. or Post-Trib.?*
3) *Does the Pastor have regular altar calls for salvation?*
4) *Is the Church preparing you for the possibility of Post-Trib. rapture?*
5) *Is the Word of God "Bible" alive or the Living Word of God?*
6) *Do they preach in your Church both the Old Testament and the New Testament?*
7) *Do they believe in the Gifts of the Holy Spirit and that they are available to whoever the Lord pleases?*
8) *Do they know the people? Do they all have Lanterns and keep them full with the wicks trimmed, in preparation for the Lords return? Do they even understand what or why?*
9) *Does the Minister preach out of the Word of God, "Bible" or other sources of information?*
10) *Are you Spirit filled?*
11) *Was Old Testament Prophecy for one time or for all times, all qualifying situations?*
12) *Who is Jesus Christ? Was He God in the Flesh?*

I could just keep on writing about the things that the Lord has shown me but like usual I have probably said enough already. If you have found any value in what I have written; then give it away, tell someone. If you have a friend or a family member that is lost or caught up in alcohol or drugs, sexual immorality see if you can get them to read what I have written. I have been there and what I have written, hopefully, will minister to them. I've been told that I make God real, believable and I cannot contain Him, nobody can. Whatever you do don't try to intellectualize God; He is, as He said; unreasonable. He is beyond your ability to reason. "His ways are not our ways nor His thoughts, our thoughts", they are; "higher" than ours. The Scriptures were written for today and its problems just like they were written from the Beginning, after the crucifixion and the problems of those periods in time. When you read the Word of God make it personal, let Him talk to you. All you need to do is receive Him and believe Him, He will do the rest. He will always be there for you and the most powerful prayer in the World is; "God help me!" Especially if you just let your engine overheat and shed some real tears, some remorse or grief. I want you to know that what I have written does not conform to common Theology but that to me is okay. Not all by any means, but some who are clergy or ministers of the Word have caused themselves a problem because of Theology. Their minds are closed; they understand God as they were taught to understand Him. How could our ancestors understand Gods Word in relationship to what was written about this time period in history. Just how intelligent are we? We keep doing the same things over and over again, thinking each time that we are going to get a different result. Winston Churchill said; "If we fail to learn from history; it is bound to repeat itself". What have we learned since the beginning of time?

Armageddon, is World War III, it starts out as a Religious War and ends up being a search for World Dominion. It ends up being a nuclear holocaust. Just keep your eyes on Israel and then when these things start to happen turn your eyes to the Bear that sits to the North. In Revelations it is the seven bowls of wrath that the Angels pour out on mankind; that the people break out with open sores, burns, hail and curse God. Those bowls is what occurs after nuclear explosions; I believe they said that it was like snowflakes that *fell down out of the mushroom cloud after the bombs detonated in Japan and the people broke out in open sores, they lost limbs and sight, some their lives, it is death, it's cancerous and then you have the radiation burns from the explosion itself. It is chapters 15, 16 & 17 in Revelations that talk of the Seven Bowls of Wrath and the Harlot who sits upon the throne when Babylon falls. I feel comfortable that I could tell you who are next President is going to be; elected in 2008. I think that I could also tell you about the beast with 10 horns; there are already, I've been told, 8 in Europe that want this and I believe that the U.S. and Russia will be numbers 9 and 10. I was just told the other day that all of those who flew on the plane that dropped those bombs, except one, committed suicide and the last one just passed away, recently.*

In 1963 when I got out of the service I had to sign a waiver that I would never tell anyone what I did in the service. I had a Top Secret Cryptographic clearance but I was enlisted, low rank and everything was based on the need to know. Two years out of the service they ran a thirteen week editorial in our local newspaper on the Gary Powers, U2 flight that was shot down over Russia and it cracked me up, they revealed things that I didn't even know and I was stationed at the base that he flew out of. When I got out of the service the only thing I would tell people, and this was based more on suspicion than fact; if you really knew what went on behind the closed doors in our Government, a awful lot of people would go to the nearest, tallest building and take the elevator to the top floor and jump off. Flying Saucers, UFO's I do not believe are alien life forms from other planets. They are either our own Governments experimentations or they are Demonic manifestations. You have no idea what mans mind is capable of and it is a good thing that we don't; or all would have been destroyed by now. We have stuck our noses and our fingers into everything and it was not intended that man go there and do those things. Artificial insemination; we have orphanage houses with millions of children just wanting a family, a mother and a father. Or are we going to try and build a superior breed of man as Hitler tried to do. They are letting gay couples adopt orphan children; what kind of a home is that to have a child raised in? If homosexuals are ordained by God and they have sex with one another then why can't they give birth to another creation of God? I don't hate homosexuals, I love them, God loves them but I cannot embrace the sin. God says it is sin and that you will not inherit the kingdom of God if you persist and embrace that life style.

His Word is alive, it's the Living Word of God and if you do not believe that the Lord or the Holy Spirit has a voice and will speak to you then you probably never will hear or learn to discern their voices. So if you are convinced that you know and understand a scripture and you do not know the voice of the Lord or the Holy Spirit then that is your opinion. Even if the Lord told you differently then what you believe you would just cast it off to the side and say; No, that's not God. I am not telling you what you have to believe, I'm only trying to present our God in the way that He has blessed me and freed me from bondage because if you do not know the Lord then you are going to end up in bondage of some nature or form. The other point again was; that you will consider your life, now and eternally, in respect to the times that we are living in. If the Seven Years of Tribulations did not start on 4/3/2007 then they could start any day or any time. I obviously am sold that it did begin then, but if it didn't then, it will not be much longer until it does begin. Just let go and give the Lord a chance, I promise that you will never regret it. If what I have written wins one soul for Christ then it was well worth the time and the money that I have put into it. I'm looking forward to a BIG reunion in the Sky, (Heavens). Just to be able to meet those who were before us, Moses, Abraham, King David, George Washington, the Disciples, etc. and the Lord; just to be in His presence. I believe it is in the Psalms; that David sings, "just one day in your court, is worth a 1,000 elsewhere".

Just today; it's the end of Jan., 2008 now, I was thinking why the Moslem faith is the fastest growing faith in America today? Why? It does not offer anything that is as desirable or a direction that Christ, Christianity offers? I now know why I hate the word religion; if you're a Moslem, you read the Koran; you believe that Mohammed was a prophet; you go to the Moslem Mosque with your rug, whatever, at certain times during the day and you kneel and bow down and chant before Ala. They have one building, one Prophet, one Book, one custom, and one God. I just looked up Church in the yellow pages of our local telephone directory; a city with the registered population of around 42,000 people. There are approximately two full pages of listing under Churches and you have just under the heading of Churches; you have 39 listings of which some are called; *Abundant Life Ministries, Because He Lives Ministries, Breath of Life Ministries, Church With Out Walls, Deliverance Temple, His Place Worship Center, Impact of the Living God Church*, etc.. Then you go to Churches-Adventist, Churches-African American Methodist Episcopal, Churches-Anglican, Churches-Apostolic, Churches-Assembly of God, Churches-Baptist, Churches-Baptist Independent, Churches-Baptist Southern, Churches-Brethren, Churches-Catholic, Churches-Christian, Churches-Church of Christ, Churches-Church of God, Churches-Church of Jesus Christ of Latter Day Saints (Mormon), Churches-Episcopal, Churches-Evangelical, Churches-Independent, Churches-Jehovah's Witnesses, Churches-Lutheran, Churches-Mennonite, Churches-Methodist, Churches-Multicultural & Multilingual, Churches-Nazarene, Churches-Non-Denominational & Interdenominational, Churches-Other Christians, Churches-Pentecostal, Churches-Presbyterian, Churches-Seven Day Adventist and Churches-Unitarian. Under all of those categories are, with but a few exceptions, several listings; just under Non-Denominational there are thirteen listings. In my twenty two years I have sat under and listened to more ministers, more different denominations, more Evangelists than most ministers have. Out of what I have listed above I could name you at least five Churches in our city that do not worship Jesus Christ as Lord and Savior. I could take you to at least five Churches that I know the Minister is Deceived and preaching a distortion of the truth. I could take you to Churches that they are more interested in the head count of attendance and the amount of money in the offering plate than they are your salvation. I left a Church not long ago that had tripled in attendance over eighteen months and never once had an alter call for salvation.

The biggest problem I have had in sobriety is that I wanted to go to the Church and tell them what an absolute fantastic job that God was doing in the Twelve Step Program that He put me into; and they did not nor would not listen. Then I wanted to go back and tell the Twelve Step Program that God has a Name; tell them about Jesus Christ and they wouldn't listen, as a matter of fact they wouldn't allow me to chair meetings at the hospital because they said I was to Religious. Today when I go to a meeting I introduce myself saying; I'm Chuck, a recovered alcoholic and I am here by the Grace of God whom I call Jesus Christ. If the old timers don't like it then I tell them that this is a program of God; as you understand Him and that is my understanding of God, so if you don't like it, leave it - they say; take what you like and leave the rest behind! You know if you found anything you like in what I say or you would want what I have; shouldn't I tell you where I got it from? You would be amazed at how many people drank or had a drinking, drug abuse problems because they had Religion shoved down their throats trying to grow up.

I guess it is this simple; I love Chinese food, but I hate to go to a Chinese Restaurant to eat dinner. The menu is so large that I spend twenty minutes trying to figure out what is what and the symbols which represent the seasoning as being, spicy, hot, medium or mild. Do I want chicken, beef, pork or fish and mixed in or with what. Do I want white rice, brown rice or wild rice? I finally give up and just order chop suey which I know I like, because I don't know the others and I can't seem to make a choice; they all sound good, but I don't want to take a chance, because I'm hungry. That is why the Church in America is going to and has lost its voice. It, the message, is all garbled up from all the different Religions and those who know, so many have Him hidden in their hearts and are afraid to talk; that they might be ridiculed or corrected. I just hope that when the bottom falls out of your world and you go running back into your heart to find Him; that He is still there. It is just like He wrote on the side of that coffee cup.

1) You can't have more than you have, unless it comes from Him; who is true.

2) You can't keep what you have unless you give it away.

3) You can't give what you don't have. That my friends, is wisdom from above!

HOW FAST ARE WE TRAVELING:

*T*here is just one more trip that I would like to take you on. The illustrations that I drew are really very interesting to consider. I by no means am educated or trained in this school of thought but it does leave a very interesting question which I will ask you at the end. Einstein, I was told, came up with the fourth dimension before he passed away. That dimension was time and on the journey that I was taken on I was led to understand or believe that time in reality is life. Time is equal to the distance traveled and the speed in which it is traveled; that without movement there is no time; it would stand still. If your heart does not beat and pump the blood through your veins and your lungs do not move in and out bringing in fresh oxygen and excelling carbon dioxide then you are dead, time has stopped.

I was stationed in Pakistan, overseas, while in the Air Force back in the 1960's and they told us that we were about halfway around the World or approximately, 12,000 miles. That means that the circumference of the earth, or distance around the earth is approximately 24,000 miles. There are twenty four time zones around the World and twenty four hours in a day. The earth makes one revolution every twenty four hours which simple math says; that if I travel 24,000 miles in twenty four hours that I am moving at the rate of 1,000 miles per hour while I'm sitting here typing this page, not even barely moving. I am moving at the speed of 1,000 miles per hour and not one hair on my head is moving. I could also print this page now and go over to the fax machine, dial an overseas operator and a fax number in Pakistan and send this page halfway around the world in less than ten minutes or I could get on my cell phone and dial a overseas operator and a telephone number in Pakistan and have a phone conversation with someone halfway around the world and there wouldn't even be a long delay between my saying something and their responding back over the phone. I could get on the Internet on my computer and talk with someone in Pakistan. I watched Desert Storm on television while it was actually taking place, almost halfway around the World. Just how fast does sound travel? What is the speed of light? Just how fast are we going at this stage in life?

It hasn't been but about two months ago that the Holy Spirit asked me; "Where have all of the birds gone?" He asked me that question on two different occasions and the second time I began to wonder, not remembering having seen any birds this summer, as usual; has God taken them home? Is it that late? As I was on my way out to the Mall I drove slowly and went on a bird watch and was happy to find out that I don't think that He has taken them home yet. You see; He let me know that the question wasn't are there as many or; less birds in the World today, it was; are we going so fast anymore that we don't have the time to see them. Are we so busy rushing from our air-conditioned houses, in our air-conditioned cars, going to air-conditioned offices or air-conditioned stores that we no longer see or hear the birds feed and sing their songs? Is time actually going faster today or is it just all of the bells and whistles; the distractions that we have in life today that make it seem that way? The Bible says that we're too; "Be still, and know that He is God," Psm.46:10. My question is; when was the last time you tried to be still? Or have things gotten so bad that you can no longer even live with yourself, in silence; or have you been playing God all this time? If you can't understand this page and do not know how to create it then trust me, you are not God. You are just another sinner like all of the rest of us, who has fallen short of the Glory of God. Thanks God for Grace; Thanks for Jesus or there would be no hope, no salvation, both for the Jew and the Greek, (All).

If you can be still, try it; if you listen real close you can hear His heart beat. We are not coming to the End; we are approaching the Beginning. The Beginning of something that you do not want to miss; so DON'T BE LATE For The "WEDDING." As they say in Alcoholics Anonymous; there is one who has all power, that one is God, may you find Him now.

I just want to say; please don't judge what I have written harshly. I am just another sinner who is saved by Grace and has been blessed by the love our Lord Jesus Christ. My heart is for those who are confined in bondage, who are lost, who are bound up in addictions and sexual immorality. There is a way out and it is not too late, you have not gone too far, it's just that the time is growing short and life has no guarantees as to its longevity. I have my problems just like all of the rest; I have a problem with the self-righteous ones. Those who say; that you're nobody, no good! Or, you just found that out! Or, who does he think he is? Those who know it all and have their noses stuck up in the air and guard their possessions with their life. I have to continually stay out of judgment and ask for forgiveness and pray for them also. There is not one of us who are any better or any worse that the other; we have all gone astray at one time or another. We are all sinners and have fallen short of the Glory of God and we are all brothers and sisters, black, red, yellow or white. I am a high school graduate and if you think that I could dream up what I have written in the confinement of this book then you have to be crazier than what some of you might think that I am. If anyone, would be so ridicules as to throw in genius; that would also fall under the last statement that I just made. The only definition that is adequate to me is that I have been "Blessed" and have had one wonderful spiritual journey over the last twenty-two years. My prayers are for you and that something that was said will help you in making the correct choice in life; to choose a different direction or course. If you know Him; have received Him and believe Him then the Bible says; "Oh death; where is your sting?", (1Cor. 15:55). To die; is to live for eternity, in Heaven, with Him.

You know we are all creatures of habit. It was easier to have said no, the first time then it is to say no, the second time and each time you do it; it becomes less of an issue regardless of what it is that you are doing. I often wondered why do battered women continue to return to the homes in which they are severely abused? Why does an alcoholic continue to do the same thing day after day, always getting the same results only each day he will say to himself; tomorrow will be different, I'll get a job or I'll only drink two drinks today, or I won't drink and drive. Each day you are either convinced that it doesn't matter, or that it will be different and it always ends up the same way. They say that; it isn't until the reality and pain of what it is that you are doing exceeds the fear of change, the unknown - which man will then change. Unfortunately most die before that happens. If you don't have faith in the now and eternal, (God), just how difficult do you think that it will be to just let go and die? Will you hang on to the suffering and pain for dear life because you are not sure of what is on the other side? Just to have the peace of knowing that whatever it is, if God is with me, it will be okay; it will work out, it will be better. . . .

BEING OPEN WITH OTHERS:

I gave a copy of my manuscript to a friend of mine yesterday. He is Jewish and I told him what the book was on and knowing the difference in our beliefs, if he would be willing to read what I have written. Being friends he was more than happy to read and give me his comments. He did tell me that I needed to understand that he was very happy with his faith and that which he believes. I told him that I definitely understood but that there were some things in my book that I would like that he sees and that the journey that I have been on with the Holy Spirit has been unbelievable. I told him that he would read in the beginning that I was not asking him to believe all that I have written. My hopes; being my friend, is that as these things come to pass he will know and reconsider based on what was written. If they don't come to pass then nothing lost, nothing gained maybe, who knows.

I decided to add this last short section because I believe that there are a lot who do not understand what the difference is between Israel, the Jewish, and Christianity. We both believe in the same God but the Jewish people still live under the Old Testament and are still waiting on the Messiah, the Prophets had prophesized was coming. As Christians we believe that Jesus Christ was the Messiah that the Prophets had prophesized about. This morning we went on another journey and I wanted to get it down on paper. I remember reading that, I believe it was three hundred and sixty three times in the Old Testament that they had prophesized as to His coming and that which He would do. I also remember them saying, and I believe there was a book written on this, that Jesus Christ from His birth through His short

Life span of around 32 years before He was crucified; fulfilled each of those prophecies to the letter in which they were written. That in itself is extremely important to understand.

Clint, my spiritual mentor, and I one evening had a conversation with a believer of the Old Testament and the Jewish customs. After discussing the differences in our beliefs the young man said; if you can prove to me that Jesus was from the linage of David, I will believe you. I wrote this back in chapter nineteen I believe; its Rev. 22:16, which is the last chapter in the last book in the Bible and it is written in Red which means it was the Lord speaking. Quote; "I, Jesus, have sent my angel to testify to you these things in the Churches, I am the Root and the Offspring of David, the Bright and Morning Star" There is also a name that Jesus was given which was; "Immanuel," which translated means; "God with us." Ish. 7:14. That was prophesied as to His coming, virgin birth. If you read John Chapter 1:1-3 it says; "In the beginning was the Word and the Word was with God and the Word was God that He (Jesus) was in the beginning with God, and all things that were made were made through Him, and nothing that was made, that was made, was made without Him." Then starting in John Chapter 14 verse 6 read through to the end. The disciples question Jesus to show them the Father. Jesus goes to great lengths to tell Phillip; "If you have seen me, you have seen the Father, for I am in the Father and the Father is in Me. The works that I do, I do not do, it is the Father who is in Me that does the works." So like I said before, they are separate, yet they are one. The only way it makes since to me is that Jesus Christ is the Heart and Soul of God. He is God in the flesh. The reason why is because the Bible says that; "what comes out of your mouth is the overflow of your heart." Jesus was the Body, the Heart, God was the Word and the Holy Spirit was the fulfillment of the Word, the carrier.

This all leads back to another interesting question. Why did God come and dwell with us and why did He give His Life up and die, was crucified? He is God; He can do whatever He pleases. You have to understand that God is Love and that God cannot look upon sin. Let's go all the way back to Genesis and what happened; God came down every day and walked with Adam and Eve and they fellowshipped, talked. He came down the one day and He couldn't find them so He called out; "Adam, where are you?" Adam replies; "We are here Lord, behind the bushes." God said; "Why are you hiding?" and Adam replied; "Because we are naked." God then said; "How do you know that you are naked?" He knew; that they had eaten the fruit from the tree in which they were forbidden. That was the tree of "knowledge and wisdom." God then replied; "In this day you shall surely die." It has been speculated that Adam lived to around eight hundred and sixty three years of age before he died. Here again you have to understand that it says in Genesis that "a thousand years to man is but one day to God." Getting off the subject for just one second that is why; theology has the creation of Adam at 4,000 BC and if God created and perfected in six days, then rested on the seventh day which it says in Genesis. Then after six thousand years the end of ages will take place and the seventh day when He rests is the Millennium or the One Thousand Years of Heaven on Earth.

Back to the Garden of Eden and the first sin of man; after God told Adam that he would surely die in this day; what did He do? According to scripture He covered them, their nakedness with the skin of an animal. God set the standard; in order to cover them with the skin of an animal. He had to sacrifice an unblemished, innocent animal to get the skin. That was the first shedding of blood which was for the covering of sin. The Jewish people have faithfully sacrificed an unblemished lamb on the appointed day. They slit the animal down the middle, laying it open, half on one side and half on the other side. They capture a small container of the blood and then the head of the household, I've been told, walks through the carcass, blood in a figure eight and then the carcass is laid up on the Alter and sent up as a burnt offering unto God. The High Priest takes the container of blood and goes into the Temple behind the veil; only he can go there and goes through his ceremonial process and then pours the blood over the Holy Seat of the Ark of the Covenant and that is the covering for that family's sins for the upcoming year. The Arc of the Covenant is the Golden Ark that they built to house the two stones tablets that Moses brought down out of the mountain with him. Those are the tablets that God carved with His finger of fire, the Ten Commandments on. It is believed that that Ark still exists and that they know where it is hidden. When the Temple is rebuilt in Jerusalem I believe that they will go back to the sacrifice of the unblemished lambs for the covering of sins. Here again you have to understand that they have been without a land for hundreds of years. Shortly after AD, God told them if they didn't repent and turn from their wicked ways that He would disburse them throughout all the World and they would be hated by all nations. They didn't and He did; it wasn't until Nov. 28, 1947 after WWII that the United Nations under the direction of the United States declared Israel a state, once again. It was May 14, 1948 that they had written a constitution and established a government. Just look at what the Germans did to them in the Second World War and Russia when they sought to get visa and leave to go home.

Why the Cross? Why did Jesus shed His blood, give His life on Calvary Hill a little over 2,000 years ago? For four thousand years God put up with their disobedience and their sacrificial offerings so He came in the flesh and dwelt with them, teaching, performing miracles, fulfilled all that was prophesied about His coming and they still wouldn't receive Him and believe Him. The Pharisees cried out for the blood of Jesus; Crucify Him! Set Barabbas, a thief and murderer, free. The only way that God could begin to accomplish that which He wanted was to shed His own blood, His life so that we could once again be in right standing with Him. You see His blood was pure, He was a seed planted in the womb of a virgin, Mary. He was not conceived or brought into the world by the mating of a male and a female. His shed Blood on Calvary, according to scripture was for the Atonement for the sins of the World, both the Jew and the Greek. One time, forever! He is referred to in the scriptures as the "unblemished Lamb of God" the "Risen Lamb of God" The Bible says that; "we are the righteousness of God, in Christ Jesus." A lot of people take that to say that we are in right standing with God due to the shed blood of Jesus Christ. Which is true but I take it literally; to me it says that; we are in right standing with God who is in Christ Jesus due to the sacrifice of His life and the shedding of His blood." You see if God had not done that, all would have been lost; there would be no salvation and life eternal in the Heavens with Him. No forgiveness of sin. Such a love for His creation is incomprehensible. The Bible also says; "that there is no way to go to the Father except through the Son." To me it says that because He (the Father) is in the Son. That is why the only way you can go to the Father is to go through Jesus, because He is in Him.

We have made the Bible way to difficult of a book to read. I can sum the whole Bible up for you in about four lines. The Pharisees questioned Jesus; Mat. 22:36-40 "Of all the commandments which is the Greatest?" Jesus replied; "To have but one God and to love Him with all your mind, heart and soul; and to put no other Gods before Him or above Him." He then said; the second one is like the first; "to love your neighbor as yourself" that; "that on these two commandments hang all the Law and the Prophets." That was regarding how it was intended that we live our lives and pretty well sums up; the whole bible. We are to walk a walk of love. Love is giving! Hate is taking! Jesus is Love; He was the light that came into the world. Satan was the darkness and that the darkness did not comprehend the light. There is good and there is evil; there is love and there is hate; there is the light and there is darkness; there is Jesus and there is Satan. Two opposites do not make a whole; are you walking in the light or are you walking in the darkness? You are on one side or the other! We are all sinners and fallen short of the Glory of God but we have the victory over evil, we have Jesus, we have His Name, we have His Word and we have forgiveness for our sins, if we forgive others, their sins.

The Lord had me draw a cross on the sheet of my notepad one day. He then told me to write on the left, top side of the horizontal line the words; Hell, eternal fire, damnation, torment & Satan and then underneath the horizontal line on the left side He had me list the attributes of Hell; like hate, murder, pride, envy, lust, greed, drugs, drunkenness, liars, deceivers, etc.. Then on the top of the horizontal line on the right side He had me write the words; Heaven, eternal life, love, peace, joy & Jesus Christ and then underneath the horizontal line on the right side He had me list its attributes; like new bodies, life eternal, no sickness or disease, joy, peace, love, happiness, etc.. When I had finished the Lord said; Chuck! What is separating the two sides? I looked and said; that vertical line that I had drawn! The Lord said; "You're right!" I sat there waiting to be told more and then the Holy Spirit got me to understand that; that is what the Lord wanted me to know. There is no neutral ground, you're either on one side or you're on the other side or you have one foot in each side. Are you being deceived thinking that everything is okay; that you are on the right side when really you're on the wrong side? This is a question? Are resentments the foundation of Judgments and Judgments the root of fear, of anger, hate, bitterness, abuse, murder, etc... The Lord said in Mat. 7:1 "Do not Judge, for as you judge you so shall be judged and as you measure it will be measured back unto you." Thank God for His Grace, His Mercy, for Jesus, for forgiveness or we would all be tossed away. You do know that in His anger, wrath, that God did that once; in Genesis, in the days of Noah and the Arc; He flooded the whole earth and killed every living thing with the exception of two of each kind which were on the boat that God had Noah build. God did say though; "He would never do that again."

I added this because last night I sought the Lord and I found Him in the field, bent over, gathering a handful of flowers. As I drew closer I got a glimpse of His face and as He turned I saw that He was crying. I cannot even begin to tell you what I felt on the inside; I am still grieving over it. He has the whole world on His shoulders and He is weeping knowing there are those who will not turn. Such Love, man has never seen or known and He says in His Word, Mat. 11:30; "You who are heavy laden with burden; take my yoke, for My burden is light and My heart is lowly."

I think that I am now finished; that I am through preaching. If you know Him, then come on; let's go give Him away, share Him with a friend, with an enemy, or go and tell your cat or your dog. He will; "never leave you or forsake you," so go out and take Him with you everywhere you go, like I said; just give Him away. Nobody wants to so whatever you do; DON'T BE LATE For The "WEDDING." By the way if you're feeling lonely and just want someone to love; go outside and wrap your arms around the nearest tree and give it a big hug, tell it you love it. I don't know if you know it or not but you cannot live without it. The leaves on the trees inhale carbon dioxide, which they have to have and they exhale oxygen which they can't use but we have to have in order to live.

I have probably driven the Pastor of the Church I go to half crazy with all that I have asked and told Him regarding this section of this book. Not only him but about everyone that I know. I wanted confirmation on what I was seeing and hearing in the Spirit. In the middle of June of 2007 I hit a lull spiritually for about two weeks. It went from a downpour to silence, so I went to the Lord and I said; "Lord! I haven't heard anything and it's been close to two weeks now. Did I take a left or right turn again when I should have stayed on going straight? Am I doing that which You want me to do? Have I been hearing You correctly? Just give me a "Word" so that I will know that everything is as it should be and that I am still on the right path; or correct my direction. Please Lord! I have to know. Thank You Lord; for hearing me." A: MEN! I am just sitting there meditating on the silence, the lull in this spiritual time and the Lord gave me two "Words". The first word was; "understanding" and the second word was; "all diligence." I immediately looked both words up in the Strong's Exhaustive Concordance and found the scriptures immediately. The first word; "understanding" was Prov. 3:5 which says; "Trust in the Lord with all your heart and lean not on your own understanding. In all ways acknowledge Him and He shall direct your path." The other words; "all diligence," is in Prov. 4:20-27 "My son, give attention to my words; Incline your ear to my sayings. Do not let them depart from your eyes; Keep them in the midst of your heart; For they are life to those who find them. And health to all their flesh. Keep your heart with "all diligence." For out of it spring the issues of life. Put away from you a deceitful mouth. And put perverse lips far from you. Let your eyes look straight ahead, and your eyelids look right before you. Ponder the paths of your feet, and let all your ways be established. Do not turn to the right or the left; remove your foot from evil." Then the next verse is Prov. 5:1 is says; "My son, pay attention to My wisdom; lend your ear to My understanding. That you may preserve discretion, and your lips may keep knowledge.

Again, all I can say is; you be the judge! For I am merely man and He is God. He is; all seeing, all knowing, all things and in all things, all places and at all times. He was; He is; and He is to come again. He is the First and the Last; the Alpha and Omega; the Beginning and the End. He is GOD, and there is no other.

A good scripture to think on, is; Phil. 4:6 "Be anxious for nothing, but in everything by prayer and supplication, with thanksgiving, let your requests be known to God; and the peace of God, which surpasses all understanding, will guard your hearts and minds through Christ Jesus."

SOME FINISHING THOUGHTS:

There is so much more that I would like to say, but I have already given you more than enough to consider. At the Church that I go to the Pastor asked me what it was that I felt the Church should be doing and I told him that his call for discipleship was in line with what I felt needed to be done. That what we need is to take God with us out on the streets. The other thing is that the Churches need to start to intermingle and have some combined activities so that we get to know each other better and come to understand that it is all one God, one Jesus. When I gave my talk at the MGB #31 last March, 2007 I was to talk on the "Wisdom of Discipleship." I never did refer to the paper that I had struggled writing, like usual I just started talking and let the Holy Spirit have His way. I started out to explain the difference between prayer and talking to God. I said that prayer is specific; it has a definite objective or request in mind. I had yet to pray my morning prayer that day so I said that; if they didn't mind I would do that now out loud so that I could show them what I was saying. This is the prayer that I pray every day since I got out of the Black Box on Aug. 6th, 2006. "Oh Heavenly Father, in the Name of Jesus I come to you in prayer. Lord I pray only for the knowledge of your will for me and the power to carry that out. Lord! I pray that the words and the actions I take will be Thy Will, not mine; that you let my ears hear and my eyes see (Spiritual eyes and ears). Lord! If there is anyone you can use Lord, you can use me. Take my hands Lord and my feet, touch my heart Lord; speak through me. If there is anyone you can use Lord, come on, go ahead, and use me. Use me Jesus; use me for your Glory. And Lord before I go into today I gird my loins with the belt of truth and shod my feet in preparation. I put on my breastplate of Righteousness and my helmet of Salvation. I pick up my shield of Faith, to stop the firry darts of the evil ones and the Sword of the Spirit, which is the Word of God. Lord! This is a day that you have made. I will rejoice and be glad in it. Thank you Lord; for hearing my prayer. A-Men:

That prayer is my heart and sets my course for the day. From here on out I am just going to talk to God; I'm going to talk out loud in my mind and if something comes up that I don't understand or am not sure of, I just stop and ask Him. I then went on to say that if you keep your focus on Jesus and walk towards Him; they will follow. For when they see you; they will have to see Him also; then they will follow. You can turn that around also; when you gave your heart to Jesus your body is now His Temple and it says in His Word that He will come and live in this Temple. That He will send God the Holy Spirit, who will live in you and abide in you forever. Now all you have to do is to read His Word and get it from the outside to the inside. You have given Him your heart, your body is now His Temple and He (Holy Spirit) lives in you and you have His Word in you that will leave only one thing. Rom.12:1 says; "Is it not only reasonable that we give our bodies as a living sacrifice unto God." Let me ask you a question; you have given Him everything else, what in the World do you have need of your body for? Give it all to God and just move over and get in the passenger's seat, buckle up and just; Let Go! Let God!

I am going to start to close this article with this; I asked my sponsor Gordy if he would bring me a copy that I wanted to add it at the end of this book. It is called;

THE MAN IN THE GLASS

When you get what you want in your struggle for self
And the world makes you a king for a day,
Just go to the mirror and look at yourself,
And see what THAT man has to say.

For it isn't your father or mother or wife
Who judgment upon you must pass:
The fellows whose verdict counts most in your life
Is the one staring back from the glass.

Some people may think you a straight-shooting' chum
And call you a wonderful guy.
But the man in the glass says you're only a bum
If you can't look him straight in the eye.

He's the one to please, never mind all the rest.
For he's with you clear up to the end,
And you've passed your most dangerous, difficult test
If the man in the glass is your friend.

You may fool the whole world down the pathway of years
And get pats on the back as you pass,
But your final reward will be heartaches and tears
If you've cheated the man in the glass.

It isn't the problems of today that drive men mad; it's the regrets over yesterday and the fear of tomorrow; that's what drives men mad. The Bible says; Mat. 6:34, "Therefore do not worry about tomorrow, for tomorrow will worry about its own things. Sufficient for the day is its own trouble." And yesterday is gone, what was done, was done and what you said, was said. You can't go back and change it; it's beyond your control. You see if you just put on blinders and take care of today, then your yesterdays will become good memories and your tomorrows will offer hopes of being better than today. You see tomorrow is going to come either with you or without you but regardless; it is you that is going to have to live with you for eternity, one place or the other. If you have cheated the Man in the Mirror, then you have cheated the Man Upstairs. You were created, in His Image; you didn't evolve from an ape. If you please Him; then you will be pleased with yourself. We never got cheated in life; we have been given a blessing, which is to have life and to choose life eternal. You may say that it just isn't fair, I was born without legs, sight or lost them in the war. Don't let it bother you, try not to anyhow. Life is only temporary and when you get up there He said that He would give us a new body. I believe that 99% of the struggles in life are; "ACCEPTANCE", or our "EXPECTATIONS". I know and see people everyday who have lost everything, families, cars, their jobs, everything; and they can sit there today and laugh not only at life but at themselves for the dumb things that they did and do. If you can't tell others about the dumb things that you have done and laugh about them then you have cheated the man in the glass. There is another prayer that I like and that is called the "Serenity Prayer". It goes like this...

God!   Grant me the Serenity to accept the things, I cannot change.
The courage to change the things I can;
And the Wisdom to know the difference.

This book is not intended to, or should it cause you to fear; unless you are deceived or think that you are standing on neutral ground; then I hope that it scares the living Hell, out of you. I am a American citizen and I am proud of our heritage and our motto's, "In God we Trust", "One Nation under God, with Liberty, Justice, and the Pursuit of Freedom, Happiness" and "The Freedom of Speech, for All"; then our strive for worldly peace and our standing behind Israel, hopefully clear up to the end. We have just made some mistakes and hopefully it is not too late, nor that we; do not try to correct them. I will leave you with one of my favorites from those who have gone before me....

Denial! Is not a river in Egypt?

To try and bring this roller coaster ride to a smooth stop; there is a scripture that I had quoted years ago and it is written on the bottom of the quote in Section III, "Attitude". The bottom, last paragraph on page five of the "Introduction" to this book, I wrote the prayer that the Lord put on my heart Christmas Eve. of 2007. Well this scripture I think is a good summation of my story, my last will and testimony. It is Psm. 40:1-5;

1) I waited patiently for the Lord, and He inclined to me. And heard my cry.
2) He also brought me up out of a horrible pit. Out of the miry clay. And set my feet upon a rock. And established my steps.
3) He has put a new song in my mouth—Praise to our God; Many will see it and fear. And will trust in the Lord.
4) Blessed is that man who makes the Lord his trust. And does not respect the proud, nor such as turn aside to lies.
5) Many, O Lord my God, are Your wonderful works which you have done; And your thoughts toward us cannot be recounted to You in order; I would declare and speak of them. They are more that can be numbered.

This happened; and for the first time I cannot tell you the exact day but it was in late April, a weekday, at around 3:00 PM until around 6:30 PM. I spoke of this to the Pastor just last week and I also spoke of it back in the Article where I wrote the letter to the Prophet. I died a second death which the Bible does not talk about as in referencing it as such. I am not going to take up your time telling you what happened and how but it was the fourth time in the last fifteen months that the Holy Spirit just took total control. The result of which I have three hours that I cannot account for; I remember my son saying goodbye as he left for work shortly after 3:00 PM and the next thing I remember was that I bolted upright in my chair looking around, trying to get a focus on what had happened and the time. I got myself collected and went out to get a fresh soda and I looked at the kitchen clock and it was after 6:30 PM. I know that I had not been asleep. Here is another coincidence; it wasn't many days later that I came across this scripture and it really jumped off the page at me, as a matter of fact I even called my sister to tell her about the verse and what it said; It is Gal. 2:20. At first I thought that this verse was kind of arrogant but the more I studied it; it is a verse of what I call, "Devine Reverence" or "The Fear of the Lord".

"I have been crucified with Christ; it is no longer I who live, but Christ lives in me; and the [life] which I now live in the flesh I live by faith in the Son of God; who loved me and gave Himself for me.

I want that you should know; if you have gotten to this point then you have read all of Section II, almost. What I want you to know is that everything that is written in Section II have been revealed to me starting as of 4/3/2007. There is nothing that I have written in this section that I have studied or researched. The dates and that information; I went to the Encyclopedia and looked up the information as it was revealed to me; in question of, could this be? I have never read Daniels Prophecy of the End of Times or the Prophecy of 70 weeks, before. I am telling you this so that you will understand that this section is not my understanding as a result of research and study; It is strictly a result of what I have seen and been told in the Spirit.

I have a copy of two prophetic tapes that had been prophesied and spoken over me at the Church I go to on Tuesday evenings. These prophetic voices did not know me from Adam; the first time I went was because the Holy Spirit raised the question in my mind; I wonder how many people have signed up and go downstairs during the praise and worship service? There was only one time slot (15 minutes) that was open, so I put my name in there; I had to find out what in the heck was going on. I had never heard of, or was interested in a prophetic ministry. In all honesty I would be more inclined to shy away from it. I have always walked under the understanding that if I needed to know something or do something; He would tell me or teach me. Well when it was my turn to go down I asked; knowing not one of the three who were there; would you like to know where I have been spiritually for the last nine months? They said no! The less they knew the clearer and better they could see and hear in the Spirit realm. I almost laughed out loud; I thought their going to miss me by a 1,000 miles. There is no way that they can see where the Holy Spirit has taken me. I left there both times with my jaw in my lap. They confirmed and nailed to the wall everything that the Lord had revealed to me. I am telling you this because one of the prophetic voices said that I had the heart of our Father. I am seriously considering taking my name off of everything in this book and making it; Author Unknown! If I do, I will provide a way in which I can be contacted, knowing as these things come into reality, if they do; there will be those who will want that I come and speak of these things for I have only told you a portion of what all that the Lord has revealed to me. I have had many visions over the years of my doing that exact thing of speaking before large assemblies and if you let me in, the biggest problem you have is not that I won't have anything to say; but that you will have a hard time getting me to shut up. In my heart I feel and believe that I have been blessed, not only to be told, but that He trusted me, and allowed me to push the pen as He spoke. I believe and know that these revelations are in preparation for me for a time which is yet in the future; but if there is anything that is good, or is praise worthy, or if one would turn to the Lord, repent and receive Jesus Christ as Lord - then you give Him the Glory, not me. I seek not fame or fortune nor do I fear ridicule, locked up in confinement, beaten, shot, banned from the bookshelves by the ACLU, deported; anything. He said in His Word that; "He would give you a peace that surpasses all understanding" and that I do have.

The other thing that I want you to know is that when I had finished Section 1, I gave a copy of my manuscript to my sister to read and when she had finished one of her comments was; Chuck! "Usually when they quote scripture in a book they give you the Book, Chapter and Verse in reference, so that you can go and read it for yourself." Well; I have never written a book before; I agreed and knew that she was right, so I went back to add that information to every scripture that I had quoted. I hadn't put one reference in my book at that point. I'm laughing; but what I want you to know is that there was only one scripture, in all that I have quoted, that I was right and knew the correct Book, Chapter and Verse. That was Luke 1:37, all the others that I thought for sure I knew the exact location of them and I was wrong. I would have told you what I quoted in reference to faith was Heb. 11: 1-2 and it was verses 11:1 & 6. I had to look up in the Strong's Exhaustive Concordance every scripture that is in this book other than Luke 1:37. Is that because I have a good memory? Or is that because He told me the Scripture? Or did the Lord honor my faith years ago when I went on my search for God? I used, at that time, to go to bed early and read the Bible sometimes I would be up until 3:00 AM reading to the point that I couldn't keep my eyes open.

I found myself straining to keep my eyelids up. I at that point would roll over and turn the lights off, then lay back down on my back and stand the Bible up on my chest and cross my thumbs over touching the inside of the back and front covers of the Bible. I would bring my thumbs back together where my thumb nails touched and then press in and pull open the Bible, which should be somewhere around the center, and I would lay it face down on my chest and clasp my hands together on top of the Bible and go to the Lord in prayer. I would always thank Him for that day of sobriety and then I would pray; "Lord!" "While I sleep tonight; Lord, I'm going to ask that you write your Words on my heart and in my mind, that I might know God." "Thank you Lord! Amen" I would then go to sleep and sometimes I would wake up in the morning in the same position that I was in when I had prayed that prayer early in the morning. Did God honor my request, of faith?

I have waited, listened and talked to anyone who will listen to me and we are now nine months into these revelations and I have heard absolutely nothing from anyone; the Prophetic Voices, the Evangelists; not anyone. I asked the Pastor of the Church that I now go too, to put himself in my position; what would he do? Either I'm deaf, dumb or crazy, or I am the only one I know of that He has told. I haven't told you this yet; but this book got started because of what happened on March the 3rd, 2007, Saturday night at the MGB#31. The last speaker that night finished early and so he wanted to share with everyone what he had just learned the previous week at another gathering. He told us how we could see and hear the voice of the Lord. Well that wasn't an issue with me because I know the voice of the Lord and I, in vision, have seen Him. It was one of the two questions that we were to ask the Lord when we got in His presence that captured my interest. The question to ask was; "Is there anything that you want to tell me; Lord?" Well of all the visions and conversations that I have had with the Lord; I had never asked Him that question. So I sought the Lord as we were told how to find him and I found Him; and as I watched Him, He came to me. When He was in my presence I asked Him; "Lord! Is there anything that you want to tell me?" It was like a ticker tape going through my mind, He keep saying; "Feed My Sheep", "Feed My Sheep", "Feed My Sheep", "Feed My Sheep". So I looked up and wrote those words down on a piece of paper as we had been told to do. It is when I read what I had written, that I started crying and I couldn't stop. Not much later we closed that day activities with communion, prayer and then personal time that you could spend with the Lord or some of the guys got together and sang hymns to the piano. It was also a time that you could console with one of the Lay People who were there for the weekend. So I asked Dean if I could have a minute of His time; I told Him what the Lord had said and I said that I did not feel that the Lord was calling me into the ministry but that I did not know the depth of what it was that He was telling me? I asked if He would pray for me that I was going to go up and get before the Lord and see if He would tell me. Everything came to a conclusion the next evening, Sunday the 4th of March and we all went back to our homes. It is now Wednesday evening and I am awoken at 3:00 AM in the morning and I had to almost tie myself to the bedpost; everything in me said to get up, go out and get this book that I had started eighteen years ago and finish it. I mean it took everything I had to keep from going out and doing that. I had only written one chapter and the title of that book was going to be "Grown Men Don't Cry"; it was about my sobriety, my rebirth and that which I have rewritten in the first chapter of this book. I got up around 6:00 AM, got a notebook and started writing this book, which I am now finishing. I had totally forgotten about that book and had no intention of finishing it. I now believe that the Lord had me write the last chapter to this book, two chapters before I got there, because He wanted Section II added to the book before it was closed.

You can call things as you may but there are an awful lot of strange, coincidental things that have been going on since August the 6Th, Sunday, of 2006. As far as I know and believe in my Heart this is the Lords. . . Wake up call. . . And it doesn't matter "When" He is coming back, what matters is "Where" are you going to spend eternity if you die tonight? I know that I am not by any means going to be alone when I get there; but I don't want anyone, not even the Son of Ben Laden to spend eternity in the place that I have seen and to spend eternity living in that; I can't even endure the thought of such.

By the way; the first four poems that you will read in Section III have the date that they were written and my name on them. I do regret having

215

signed my name on them because like this book, I know who wrote them, I just pushed the pen. The first poem "Life For a Dream" He wrote for my oldest son who had chose to pursue a life style such as I had. That night, as he was about to leave the house to go back and try to patch up a broken relationship; as I was going out to the back porch to attempt one last time to stop him from going, I noticed a pad of paper sitting on the dining room dinette as I went through the room to the kitchen. Well I couldn't stop him and change his mind, as he left the house. I was just sitting at the kitchen counter, head down, depressed, knowing that once again I was going to have to try and put the pieces back together when he returned home. I, like I said, was just sitting there staring at the kitchen counter and the Holy Spirit said; "Go get a pad of paper." Like a robot I got up and walked out to the dining room and got that pad of paper that I had seen and then returned to the kitchen. I set the pad in front of me on the table and resumed just staring blankly in front of myself. The Holy Spirit then said; "Go get a pen." So I again, like a robot got up and went over to the drawer where we keep pens and pencils, got a pen and returned, set the pen down beside the pad of paper and resumed my position of just staring blankly into space. The words started to come so I picked up the pen and started to write. My son returned home just as I had finished, so I signed my name to the bottom, tore the two pages out of the notebook and held them up in the air; with my back turned to him as he entered the back porch. He said; "What is that?" I said, with my back still turned to him; "It's for you!" So he took the papers out of my hand and asked me; "Who wrote this?" I said; "I did." He stood there and read those two pages and when he had finished, he said; "Dad! This is me!" Still not looking at him with my back still turned to him I said; "I know!" He then said; "I didn't know that you knew how to write poetry? I said; "I don't." He then said; "I thought that you said that you had written this?" I then, with my back still turned to him, staring blankly down at the counter, said; "No!" Then I raised my left hand up and pointed my thumb upwards towards the heavens and said; "He did!" That has been eighteen years ago now and it hasn't been but about five months ago that he asked me if I still had a copy of that poem, and I gave it to him plus this a copy of this manuscript and told him that I thought he might find this quite interesting reading even though he has since graduated from college and is married now. The second poem "Sweet Surrender", He wrote for me; that poem is all about my rebirth on Sept. 10/11 of 1986 in South Georgia and my early walk into a new world, sober. I remember when my wife picked me up from the Hospital after my thirty day re-habilitation program. She drove the van as we headed home, the first time in thirty days for me. I remember seeing a squirrel jump from the limb of the tree on my side of the road, over to the limb of a tree on the other side of the road and you would have thought that I had just witnessed Gods creation of man. At forty five years old I had never thought of or seen such a wonderful sight, as I witnessed a creature fly from one tree to the other one. They say when you start drinking to cover up your feelings, that you quit growing emotionally. I was a forty five year old man with a fourteen years old set of emotions. Everything was real for the first time and everything was new. I am soon to be sixty seven years old on the outside but I am now only about eight years old on the inside. That is good! Because He says, speaking to the Disciples; "Least you become like one of these", pointing down to the little children who were playing beside them; "You can't enter the Kingdom of Heaven." Praise God! I'm getting closer.

I will tell you what Smith Wigglesworth would have told you. Get the Word of God on the inside and don't be moved by what you see, don't be moved by what you feel; only be moved by what you believe! The World says to see It, is to believe it; I say to believe it, is to see it. When you read the Word of God, don't be concerned as to whom the Lord or Disciples are talking to and what they did and that is why what was written was written. If the shoe fits, then wear it, or trade it in for a better pair. Are you a Pharisee or a Sadducee; or which of the seven churches of the time do you belong in? In other words, make it personal, He wrote it with you in mind. We are all sinners and have fallen short of the Glory of God, even the Pope, which may be hard for some of you to believe. In that one word "believe", will determine everything in this life and your future eternal destination. You can have all the head knowledge in the world but if you don't believe it and have faith in it, then it is only knowledge, not wisdom. The Bible says; "By the stripes of Jesus, you are healed." So tell them to leave, tell your body to get in line with the Word of God, tell your flesh to shut up and the start praising the Lord for your healing. I don't care how you feel the rest of that day and the nest day or the nest day. When you get up just continue to praise Him for your healing. You will be amazed before you are half way through. Even if you're healing doesn't come right away you're not going to suffer as much and you're going to have hope. Last; you are saved by Gods Grace; the shed blood of Jesus Christ, His life, death, burial, resurrection and most important of all, is your faith. The Bible says, Rom. 10:9-10; "That if you "confess" with your mouth the Lord, Jesus Christ and "believe" in your heart that God raised Him from the dead, you will be saved." For with the heart one "believes" unto righteousness, and with the mouth "confession" is made unto salvation." There are those two words again, "Believe" and "Confession" or what you speak out of your mouth. I'm glad you made the right choice, because the Wedding Ceremony is soon to begin and the party; the Celebration is going to be unbelievable and will last you a lifetime, eternal.

I had just put the computer up and He has started telling me something else, again. Do you know; that in all the genius of man we never have nor never will come up with a synthetic blood. The Bible says that; "life is in the Blood!" Jesus said; that at the end, "His Blood would cry out from the stones." Blood carries oxygen; nourishment, water and healing throughout your whole body. It touches every aspect of who you are. Healing comes from the inside of you, your blood, not from the outside of you. Medicines don't heal you; they just take away the pain, while your body heals itself. Oh, yes they can give you anti-bodies that will build up your immune system so that when germs enter in; your body is prepared and can destroy them before the infection sets in. You can go to the blood bank at the hospital and give a pint of blood and they will pay you thirty or thirty five dollars for it. Go home and four or five weeks later you can return and do the same thing all over again. Blood is the only thing that replenishes itself. They have come up with medicines that will help deter the growth of the infection, cancer but it doesn't heal it or destroy it. The only way they can offer you help is to kill the cells that are infected with the cancer or cut them out of you. That is why the "Blood" of Jesus and the trail of Blood that runs from Geneses to the Cross is so important to understand. If you do not understand the Blood; then you really can't understand what Jesus did when He died, gave His life for you.

I have just removed some of the additions which I had just inserted into my book because I have just been given this addition to this section. For the last two weeks I have just been kind of beating the ball back and forth. Every time someone asks a question or makes a statement regarding what I have written I add another paragraph or two in answer. Just the other night I was asked the question, or the statement was made that this was my opinion; that Sunday was the seventh day of the week. It is just this simple; The Jewish people have Saturday, I believe, being their Holy day. In America we have Sunday being our Holy day, even though that is a farce; how many businesses are open seven days a week anymore and a lot of them are open 24/7. You can make Sunday any day of the week you want to. The illustration that I drew on page 114 is correct. Just remove the names of the days from underneath the boxes. God did not rest for one day and then work six. He worked six days and then on the seventh day He rests. So the beginning of the work week is day one and the end of the work week is day six and the next day is seven, and it is to be set aside and made Holy. The whole world to my knowledge uses Gods standard of a seven day week. So a week consists of six days and then you take one day off and rest; day seven in all reality is not a part of a week; it is day that is set apart from each week and was meant to be kept Holy, in worship and honor of God.

The new addition to my book is this; The Lord got me thinking this morning about why He spoke in parables when He taught the multitudes on the Sermon on the Mount. Why didn't He just come out and call things that were as though they were. How else could you speak the truth, Godly reality, to all generations in time, other than to speak in Parables or in association with the truth? If He had spoken directly in relationship to that period in time how many of us would just say; boy they must of have been dumb back then or really bad, thank God I'm living in this generation. Are we really better off today than they were two thousand years ago? They had a need for God back then, even though they didn't listen very well. Do we have as much a need for God today as they did two thousand years ago; or have we become so intelligent and greedy that we no longer need a God? For heaven's sakes, why do we need a God, we can fly to the moon and mars. We can split the Atom! We still don't know how to dispose of nuclear waste and we can destroy the whole world with our nuclear weapons of war, but let's don't talk about that. The Lord said in His Word; "If He didn't return; all would be destroyed." We have progressed in time intellectually as far as advancements in technology but I believe that we have regressed in time spiritually. How long will it be before we are living on dirt covered garbage, trash pits with worn out, broken down, abused whatever's? But then again it was all done in the name of prosperity, wasn't it. How much would it really cost to make a vehicle that would last you a lifetime? How many miles per gallon of gas could you really get if the technology that is available were to be used? Then I got thinking about how many stuffed trophies of animals and fish are hanging on the walls of offices, homes and in the cabins around the world. We have dug into, torn apart, reassembled, killed and destroyed almost everything that God had created and we are nearing the time that we are going to turn our hate, our lust and search for power against each other under the names of Religion and Peace. We; under the name of Christianity, can't even agree on the interpretation of the scriptures. Some Churches you can't become a member of unless you are baptized and come out speaking in other tongues and then there are Churches that will tell you that you will have to leave, get rid of the Demon that is in you; if you stand up and speak in other tongues. The Lord has kept telling me this over and over again, "You're going the wrong way," "turn around." Then He kept telling me that; "Heaven, is in your heart." "Heaven is in your heart." I now think that I understand what He was saying. I in my heart believe that I have turned around and I know that many of you have also; but those of you who haven't yet I'm going to ask that you, please, for your sake, not mine; just stop right where you're at, right now; turn around, close your eyes and look on the inside from here on out. Heaven is; in your "Heart" and 95% of what you see and hear on the outside of you is a lie or a distortion of the truth anyhow. Just give "Jesus" a chance; you have everything to gain and nothing to lose . . . .

Just last night I figured it out; I had commented to the Pastor on Monday after intercessory prayer; that my household was coming under attack, spiritually, though I have no fear, I need as much help as I can get in prayer over my family and household. I kick myself; for the last three weeks I have had an absolute horrible time trying to deal with resentments. Little he, the *one downstairs threw everything he had to try and get me to start cutting down with my tongue. Thank God I did not speak them out of my mouth, but I had to ask for forgiveness almost every night for something. I have just removed two pages from the end of this book because I was voicing my opinion on the issues that I am not happy with our Governments decisions, or lack of decisions on. I told you up front that this book is not about Politics or Religion, so I removed what I had written. The reason that I have his attention is because I know that he does not want this book published, especially as written; so I am now going to close. If I have more to say, or the Lord puts it on my heart, then I will write a sequel to this book.*

I am inserting this section now, it's Saturday the 9th of February, 2008 at 10:30AM and I have been up since 4:00AM; which is normal. Yesterday, Friday afternoon, I received a call from my publisher and they wanted to know if they had the final edition to my manuscript; that they were now ready to begin the publishing of my book. I said, no; that as I was speaking I was just making some last minute corrections and that I should have the completed copy to them by late afternoon. I sent them, e-mail, around 4:45PM, what I thought was the completed version which included everything outside of this paragraph that I'm adding now. Before I closed the day yesterday I went to the Lord again and told Him that I felt that I had everything finished the way that He wanted it, but if there was anything else that He wanted me to say; that He had to let me know because I told them to check first thing Monday and if nothing new was there, then they now had the completed manuscript. I again said that; You know how to get my attention and I know that you will let me know, Thank You Lord, Amen. Well this morning I have not been asleep again, as usual; we went on another trip and at the end I asked the Lord, do you want that I put this in the book? The answer came quickly and the Holy Spirit said; "Yes". I have gone to all of this explanation to tell you this because, in all honesty, I'm a little reluctant to add it. I think that I understand but I'm not sure; so I'm just going to turn it back over to the Holy Spirit and let go. It all started with the Holy Spirit raising a question, which He has raised several times before and I've thought on but never really came up with an answer that I felt comfortable with. The question was; why, what comes into your eye, what you see, gets twisted around and turned upside down and recorded in the back of your eye? Why is it upside down and is it the opposite of what it appears to be? Then; this is going to get weird now - He said; that I am already in Heaven, that the end has already happened and is over with? That even though I'm up there; I'm back down here? I believe that was His way of answering my request that I'm on His side of the fence when this is all over. He said; what you see coming in from the outside is like an illusion, that you are like, looking into a mirror and what you see is actually behind you; that we are in and walking towards Hell, all the time thinking everything is okay, there's no problems. When the end of ages comes or your life comes to an end you will pass from death to death or from death to life, eternal life in Heaven. You will either just pass through the mirror or illusion or you will bang smack into it, fall down, turn around and find yourself in a flaming infernal of fire and torment. Then, that the Lord had kept saying that; Heaven is in your heart! That it is on the inside of you, on the other side or behind you. He has shown me this several times before but this time it made a little more sense. At the end we see Hell, the fire and torment coming right in front of us; that we turn our eyes inwards, into our hearts to escape the reality and one of two things are going to happen. You are either going to be consumed by the infernal of fire or you are going to ascend through a tunnel in your heart and appear on the inside on the other side which is Heaven. Is that the rapture or is it those who receive Jesus as Lord after the rapture? In other words you don't die out of yourself; you pass through your heart into eternal life. The Bible says that "the path to Heaven is straight and narrow and so are its gates; but the path to destruction is wide and so are its gates." The Bible also says; "there is no other Name in the Heavens or in the Earth by which you must be saved, then the Name of Jesus Christ." To me the reality of what I have just written is this; when you die, or if your still here when the end comes, the only way that you are going to walk through the illusion or escape through the tunnel is through Jesus Christ. You are going in through Him or you are not going there. There is no other way! So I am going to leave you with a Holy Spirit question; the same question that He asked me three times in Nashville, TN on 7/7/07. "Have you truly given your heart to Jesus?" Have you asked Him to come in and be Lord and Savior over your life? Do you believe, in your heart, that God raised Him from the dead into the Heavens and seated Him at His right hand and made Him Lord over all of Heaven and Earth? Do you believe that He; Jesus Christ, came, died and shed His blood, gave His life so that you could have life? Are you willing to confess that Jesus Christ is Lord? That He died for you? I think that I'm up here, yet down here to beg you; please, don't take a chance, you will never know when that window on your life or life itself is going to shut for eternity. Life is only temporary, death is eternal.

Read Mathew; New Testament of the Bible starting in Chapter 24; it's titled "The Great Tribulation" and it's written in red, the Lord speaking; it is also in Mark & Luke. Then look back at what has been written in this book. Why would the Lord tell us these things if we are not going to be here through at least most part of the Tribulations? This book started out that I wanted to reveal a side of God to you that people either don't know or don't talk about. The Lord changed it and I believe that it now has been written with two intentions in mind; one, it is the Lords wake up call to the Church and number two and most importantly to me is that it is an Alter Call to those of you who have not received Jesus Christ as your personal Lord and Savior. If my testimony has not made God real, believable; then I don't know what will. Please give Jesus a try, you can't lose and you have not gone too far, even if you're on death row, a mass murderer, if you seriously repent and have sincere remorse over what you have done to others, forgive and ask to be forgiven. If you believe Him and receive Him, He will walk with you all the way to paradise and for eternity. Yes, you will have to pay the price for your mistakes but life is only temporary and death is eternal. I have just given you my God; His Name is Jesus Christ. I know what I have just written is true, what I have seen in the Spirit, and I can neither contain Him nor can I live without Him. I walk in miracles, visions and now revelations of the Holy Spirit. I know the voice of the Lord and the voice of the Holy Spirit and I have seen their ways. He is not only my Lord and my Savior; He has been my helper, my comforter, my healer, my teacher and my best friend. He has never let me down; He has chastised me, but I deserved it and He did it because He loved me. So please believe me; like I said on page five, if I could just breathe Him onto you, I would do it.

I just this morning revised that last paragraph to make it more of a questionable issue rather that a statement and it wasn't ten minutes ago that I sent it to the Publisher. I just had a conviction come over me and that was; Is the Rapture the 144,000 Jews, at the end? That everyone who is still alive is going to be here all the way through the end, all of the Greek as the Bible calls it? I don't know but I wouldn't take what has been written lightly if I were you.

LATEST NEWSFLASH:

I don't know if this will make my book or not; the finished edition of my manuscript was sent to the publisher on Monday the 11th of Feb., 2008. It was last Friday the 15th that I got on the internet and Googled "Prophetic Voices"; the first site listed I clicked onto and he had written a book titled; whatever! It was about the End of Times, by an American Author. I removed the names, because I will not pass judgment. You could print a copy of his book, no charge; so I did. It was like 270 some pages long, and I read the first 90 pages the same day; I was happy to find out that finally someone was hearing or seeing what I have been hearing and seeing. It ended up over late Friday evening and early Saturday morning I sent him over eleven pages of an e-mail response in wanting to open a channel of communication with him. Just yesterday I tried to delete the e-mails that I had sent to him; though we are in the same period of time as to the Tribulation period; he opens his book with "this may be already happening by the time this book gets out!", then I read on his website that "News break", the mid-tribulation period, the battle of Armageddon started on 2/8/2008. His book causes panic, it creates fear and the battle of Armageddon did not start on 2/8/2008. My book is the opposite; my book says there is nothing to fear, but it is time to wake up to the reality that we are either in or soon to be entering the "Seven Years of Tribulation" period. I am convinced, myself, that there is now only six years and a little over one and one third months left until the end of times; but that it is not too late, that salvation, life eternal is still an open invitation. The Bible says; that there will be false prophets in the World during this time, to beware of them. Then like I said also; it doesn't really matter "when", what matters is, "where"; where are you going to spend eternity. So please, as you begin to hear these things, do not panic; just be calm and deal with the issues at hand. He will be there for you, like I said He would, if you will repent, turn and receive Him into your heart and believe Him. Ask Him for help; but you will have to turn from your wicked ways.

The other things that I wanted to tell you is that I am on a mailing list of Lou Engle's Prophetic Ministry and I have been receiving e-mails on a continuing bases that are not speaking directly in relationship to The End Times, but are of a matter of urgency. They have to do with the upcoming election of 2008 and the issues of Abortion, Homosexual or the gay right, movement and prayer in our schools. And his call to rise up an Army in the Youth; Lou is a powerful speaker, and very influential in the Prophetic arena. His latest e-mail was about the legislation that just got passed in California and a call for twenty-one days of prayer based on Joel 2:12 "to blow a trumpet in Zion, consecrate a fast, call a sacred assembly, and gather the people...and it will come to pass and I will pour out my Spirit on all flesh." The bill or legislation that was passed in California was called Bill 777 that declares, in public schools, a male student can declare his gender as female and then can use the public bathroom of his declared gender.

The proposed Federal Government Legislation that I told you about; that it was under the hate laws, that the Churches would no longer be able to preach Sodom and Gomorrah, that Homosexuality was a sin. That bill did not pass by a small margin this go around but I think that you will find that it will pass in the next assembly of Congress.

It wasn't five months ago, my wife and I were babysitting for our grandchildren and I was seated in the front of the television, which was on, in the easy chair; and it was one continual episode of SpongeBob. I finally got up and changed the channels and I ended up on a news interview program; I don't remember the name of the host; but I know that I have seen his show before. Anyhow he was interviewing a school teacher from Boulder, Colorado and the teacher said; that they had just had a mandatory assembly of twelve to fourteen year old students, (Junior High), and they were taught that it was time that they began sexual experimentation, one with another; and that it was okay for boys to experiment with boys and girls with girls or boys with girls, either way. It was also a time that they began experimentation with drugs (sorcery), but to do it cautiously, always with others present and only to start with marijuana and in small doses. When the TV host heard this he came up out of his chair wanting to know if they fired the principal on the spot and the teacher said; no, that he didn't know that he would even be fired. The TV host almost missed his chair when he collapsed back down; in disbelief.

You know I told you that I pray every morning that, "He will let me eyes see and my ears hear"; for a person who does not watch television, read the newspaper and no longer is even out in the world that much anymore, always, seems to pick up on these things and when I tell, even my friends, they in disbelief say; well I didn't hear or see that, I'll believe it when I read it or hear it. I just smile and say; why in the world would I make that up, if I hadn't of heard it on the radio or seen it on TV, I wouldn't have told you so; and that you never will hear it again or read it in the newspapers, that will be covered up just like the twenty mile deep hole that they had dug in Siberia, Russia and the screams of torment were so ungodly that they couldn't get anyone to go back down and work that mine anymore. They wouldn't even allow scientist to go down and study the sounds; and that got shut up so fast you wouldn't believe it. I am telling you that if you did really know what went on behind closed doors in our Federal offices, Government; a lot of you would just go to the tallest building, take the elevator to the top floor and jump off.

If this isn't the "End Times" that the "Seven Years of Tribulations" started at midnight on 4/3/2007; then it started just before or it is very soon to start, one way or the other. I do know for sure that we are not into the last half "The Battle of Armageddon"; yet. Just keep your focus on Israel and the Temple being rebuilt, that one year covenant being signed. That is scripture and that has to happen! Also don't fall trap to those who will come and say that they are the Christ, regardless of what signs and wonders they may be able to perform; He will appear, in the skies over Israel, just like it is written and by that time there will be Billions who will have fallen from the devastation.

I will tell you of one other vision that the Lord gave me; this was about three months ago. The vision was a fishnet that was stretched from Madrid, Spain over to Libya, North Africa or across the mouth of the Mediterranean Sea. It went from the edge of the water to the bottom of the Heavens and I saw the grey clouds as they rolled in and gathered as they were caught up in this fishnet. The clouds started turning black and they just kept coming and coming. It ended up being a deep black sea of clouds and like molasses as they turned over and rolled in and out slowly one with the other. On occasion there was a slight edge of rich blue that formed around one of the clouds as it rolled and twisted. That was the sun that just barely snuck in through the depth of the black turmoil. The clouds kept building and building and they had pushed the fishnet out to where it appeared that it might just break at any moment. And then I heard a loud bang and say a large ball of fire flash; then the fingers of the lightening just skirted across the top of this, now sea, of rich pitch black clouds. I then heard a voice speak out of the Heavens, whether it was an Angel or the Lord, I don't know, but the voice said; Chuck! "This is a storm that man has never seen before or will never see again; it is but a time, a time and a little over a half time and then that net will break." That puts us around October of 2010 which according to what I have heard and seen in the Spirit is the three and one half year mark of the "Seven Years of Tribulations".

In the Bible in Matthew, Mark and Luke there is a section that is titled "The Signs of the Time and the End of the Age." In Luke 21:8, under this heading and written in Red, the Lord speaking, it says; "And He said; Take heed that you not be deceived. For many will come in My name, saying, "I am He, and The time has drawn near." Therefore do not go after them. I heard on the radio going to Church, just about one month ago that there is now one in North Korea; that claims that he is the Christ and that there is one in London who also claims that he is the Christ. That the Jehovah Witnesses and the Mason Lodge are listening to the one in London and have his picture up in their Churches. I was also told by a Christian Psychologist, who is a friend of mine, that there is one in South America that claims that he is the Christ and that he has a large following at this time. I have a friend of mine that always says; Chuck, that is what you believe! I haven't heard or read of that anywhere. I just smile and tell him that; you probably won't read or hear these things on the common news media, or if you do they will be shut up so fast it will make your head spin. The news media today is Political and it is "Left"; and if you are Political and especially "left" you are not going to report anything that would be considered "Religious" or Christian other that the Church Service scheduled on Sunday mornings and the times.

Just don't listen to false Prophets and Teachers, give your heart to Jesus and read His Word for yourself and pray. You work out your own salvation; by going to the Lord with fear and trembling. He will be there for you, He said that He would and He already knows the exact hour, the day that you are going to do that. Just don't panic and live in fear and turmoil, the enemy is great at creating that. Like I said earlier; if it doesn't happen for another 1,000 years; what have you lost, you're going to have a better life while you are here and an eternal life in the Heavens with our Lord "Jesus Christ". I don't even know you but I love you; I love you because He loves you, and what is good enough for him is more than good enough for me.

THE CONCLUSION:

It is now Friday 3/7/2008 at 6:00 AM and I have been up since 2:30 AM, reading the Bible and falling in and out of sleep. It is now almost one year to the date as to when the Lord got me to start in writing this book and it will not surprise me to find out that it will be on the market as of 4/4/2008, exactly one year since the Lord gave me the vision of His speaking to the World. Yesterday, Thursday, is the Pastors day off from the Church but I bothered him anyhow; I called him on his cell phone and left a message that I couldn't find in the Bible where common Theology got the interpretation of the Rapture from. Last night around 9:00 PM I got a return phone call from the Pastor and he told me that it was in the Book of 1st Thessalonians starting in Chapter 4:13-18, which is titled "The Comfort of Christ's Coming" and then Chapter 5:1-11, which is titled "The Day of the Lord". I went out, I was already in bed, to the living room and got my Bible and read from Ch. 4:13 all the way through 5:28, which is the conclusion of Paul's letter to the Church in Thessalonica. I read it about three times and then went to sleep for the night as I had not gotten but about three to four hours of sleep each night in the last two days. When I got up, dressed, and out in the living room this morning at 2:30 AM I took the Bible with me and read that section again about three times and then finding myself getting tired I went to the Lord in prayer and asked that the Holy Spirit give me interpretation of those scriptures while I slept. I awoke around 4:30 AM and reread those versus and this time I went and read the end section of the book, where is gives definition of the Scriptures and is titled "Truth-In-Action"; I then went to the beginning of the Chapter and read the; "Introduction" to this Book which is quite extensive. This is the "revelation" or the reason that I feel, now comfortable, that this is the final conclusion to this book.

First in the "Introduction" it was written; "That throughout the history of the Church, there have been those who deprived the return of Christ of its intended force by setting dates or specifying limits. Those of any age who do so are claiming to know more than Jesus Himself:" "But of that day and hour no one knows, not even the angels in heaven, nor the Son, but only the Father" (Mark 13:32). It was also written in verse5:19-20; - 19) "Do not quench the Spirit." - 20) "Do not despise prophecies." My point is this; Section Two of this book is prophetic and of the Holy Spirit, the Lord and number two when the Lord gave me the vision of His speaking to the World; that He now knew the hour and the day in which He would return, but when the Scriptures were written He did not know.

The second point being that in reading Chapter 4:13-18, "The Comfort of Christ's Coming", it says; 13) But I do not want you to be ignorant, brethren, concerning those who have fallen asleep, (already passed away?), lest you sorrow as others who have no hope. 14) For if we believe that Jesus died and rose again, even so God will bring with Him those who sleep in Jesus. 15) For this we say to you by the word of the Lord, that we who are alive and remain until the coming of the Lord, (when Jesus appears in the sky.) will by no means precede those who are asleep, (we are all going together!) 16) For the Lord Himself will descend from heaven with a shout, with the voice of an archangel, and with the trumpet of God. And the dead in Christ will rise first. 17) Then we who are alive and remain shall be caught up together with them in the clouds to meet the Lord in the air. And thus we shall always be with the Lord. 18) Therefore comfort one another with these words.

I know that I have been in the 3rd heaven once; that was back in July of 2007, when the Holy Spirit totally took over and I have three hours that I cannot account for. I remembered, it was about three weeks after that experience; that I went up through a layer of clouds, into the first heaven, and there was a farm and some animals. I kept going up and then went through another layer of clouds and there were the people, which would be the second heaven. I then found myself on a glass elevator and was continuing to go upwards and the people, now below me, were waving, as I kept going upwards. I remember going through the 3rd layer of clouds, which would be the 3rd heaven, and all that I can remember is that it was a beautiful medium, rich, without clouds, blue sky, or room, and it was like a dome lit area. If that was the Glory cloud of the Lord, I don't know. I cannot tell you anymore about that experience other than for some reason I feel comfortable that the Lord had a meeting and that Moses, King David, Abraham and Paul, the disciple of Christ and I believe Peter, the disciple of Christ were there; also. This I do not know for sure and cannot say with certainty but in the spirit I believe it. My point being; are the "dead that are in Christ", those that I saw in the second heaven, that day. Paul writes about those who are asleep and also about those who are dead in Christ? I think that the word asleep that he uses has different meanings in his writings to the Church in Thessalonica. In some cases it means being literally asleep, in other cases it means out of fellowship and in other cases I think that it means deceased?

Based on those scripture alone how can the; "Rapture" be anything but a Post Tribulation rapture of the Church. In verse 4:15 it says; "For this we say to you by the word of the Lord, that we who are alive and remain until the coming of the Lord, will by no means precede those who are asleep," If souls are going to be won for the Kingdom of God up until the Lord returns, the Church has got to be here in order to do that. Paul is trying to comfort us in letting us know that we will be okay; not to worry. Hasn't the Lord been saying that in this whole book so far! Do you realize how many are going to perish (die), in the last days of the Tribulation period, over three fourths of the World's population will be destroyed by the End of Ages. How many are just going to perish, die, just due to heart failure. And then why does the Bible, (Lord), tell us that Christians are going to be persecuted in the End, if the rapture of the Church has already taken place, prior to the End; then who is going to help those, or win those for Christ, if no one is still here in the Church," body of Christ"?

Then in Chapter 5, the last chapter in 1 Thessalonians, titled "The Day of the Lord" it is written as to how we are to conduct our lives in the last days, or in not knowing when that day will occur, as Paul is writing. In verse 5:1, Paul writes; 1) But concerning the times and the seasons, brethren, you have no need that I should write to you. 2) For yourselves know perfectly that the day of the Lord so comes as a thief in the night. (The Church in Thessalonica was very well groomed, you might say, in the Lord. They were knowledgeable and for the most part obedient to the Words which had been spoken to them.) Then in verses 3 through 11 it says; 3) For when they say, "Peace and safety!" then sudden destruction comes upon them, as labor pains upon a pregnant woman. And they shall not escape. 4) But you brethren, are not in darkness, so that this Day should overtake you as a thief, (I believe that Paul is now speaking about the Mid-Tribulation period in time. The Lord comes as a thief in the night because there will be many who are not aware of the Scriptures and do not know the Lord or will be ready and then there are those who just don't believe). 5) You are all sons of light and sons of the day. We are not of the night nor of darkness. 6) Therefore let us not sleep, (fall out of fellowship or away from the Lord.), as others do, but let us watch and be sober. 7) For those who sleep, sleep at night, and those who get drunk are drunk at night. 8) But let us who are of the day be sober, putting on the breastplate of faith and love, and as a helmet the hope of salvation, (which are parts of the armor of God). 9) For God did not appoint us to wrath, but to obtain salvation through our Lord Jesus Christ, 10) who died for us, that whether we wake or sleep, we should live together with Him, (In other words, if it is evening and you are asleep, you do not have to worry, that you will be okay). 11) Therefore comfort each other and edify one another, just as you also are doing.

Paul then goes on to write starting in 5:12, which is titled, "Various Exhortations", again as to how we are to conduct ourselves. 12) And we urge you, brethren, to recognize those who labor among you, and are over you in the Lord and admonish you, 13) and to esteem them very highly in love for their work's sake. Be as peace among yourselves, (Paul is talking about the Ministers and Prophets, the leaders in the Church). 14) Now we exhort you, brethren, warn those who are unruly, comfort the fainthearted, uphold the weak, be patient with all. 15) See that no one renders evil for evil to anyone, but always pursue what is good both for yourselves and for all. 16) Rejoice always, 17) pray without ceasing, 18) in everything give thanks; for this is the will of God in Christ Jesus for you. 19) Do not quench the Spirit. 20)

Do not despise prophecies. 21) Test all things; hold fast what is good. 22) Abstain from every form of evil, (Paul is now defining the conduct that we are to perform).

In opening this Article, I explained how this all came about. It was a friend of mine who lives in California that I spoke with just last weekend and he; being interested in the End Times, asked if the Lord had revealed anything to me regarding the, "Rapture", of the Church. He wanted me to send him a copy of my manuscript, which I have just done. What I want you to know is that it was 3:30 AM, on 3/7/2007 that the Holy Spirit awoke me and wanted that I go out and start to finishing this book, which I had begun eighteen years ago. It was around 3:30 AM, on 3/7/2008 that I asked the Holy Spirit to give me the interpretation of these Scriptures; as I was about to drift off into a short nap this morning. What is rather exciting, if you do not believe in coincidences; it was One Year, Zero Hours to the exact day that I was called to write this book and then when it was finished. Keeping that in mind; you might want to re-read some of the Articles that have been written in Section Two of this book. What is most revealing, to me, was where in the Bible they quoted Mark 13:32; which said that only the Father knew the Hour and the Day in which the Lord would return. Then; how I wrote that when the Lord gave me the vision of Him speaking to the World that He now knew when He would return. If the Lord does not want that one soul should perish, or that one would be ignorant of, or left behind; do you not think that He would tell someone?

I was up early this morning again, around 2:30 AM, and re-read those chapters again about the Rapture. I then drifted back into sleep and around 4:00 AM I awoke and the Lord got me to thinking about the Crucifixion, what He got me thinking on was that it was the week of Passover and the

Crucifixion of Jesus Christ that the Lord gave me the vision of His speaking to the World; that happened on late, the evening of 4/3/2007, a Tuesday. It was Wednesday 4/4/2007 that I got up and made the journal entry of the Lord speaking to the World the previous evening and it was at the Passover Service at the Church on Thursday 4/5/2007 that I went up for prayer, seeking the answer from the Lord of "Yes" or "No", that it was Him speaking in that vision. What I am asking is; the fact that the Seven Years of Tribulations began at midnight EST on 4/3/2007 significant with the fact that it was Easter week in which we celebrate both the Passover and the Death, Burial and Resurrection of the Lord. In other words is the Resurrection of Christ and the Beginning of the Tribulation period significant in time? The Lord says; He is the First and the Last. He was the first to ascend up into the Heavens and He will also be the Last, at the End, when we are all caught up together in the clouds. Well was this the First, or the Beginning of the Seven Years of Tribulations?

What the Lord was stirring up was the fact that this year, 2008, is the earliest that we have ever had Easter, fall on. Which brought up the question; what day does 4/3/2014 falls on and when we will celebrate Easter that year? So I looked up under Calendar in the Book of Encyclopedia the Table of years and charts where you can see in any given year the month, date and the day of the week. On 4/3/2014 it is a Thursday! When will the Passover occur in the Year of 2014? And; is that even significant, if the number in my illustrations representing Jesus Christ is "4" and the 4th day of the week is on Thursday and then the Passover day also being on a Thursday, is that significant enough for His return? In other words; on 4/3/2014 a Thursday, will the Shadow of Death pass over the Church and that's when the "Rapture" of the Church takes place and Satan and hell will be spewed out of Gods mouth? I will leave you with those thoughts!

IN SUMMARY

*I*f you take Article Two "The Revelation of the Number Seven" and then Article Five "The Significance of Numbers in the Bible". On the Illustration of the Number Seven; I show that the Number "7" represents God and the Number "4" represents Jesus Christ and is seated on the right side of the triangle, (Triune or Trinity). And that the Number "3" represents the Holy Spirit and is on the left side of the Triune or Trinity. I then have the Number "8" representing Satan and the numbers "6" and "1" representing man and woman.

The reason that the Number seven is the House Number in gambling is because there are only three ways that you can make a "6" with two dice. You can have the combination of a (5+1 or a 4+2 or a 3+3). There are also only three ways that you can make an "8" using two dice. You can have a (6+2 or a 5+3 or a 4+4). But there are four ways that you can make a "7" using two dice. You can have a (6+1 or a 5+2 or a 4+3 or a 3+4). Not that gambling in any way is associated with God; but is that why "7" is God's Number and there are "7" days in a week? In all reality there are only three ways that you can make the number six and there are only three ways you can make the number eight; but there are four ways that you can make a seven. Yet the number "8" is greater than, or above the number "7".

God is a "7" because it is the combination of both "3", the Holy Spirit and "4", Jesus Christ which completes the Triune or "7" which is God. The Number "8" represents Satan because Satan put himself equal to or above God. Remember if Jesus Christ, "4", was God in the flesh and lived with us; then 4+4 equals "8" and that would make an "8" Satan equal to a "4", Jesus Christ or it would be an "8" Satan who put himself above God who is a "7". Either way that you look at it! Also remember that Jesus Christ was resurrected and is now in Heaven and seated at the Right Hand of God.

With the Number "3" representing the Holy Spirit and the Number "6" representing Man then 3+3 equals "6" or Man and it is the Holy Spirit who will come and lives in you. The Holy Spirit is who is here on the Earth where man is. And remember it was Satan "8" that was cast out of the Heavens because he put himself above God. You also need to remember that God is a Triune of "4" Jesus Christ, "3" the Holy Spirit and "7" God. That is why mans number is "6" because we are under God "7"; or less than.

The Number "1" represents Woman because in Genesis God took "1" rib out of the body of Adam, while he slept, and created woman. Woman was created to be a companion to man. Man and Woman are opposite, yet the same, creations of God or Human Beings. And it is only the mating of a man and a woman that can create another creation, of God, a male or a female child. Even though man and woman both have 12 ribs per side or twenty four ribs. I think that is written to show the bondage that God had created between male and female. That one was made from the other because it was intended that they be bonded together in the covenant of matrimony or marriage and through having sex they could create another creation of God. If you think that God approves of Homosexuality, that He won't spew you out of His mouth; then why can't a man and a man or a woman and a woman or a man/woman and an animal have sex, mate; and create another creation of God, a child, male or female? Why does God go to great lengths in the Bible to specify the Covenant of Marriage and marital vows and the specifics of the breaking of that Covenant and how it is that you are to live your lives if you do so? Why does He use Sodom & Gomorrah as an example of His hatred of sexual immorality and then in Col. 9:10; does He specify that "You will not inherit the Kingdom of God", then lists the life styles that He is talking about and it clearly specifies "Homosexuals". It is not difficult to determine if you were created a male or a female; just look! And where did "Aids" come from?

The Number "14" is significant because if "7" is God, (the Number of Perfection and Completion), then 7+7 equals "14" or two. And two represents the two creations of God, "Man and Woman". It also represents the two elements of Life which were created; that is, "Man and Time". It also represent the two manifestations of God, "Jesus Christ and the Holy Spirit", it also represents the Old Covenant and the New Covenant of God; the "Old Testament" of the Bible and the "New Testament" of the Bible". It also represents the Significance of the Number "7" which is, "Perfection and Completion". Again; just read, Mat 1:17 "So all the generations from Abraham to David [are] fourteen generations, from David until the captivity in Babylon [are] fourteen generations, and from the captivity in Babylon until the Christ [are] fourteen generations. That again was written, "14", to tie "two" together; both the Old and the New Testaments of the Bible. It was to show the linage of God from Abraham the Father of Israel to Christ, who was the Messiah or "God lived with us" or God in the Flesh, the Father and Savior of all mankind. The Messiah who the Prophets had prophesized was coming and who Jesus fulfilled all of those prophecies to the letter in which they were spoken, or written. It also shows the linage of King David and his significance in the History of God's Creation; man.

The Numbers seven and fourteen are not just another two numbers that are written in the Bible and used; they are significant, very significant numbers in understanding God and His Divine organization of all things. All of the numbers in the Bible are significant of something but these two numbers are significant in understanding Gods order of things. Everything in Creation is in Two's and Seven is the only number that represents God. Even in the Beginning, God created and perfects in what; "6", (the number of man) days and then He does what; rests, on the 7th, (the Number of God), day. It never in the Bible talks about the eighth day. The eighth day is the Millennium or the 1,000 years of Heaven on Earth. Man was allotted 6,000 years for perfection! That is why it says in Genesis; that, "1,000 years to man is but one day to God". Theology has the Creation of Adam at the year of 4,000 BC and in the year of 2,000 AD we reached the number 6,000 but it still leaves the one cycle of fourteen, or two "7's", the perfection of both "Man and Time" and the last "7" is the Seven Years of Tribulations and they started just when He said they did; At midnight EST on 4/3/2007, which was the perfection beginning number of "777", and will End of 4/3/2014 which is the completion number of "777". That is why 7/7/2007 was a day of perfection in the cycle of perfection. And I believe that you will find that 4/3 and 7/7 will be significant days of each of the remaining years until the End.

And here I thought this was all over with; the revelations, because it is now 3/21/2008 and I had closed this Book almost three weeks ago, now. I am again beginning to feel in the Spirit that something big is about to take place and I believe that it will manifest itself on 4/3/2008. This last Article was not a result of my study of Numerology of the Bible; it was a revelation. The Lord has put someone in my life; who has been extremely inspirational and is what I define as a Christian who walks in "Devine Reverence of the Lord" or in the "Fear of the Lord". Her name is, call her Susan, and she operates in many of the same gifts that I operate in. It was her talking with me about the significance of dates and numbers in regards to the "Days of Celebration", the festive days, or significant days of worship in Israel; just yesterday. That is what led me to this revelation, or the writing of this Article which I am happy; that it will be included in my book.

I just last night went and read the footnotes in Daniel Chapter nine regarding the Scriptures about his prophesy of "70" weeks, which I drew the sketch showing that Prophecy in relationship to the "Seven Years of Tribulations". I now understand why the Pastor kept saying: Chuck, you understand that this isn't common Theology don't you? Theology has the weeks being years but they have the seven weeks being a multiplier of time, in other words it is 7 years times 62 years. I wasn't left with the impression that they even have figured that prophecy out yet. I do know that it used the phraseology that "this school of thought" says, etc. That means that there are several different interpretations of the Scriptures. That also means that there are several schools of thought or teachings of Theology. Why would you think that man would ever agree on anything now? Man has never agreed on anything since the beginning of time. Just look as Cane and Able for example. It has been an ongoing saga of who has the greenest grass, the biggest house, the best and fastest car, the most money and so forth and so forth ever since the beginning of time. You work for your employer for a paycheck at the end of the week and you will do the best that you can to do what you are told to do to make sure that you do not lose your job. You don't go to work because you agree with the Company's business philosophy and in a lot of cases you don't even like some of the policies that they have imposed on you. You are in servitude to your employer because you need a paycheck to support your personal desires and raise your family. I am telling you that man has never agreed on anything since the beginning of time it has always been a struggle to get one's own ways. We just gather in groups, which have "some" thoughts that bond us together in opposition of our adversaries or opponents.

I was just thinking, being now Easter, on the Celebration of Passover and the Life, Crucifixion and Resurrection of Jesus Christ as to common Theology and the days that we celebrate when those events occurred. Theology has the Lords Last Supper, on the day of the Passover Celebration, because Jesus Christ was the Passover Lamb. Then the day that He was crucified was on Friday, (Good Friday) and then Sunday is the celebration of the Resurrection. How can that be? That meant that He would have arisen from the grave on the second day; not on the third day as the Scriptures say. From Friday late afternoon, the Crucifixion, to Saturday late afternoon is one day and from Saturday late afternoon to Sunday late afternoon is two days; which means it would have been on a Monday that He was resurrected, wouldn't it? And if Jesus was the Passover Lamb then He would have had to have been crucified, died on the day before Passover. If He died, which it is written that He did; then He would have had to have been crucified, died, the day before the Passover Feast or Celebration, because death passed over Him, it couldn't contain Him and Passover is on a Thursday.

In Israel, the day ends at sundown and that they have Saturday being their Holy Day or our Sunday; day of worship. I have heard this or just read it recently that they hurriedly prepared the Lords body for the tomb and buried Jesus, laid His body to rest in the cave, just prior to sundown because at sundown was the beginning of the Passover feast. That they were not allowed to even bury, the dead, on the day of Passover; that all things stopped. That would mean that the Lords Supper would have been on a Tuesday; Jesus knowing that He was the Passover Lamb and wanting to set the significance of communion and what it represented, being His blood, His flesh, His life and death, knowing that He was going to pay the price, with the sacrifice of His life, the shedding of His blood the next day for the sins of all mankind. Which would make it a Wednesday that He was crucified; not on a Friday. Then the Israelites, the followers, believers of Christ hurriedly prepared His body for the grave before sundown because of the Passover Feast which would begin at sundown Wednesday night and celebrated on a Thursday. That would fall in line with the fact that the shadow of death passed over Jesus that night because He lives, He was resurrected from the tomb on the third day, into the Heavens. That would make the resurrection of Jesus on a Saturday, which Israel celebrates as their Holy day and it would fit into the Scriptures as to; it is the seventh day that the Lord rests. If He was resurrected on a Saturday then it would be on a Sunday that the Lord rests, His work was finished, He took the keys to Hell out of Satan's hands, arose into the Heavens on the 3rd day, Saturday and He rests on the 7th day of the week; Sunday. I don't know; but once again, that makes more sense to me than either the Greek or the Jew or common Theology does.

Based on that last paragraph that I had just written; I will leave you with a question? It was 4/3/2007 late evening on a Tuesday that I had the vision of the Lord speaking to the World. It was that Tuesday that I had the vision of the Lord speaking to the World, (The Last Supper?) and it was on Wednesday 4/4/07, (The day of the Crucifixion) that I made the journal entry . It was on Thursday (Passover), that I went up for prayer seeking the answer from the Lord "Yes" or "No"; that it was Him speaking that night. It was on Sunday, now 4/8/2007 (The day the Lord rests), that I went to the Lord, knowing that the answer had been "Yes" every night, but still unable to take myself out of the picture. I said; Lord, I am going to go on a water fast for three days and stay before you, if I awake on Thursday morning and have not heard the word "No" then I have to assume that Your answer has to be what I have heard every night so far, "Yes". Thursday morning was different; I didn't seek the Lord this time, He woke me up at 3:30AM and this time I went up through an opening in the bottom of the clouds and was immediately standing right in front of Him. I went to my knees and He laid His hand on my shoulder and said; "rise and look into My eyes", I arose and

242

looked into His face of total composure, peace and He said, clearer than ever, "Yes"; then the vision went away. At 5:30AM that morning I was awoken by the Holy Spirit and He said very clearly, "3" times; "The thousand years ended on Wednesday". Point being this; the only Wednesday that was of any significance, because I had been journaling since 4/1/2007, was Wednesday 4/4/2007 when I made the Journal entry of the Lord speaking to the World, the previous evening. It was the week in which we celebrated Easter; was that a Wednesday that Christ was crucified on instead of a Friday? Also it was exactly "7" days that I stayed before the Lord seeking the answer "Yes" or "No"? Did the beginning of the "Seven Years of Tribulations" start on the day of His crucifixion which would have been on Wednesday 4/4/2007, instead of on a Friday? If it is Midnight EST of 4/3/2007 what time and day is that in Israel? Would that be around 12 Noon on Wednesday, about the time that Jesus was condemned to Death, His crucifixion? I will leave this all up to you to decide!

Just two more interesting occurrences; it was also "7" years that I sat in what I described in Chapter 15 of Section One; "The Black Box", without God. Then my sobriety date which started on 9/10/1986 at 11:40PM, a Wednesday ("3"), the third day of the week and ended on 9/11/1986 at around 12:25AM, a Thursday ("4"), the fourth day of the week; that I passed from 31 years Alcoholic (Life in Hell) at midnight on my knees crying out to God for Help (Death) into rebirth (New Life); a New Creation in Christ. Then if you just look at the year itself, 1986; If "8" is Satan's Number and "6" is the Number of man, then I went from "8" Hell, through "7" God, into a New Creation "6" or back to "Man" or new life. The number "7" is what falls between the numbers "8" and "6", doesn't it? Are these too, just strange coincidences?

I am going to finish with this true story about what happened just last week. On one of the Prophetic Tapes that I have, which are the Words that were spoken over me late last summer and last fall; they saw that the Lord was girding me up to where I would say in just a few words what before had taken me pages and pages, sometimes chapters to say. Well I have started a sequel to this book and the Title of that book will probably be "Un-preached Sermons regarding the End of Times" and I am now entering those Sermons as they come, onto my computer; to later be organized, formatted and put into book form. I had started one of the Articles, Sermons, venting due to my frustrations of trying to get anyone in the Ministry to listen to what I am saying in Section Two of this book. I then enter into a period of peace and I wrote a lot of good things which I wanted to keep for later use. At the end, page twelve now; I explode! What I wrote was with venom, anger, almost every fourth word I spelled in all bold letters and then I say; you go read this and you tell me what the Lord is saying! I then skip to a new paragraph and I type; "Wow", where did that come from and then go on to explain how I started out just venting, then wrote all those good things and now I explode into anger and speak with venom. I then type; I just reread the title that I had given this Sermon, "A renewal of Concern:" and I type in, maybe that is the Lord saying something to me? I then fifteen minutes later type in; I now believe that it is the Lord that is saying something to me!

I came under the Conviction of the Holy Spirit; over having written in venom that last page. Before it was over, I highlighted everything except the Title and the last three lines and then hit the right side of the mouse and selected the top option "cut", hit the enter button and deleted everything that had been written. I then continued the new paragraph which I had started explaining what was happening. After that had been done I changed the Title of this Sermon to: "This is Really Funny:" and that was not good either, that got changed again to; "Is This Really Funny?" I then typed the last paragraph onto this page that is left, asking the Lord to forgive me for having written words in anger. Now just sitting there in my chair I noticed that I had printed one copy of that Sermon, read it, and was going back in to make some adjustments which ended up including that last paragraph which was written in anger and I thought to myself; good I'll just bury it off to the side of my chair and later I will go back and re-enter the good things that I had written, which I wanted to keep. That was not any good either; He told me to dispose of them. I struggled with myself for about ten minutes and then finally consented and decided that I would take and fold them, (eleven pages), in half and put them in an open trash bag which was sitting out in the kitchen. It ended up that He made me take them into the den and shred them. I had run three copies of the single page that now remained and He made me take two of the copies and shred them. The third copy He made me take to the Pastor of the Church and give it to him to read and then ask him to ask himself the question as to "Why did I do this?" It is now about one hour that has elapsed and I find myself sitting in my easy chair in tears; asking the Lord to " just rip this out of me"; that this is not a 98% deal, You either take all of me or none of me, I won't settle for less! Then the next day I have to go up and ask the Pastor, giving him that one page which is left, if he will forgive me? He asked for what? I said that it was something that was never said, never read nor ever would be, but it was something that I had written in anger and that this was between the Lord and me, but it had included you. He laughed; and said that he already had forgiven me for a lot of what I had written; so sure, he then forgave me. I thanked him and told him that I was really sorry and that I appreciated his forgiveness.

Two days later now; it's Monday intercessory prayer time and afterwards I asked the Pastor if he had come to any conclusions as to why I had kept this page and filed it to disk. He commented that he really didn't even understand, for sure, what that page meant? I then explained everything to him that I have just told you; about how I came under the conviction of the Holy Spirit and all of the things that He made me do. I then said; Pastor, let me ask you a question! Do you think that He would allow me to write Section Two of this Book; where in all reality I am telling you that, this is what the Lord has spoken, and what He has shown me in vision. Then to have it Published and put out on the market for others to read; He also put someone in my life who for a minimal fee will help me construct a request to the US Government seeking a Federal Grant of 200,000 dollars to get this book written in different languages and then travel around and do Author Signings to promote the Book stores into carrying my works on their shelves and getting it out into the public's hands to be read?

Do you think that He would allow that, and to do that, and never say one word; if it wasn't Him who has been speaking? If He convicted me over twelve pages that He knew would never be published, never spoken out of my mouth and never read by another human being; would He allow me to publicly go forth with Section Two of this Book and never say; one word? The Articles that are written in Section Two of this Book were just an ongoing of Revelations which I would finally conclude and then two or three days later start another Article because of something someone had said or a question that someone had asked of me. You ask me a question and anymore within two hours the Holy Spirit is taking me too or revealing the answers to me.

That one paragraph just summed up what has been one year of the Pastor and I talking about the things that have been written in Section Two of my Book and in which we never came to any agreement on the contents of; as a matter of fact many times he would comment. You do know, don't you; that this not of common Theology? That, my friends is the fulfillment of that Prophetic Word that had been spoken over me almost five months ago. The end result; I told the Pastor to just forget Section One for now and read Section Two of my Book. Because as time goes by and if these things do come to pass as they have been written then He would know who to call and He knows how to get a hold of me; because I know a whole lot more than what has been put on paper and that I will be more than happy to come and speak with him so that he can prepare the Church for the things that they are going to be faced with. The Church in America is asleep and they are in no way prepared for the on sought of the people who will be running to them for help. Plus they are not prepared themselves for a Post-Tribulation rapture if that is what will happen and I am almost positive that it will be. And if you too are here clear up to the End, with me, and you know the Lord and Love Him then we will be in Paradise together when this is all over; but you too will know what it is that eight and one half years after the fact I cannot still adequately define for you. You too, will know Hell, when you get there! Because if you do not have "The Fear of the Lord" and are walking in the "Kingdom Dynamics" that have been provided that you do; you will walk or be crawling on your knees, pleading with God to help you, before it is all over.

That day before I left I told the Pastor also; Pastor if I am standing beside a body of water and the winds are howling and the waves are rolling and I hear a voice crying out "Help Me!" "Help Me!" and the Lord say's go and get him; I will walk out on the water and pick him up and bring him back to safety. The Pastor said; the secret to what you just said is; that the Lord said, go and get him! That is not the secret; the secret is twofold, number one do you even know that it is the Lord that is telling you to go and get him?

Do you know the voice of the Lord? But number two is more important than the first one; number two is what do you believe? If you know it is the Lord speaking; are you going to run around trying to find a boat in order to manage the waters and get out to that voice that is crying out for help, and then saying that you find a boat, are you going to start crying out for help yourself, in order that you can manage the boat through the rough waters to get out to him? Or are you going to lift up your hand and say: "Peace, be still!" and calm the waters, and then walk out on the water and pick him up and bring him back to safety. If you remember, I said way back in the beginning: Will you receive Him? Will you believe Him? Knowledge is one thing but faith, believing is another. Remember, He said; "If you can believe, all things are possible to him who believes." He also says; "The things that I do, you will do also, even greater things will you do!"

Who was it that cried out for the blood of Jesus? Was it the Moslems? Or was it the Romans? Or was it His own people that cried out; set Barabbas free; crucify Jesus?

Please don't misunderstand; you don't know how much I have appreciated the time that the Pastor has provided for me, listening to me and asking the questions that he has asked. It has been a process of edification for me and the questions have led to many revelations in themselves. He has done a wonderful job in developing the Love that is in his Church. I told him that there is more love in his Church than I have seen anywhere, before.

I opened this book this way and it is important to me that it be closed this way. The question isn't "When", the question is, "Where are you going to spend "Eternity?" and your loved ones! I am; as He is, not interested in statistical accuracy, only souls. He does not want that one soul should perish, nor do I, I've been down there and you do not want to go there. That I can promise you! Just look out your window and see if you can see what has been described for you in this book. Keep your focus on Jesus but keep your earthly eyes on Israel, they are His chosen ones; from the Beginning and they will set the stage for His return. Watch for the news that the Temple is being rebuilt and that one year covenant has been signed and you will know the time.

In closing I just want to try and help you if I can; so if there is anything you might want to ask or say just drop me a message when you have the time. Even if you think I'm crazy I would enjoy your comments. This is an E-Mail address in which you can reach me, let me hear from you. . . .

CHARMCCUEN@AOL.COM

I am again laughing; my one sister told me that I had a lot of John the Baptist in me and I was just given the name of the ministry; it is "Prepare the Way." If you have and would like to help support this ministry your contributions would be most appreciated and blessed. I am trying to find a way that I can get this book marketed properly and would like to have it published in more languages.

All proceeds from this book and any donations or correspondence send to:

An Apostolic Church:
Preparing The Way; Ministry
P.O. Box 1526
Elkhart, IN 46515

Date: 7/14/2008
To: T.V. Evangelist

SUBJECT; PROPHETIC VISIONS AND REVELATIONS OF THE HOLY SPIRIT.

My name is Chuck Mc Cuen and I am 67 years old. I am not a known voice in the Prophetic arena but I do come in with substantial credentials of 22 years of walking in miracles, visions and conversations with the Lord. I have been told that we are on the very same line in what we are seeing for the future of America and I wanted that you hear my prophetic word, in hopes that we can get together and discuss these visions and revelations further.

I see Obama as being the next to take seat in the oval office and I do not believe that he will complete his first term in office whether it be an successful terrorist attack, assignation, or natural death. Although the elected party has no bearing on what I have seen is going to take place in the next election. I think that Hilary Clinton will either assume the Oval Office or be elected in 2012 the year of the fall of Babylon which is the United States.

In an End Time vision of the Lord speaking to the World He spoke first to the World then the United States and lastly to Israel. The United States was called Babylon and told that we were going to fall. The Lord said that the Church in America is asleep and He told the Ministers to take off their Religious apparel and to start preaching the day of the Lord. He spoke harshly against our Government and the ACLU.

In 2009 no later than 2010 the United States is going to make the worst mistake in its entire history. We are going to become a Socialistic Religious Nation and almost overnight. Under the hate laws they are going to pass into law that the Church can no longer preach Sodom & Gomorrah or that homosexuality is a sin. That takes away the Church's voice and their First Amendment Right to the Freedom of Speech. Then they are going to pass into law gay marriages and gay social security benefit for survivor right packages and also gay healthcare programs. We as a Nation will have then re-written the Bible and say that we know better than what God does. This is already happening on the West Coast and you also have with the Pope's approval of announced homosexual Priests still ministering in the Church's in California. The hate laws are in all reality going to take away all citizens First Amendment Right to the Freedom of Speech. If you speak against anything it will be considered hate. So in all reality we will be under a dictatorship, Socialistic and a Religious form of Government.

In Vision I saw a ball of fire fly down from heaven and totally destroy Washington D.C., I believe that it will be a successful terrorist nuclear attack and that Washington D.C. will be flattened. Our Nation will be run from Camp David and from Air Force One and later when we fall we will move our Nations leaders overseas along with Russia and we will become the two remaining Nations to form the Roman Empire or the Beast with 10 horns. I am told that there are already eight European Nations that want this confederation. The United Nations was all but done away with when we went to war in Iraq. We will go to bed with Russia and provide them with all of the technology to make Stealth Bombers and advanced nuclear technology that we have.

The next couple of years I believe that there will be war or the threat of between Israel and Iran, those problems will spark the American Economy and I believe that there is going to be a great outpouring of the Holy Spirit and a large revival in the interior of our Nation which will put us into a false sense of that everything will be okay. I believe that there will be some efforts to settle the economy and lower the fuel prices but not with any great success we are on a downhill landslide and it is going to get worse. The solution to this disturbance between Israel and Iraq and the rebuilding of the Temple is going to bring a false sense of peace that won't last long.

There is a storm brewing; a storm like man has never seen before. The Lord gave me a vision and it was a fishnet that was stretched over the mouth of the Mediterranean Sea from Madrid, Spain over to Libya, North Africa and the net ran from sea level to the bottom of the clouds. The sky turned rich black and the clouds began to roll in turmoil with just slight slivers of light that rounded the edges. I saw a ball of fire explode (lightning) and the fingers of fire just skirted across the top of this sea of Dark Black Clouds that ran and extended forever. The net was pushed out to the point that it looked like it could burst at any time and the Lord spoke. He said; Chuck! This is a storm that man has never seen before and it is yet but a time, a time and a half time and the net will bust.

The United States is broke as I speak and the American dollar is at an all time low. We will come under terrorists attacks on a more frequent sequence in the upcoming years. Inflation will become a nightmare and a potential World financial collapse. I believe the Israel is going to go to war with Iran and that the United States will have to back Israel which is only going to drive us further into debt. When we fall, we, I believe will be taken over by the Chinese because of our inability to function without them as a material supplier to build weapons, material to assemble products for sale and we are I am told approximately 40% vested to them at this time due to unpaid debts. We are no longer a manufacturing giant we are an assembly plant of foreign made components. The Social Security fund is broke and there is no Gold or Silver to back up our currency. The Lord says that in the End it will take a whole weeks income to buy one loaf of bread.

Russia will be the supplier of the nuclear weapons and weapons of war that will be used against Islam. They never have disposed of their nuclear build up of years ago. They along with the other 9 nations will take on the fight against the Arab Nations and Islam as in defense of Israel but in all reality Russia is seeking World domination. The intent is to destroy Islam then over power the other nine nations which is no battle at all and then all that is left is the far West or China and Japan. China sees this happening and they march towards the Euphrates in opposition and when they reach the banks the Lord appears in the sky and all will, Praise the Lord, come to the End of Satan and his reign on the Earth. The Lord will appear in the sky over Israel just as it is written. The End the last year will be a nuclear holocaust and like the Lord wrote "all would be destroyed if He didn't return. Two of the bowls of wrath that are poured out at the end are the effects of nuclear explosions they happened in 1945 when we dropped the Atomic bombs on Nagasaki and on Hiroshima in Japan. Large hail stones and people broke out in open cancerous soars due to the fall out of the nuclear explosions. By the way there are already three in the World who claim that they are the Christ. One in North Korea, one in London who I heard the Jehovah Witnesses and the Masonic Lodge are following and that there is one in South America who has a large following. The sea turning to blood red will be the release of the nuclear waste that we have been burying in the Oceans for decades. I believe that all of the sea life will be destroyed due to this waste we have buried.

Signs to look for - This is Vision and Revelation; The Seven Years of Tribulations I envision may have begun at 12:00 Midnight EST on 4/3/2007. That is all based on two facts with one being that was the night that the Lord gave me the vision of His speaking to the World and when he finished speaking to the World, then the United States and lastly to Israel He says that He is now going to prepare for His return that He is finished. Midnight EST on 4/3/2007 a Tuesday would be 10:00AM Wednesday morning in Israel and 4/3/2007 and is the week of the Passover and the Crucifixion of Jesus Christ. According to what has been revealed to me the last supper was on a Tuesday and then Jesus was Crucified on Wednesday, not Friday and they hurriedly prepared His body for the tomb because the day ends in Israel at sundown and Thursday begins and it is the beginning of the Passover feast and nobody is allowed to do anything including burying the dead. That means that He would have arisen three days later on a Saturday and then on Sunday the 7th day He rests. The Holy Spirit has convinced me of this regarding the last supper and the crucifixion as in we have been celebrating the wrong days and it makes sense. I stayed before the Lord for seven days, including a fast in question of the Vision of His speaking to the World and my journal entry of that. It was the morning of 4/11/2007 that I was awoken by the Holy Spirit and three times He said; "The thousand years ended on Wednesday!" That according to my journal had to be on Wednesday 4/4/2007 when I wrote in my journal the Lord speaking to the World the previous evening around 10:30 PM.

Bottom line Israel was re-instated as a Nation by the United Nations back on Nov. 28, 1947 at the end of WWII. They had written a constitution and established a government on May 14,1948. So if you add 62 years to that window, which is spoken about in Daniels Prophecy of 70 Weeks. You come up with the dates of Nov. 28,2009 to May 14,2010. I feel absolutely comfortable with believing that the one year covenant to rebuild the Temple, spoken about in Daniels Prophecy of 70 weeks, will be signed on 4/3/2010 or on 5/14/2010 with an outside date of 7/7/2010, which all fall within that 62 year window. When that one year covenant is signed we will be precisely three years into the Tribulation period. So that means regardless of the date in which it is signed it then is correct to assume that the Seven Years of Tribulation has started and that there is now less than six years remaining. This is all vision and revelation and I will back it up with scripture. Read Daniels prophecy of "70 weeks" and his prophecy of "The End of Times" up to where he talks about the 1290 ant 1335 days and then look at the attached chart that I sent along. I had never read these prophecies before and it was the Holy Spirit that took me there and then told me that the 7 years were the 7 years of Tribulations. It may not conform to common Theology but how can you deny that everything fits perfectly together in all of the windows. After the vision of the Lord speaking to the World, seven days later I was awoken at 5:30AM and the Holy Spirit repeated three times that the "Thousand years ended on Wednesday".

Israel will sign a one year covenant with Islam I believe on 4/3/2010 to allow them to re-build the Temple and we will be 3 years into the Tribulation period. That will be a concession which will be at the end of this war with Iraq. It has to be Islam because sitting about two feet outside of the old Temple Wall is one of the World's largest Moslem Mosques. The 1290 days is from the time of the beginning of the 7 Years of Tribulations until the Temple falls again, according to prophecy. The 1335 days is from the time the Temple is built until the end of the Tribulation period. That means that the Temple is built 57 ½ days before mid-trib. and that it will fall 12 ½ days after mid-trib. which means the Temple only stands for, guess what, 70 days.

Jack I would love to meet with you and explain this spiritual downpour that I have been on ever since 8/06/2006 a Sunday at 1:00PM in the afternoon. Jack I am not telling you that "I Know" what I am telling and have told you is all Prophetic but the evidence and the foot prints of the Holy Spirit on what I have spoken is undeniable. There is so much more but I know that you don't have the time to read about it.

The only argument that one can come up with is that the Bible says that nobody knows the hour or the day in which the Lord will return not even the Angels in Heaven, only the Father knows. Number one I don't claim to know the hour or the day in which he will return and number two the Holy Spirits answer to that statement is: When the Lord gave me the vision of His speaking to the World He closed speaking to each section with the words that He was now going to prepare for His return, that we were to turn and receive Him and Believe Him or that we would perish in the lake that burns forever. When He finished speaking that to Israel He said; "I am finished!" and He slams the door shut to Heaven. Everything since that night with but a few exceptions has been the Holy Spirit. The Holy Spirit said in answer to the question that nobody knows the hour or the day is that the Lord now knows the hour and the day whereas when the Bible was written He didn't. With God being Love and that He does not want that one soul should perish; do you not think that He would tell someone, especially in America with all that is going to happen to our Nation and the fact that we are sitting here thinking that we our wonderful and everything will be okay.

Given the opportunity I can tell you much more and believe that I can be convincing as to its being authentic and as to why me. I walk in 3 Divine Miracles of deliverance from Alcohol ½ gallon a day habit /Drugs, Sexual immorality, Gambling, Smoking a five pack a day habit and then I spent 7 years totally separated from God convinced by "him", knowing or thinking it was the Lord; that I had committed the unpardonable sin. All three miracles involved having been spoken to or in conversation with the Lord and the Holy Spirit. All three I went from total defeat to victory in less than thirty minutes and no withdrawals. I walk in 3 Divine miracles of deliverance, visions and

I know the voice of both the Lord and the Holy Spirit. I now walk as of 8/6/2006 in Prophetic Visions and Revelations of the Holy Spirit. In July of 2007 I was taken up into the 3rd Heaven and in the Spirit I know that I sat in a meeting with the Lord and several others who were there also. This year in April I saw just a glimpse of the Glory of the Lord and the Holy Spirit told me it was coming to bury my head. I bent over, with my face buried in my lap and my entire body was shaken violently as I bawled out for Mercy, crying I pleaded with the Lord to have Mercy on my soul. Years ago the Lord spoke to me through a stone which has never left my bedside since. Jack that is my credentials please give me an ear there is much to be done in our country, our Nation, before the Church is driven underground and we the people lose our First Amendment Right to the Freedom of Speech. The Lord needs a voice while there is still time to prepare the Church; it is asleep and not ready at all for what is coming just around the corner. Even if the dates are wrong I know that the events or feel comfortable are correct and are going to take place. My heart of concern is that if this date is the truth there are many in the Church who are convinced that they the rapture will occur and that they will be out of here before the Tribulation period even begins. There is no where that I have read in the Bible that specifies when the Rapture will occur and it leans in my opinion more to a Post-Trib. Rapture of the Church or when the Lord appears in the sky or soon after. The Bible says that Christians will be persecuted in the End. My interpretation of persecution is to be beaten and imprisoned because of your beliefs or refusal to conform. Even if I am off a few years I know that what I am seeing has substance and isn't it better to prepare for war then to laugh it off and say it isn't going to happen to us. The Lord cautions us not to be caught sleeping and we are asleep. What we need is End Time Revival and to drive Religion out of the Church and get into Kingdom Living here at the End. We just need to get the message of salvation and the name of Jesus Christ out onto the streets and quit sitting around patting each other on the back in the Churches and getting out feet tickled.

One last note and that is this coming Aug. 16th, 2008 and Lou Engle the Prophetic Voice in America; his last call for revival in the United States will occur in Washington, D.C.. I was at his first call in Nashville,

TN on 7/7/07 and had fasted for forty days prior. Later in Aug. of 2007 the Lord gave me a vision and it was three Angels with short scrolls. The first Angel read the date and it was 8/16/2008 then the second Angel read the place and it was Washington D.C. and lastly the third Angel rolled down his scroll and read a number and it was 5 million. The Lord then gave me a vision of Washington D.C. and the mass of humanity and at the end of the day all 5 Million were just standing there shouting to the music, or the band playing the name of Jesus. It was just back and forth, Jesus! Jesus! Then again Jesus! Jesus!. This was a powerful vision Jack. Just three weeks ago I received some trash mail from Switzerland about reincarnation and that I had a hidden treasure waiting for me to claim from a previous life just send 27.50 to find out the information. I was just ready to pitch it when I read that this July 4th, Independence Day was a critical day for me and that bothered me with all that the Lord has been showing me regarding our Nation. So in thinking things over I decide since I am going to Lou Engles call on 8/16/2008 in Washington D.C. that I will go on a fast. I decided that since the fast last year was 40 days and that was kind of significant with scripture that I would do another 40 day fast and that I would start it on 7/7/2008 after the 4th of July. Three days later I do the math and find out that my 40 day fast will end at midnight on 8/16/2008 in Washington D.C.. That is prophetic in itself and very typical of the Holy Spirit in His ways. I was awoken the morning of July 5 with our Nation on my mind and sat up and took some water and looked at my digital clock to see what time it was. It was 333 on my clock, the number of the Holy Spirit. The Triune, according to revelation, is 743, with "7" being the number of God and "4" being the number of Jesus Christ and "3" being the number of the Holy Spirit. I went back to sleep and was awoken again with the Nation on my mind and sat up and got a drink of water and I looked at the clock to see what time it was and it was 444 exactly, the number of Jesus Christ. Jack that is too many of what some people call coincidences, which I don't believe in the first place. I am praying for and believing that on 8/16/2008 you are going to witness the beginning of a full blown End Time Revival of the Church in America and it is going to be orchestrated by our youth. I believe that the Holy Spirit, the fire of the Holy Spirit is going to be released. You are going to see full body part healings and people raised up off of their death beds. You are going to see the chains of bondage of drugs, alcohol, tobacco, sexual immorality all forms of bondages start to be broken and people beginning to walk free from bondage. The outpouring is already beginning to happen but 8/16/2008 I believe will be climatic. They are already going wild down in Lakeland, FL and in some other areas. The Evangelists are winning souls by the thousands and have been overseas with their crusades. Just look at the signs they are too staggering of a number to even quote anymore. The fires in California, the floods in the mid-west, the crazy weather patterns and hail and reported tornadoes all over the land. What just happened in China and now the upheaval between Israel and Iran and we are still at war in Iraq. The threat of terrorists attacks and that there are now three in the world who claim that they are the Christ, etc..........

In vision I saw ABC, NBC, CBS television at this gathering in the evening and that it was being televised across the nation. I saw the headlines of the next day papers and they read 5 Million Cry Out for Jesus in Washington D.C. on 8/16/2008. Another thing that is significant is the date itself. Again according to revelation of numbers "8" is the number of Satan, he put himself above God who is a "7". You have the "8" month, 16th or "8"+"8" day and the year "8". That is the day "Satanic" and we as a Nation or 5 Million hopefully plus; are going to cry out for "Jesus". Spread the Word and get as many there as you can. This has to be another written revelation. I had not seen the date of 8/16/2008 until just now.   Jackthere is nothing to fear because "Greater is He who is in us then he who is in the World" and "We can do all things through Christ who strengthens us";also, "God did not give us a spirit of fear but of power, love and a sound mind." It is just that the deception in the United States is at an all time peak and it is scary. This all started back after WWII, then in 1962 when we re-wrote the separation of Church and State and took God out of both our Government and our Educational Institutions. Everything has just plummeted straight downwards and quickly since that date. You know it doesn't matter when the Lord is going to return; what matters is where are you going to spend eternity if you fall over dead in the next ten minutes from heart failure? The question never has been when it always has been where and no one seems to ask or minister salvation anymore. I am a Church hopper and you would be amazed at how few, almost never anymore preach the message of salvation and have an altar call. If you come up to me for prayer and healing the first thing I am going to ask you is have your given your heart to Jesus and believe that He arose from the grave into the Heavens? If you aren't saved what good is healing going to do for you. I need help in praying and working to break this bondage of Religion off of the Church so that they can operate in the gifts and move in this End Time out pouring of the Holy Spirit. We also need the Church woken up to the message of salvation and that we are at war and have been for a long time and losing. Only now it is End Time War and it is going to get hectic in the good ole U.S.A. at the End.

A friend and a brother in Christ: Chuck Mc Cuen

SECTION THREE
POEMS & QUOTES

LIFE FOR A DREAM

Where am I at?
What went wrong?
It seems like only yesterday,
Laughs, good times, a song!

Now when it's bleak, times are bad; but for a cry.
I look back at the past and wonder why?
Depression is hell–Oh! The worry and fear.
To think it all started with just one beer.

A good student was I and active in sports.
A scholarship possible–great things of all sorts.
What made me change? Was it a friend? Was it a girl?
Maybe I was just bored and wanted to give live a good whirl.

I know I got tired and started to run.
I quit eating regular, gave up sleep to have fun.
There just isn't enough time, don't you know!
A young man in search has to stay on the go

The first time I drank was to gain courage, relieve the pain.
Impossible! It only got worse. The next day it was back all over
again!
Everything made sense, now it's gone.
Maybe it was bad booze, a curse or bad Oman.

I just wanted to live, not lose.
Everyone else does–Why can't I drink booze!
Are they really happy? Or is it just me!
The pain–Feelings are felt but not easy to see.

261

I wanted to kiss her, not hurt her.
I wanted to laugh, have fun—not yell and scream.
Instead here I sit, without hope, not a dream.
This can't happen to me, for I'm a good student—Can't you see.

I remember the promises—Never again!
But things didn't go my way—I just couldn't win.
It only got worse and drinking become more.
I even did drugs and tried robbing a store.

Did you ever hear the sound of a steel door slamming shut?
To be cut off from life, with gangsters, murderers—the lot.
Poor me! What did I do wrong?
Will I ever laugh again? Have good times and song.

Then I awoke—God what a dream!
I fell to my knees and said Lord help me! I don't want all of those things.
He smiled, I felt warm and then I knew it was okay.
He said very clear in my mind—Just take care of today!

Rather than running now when things seem bad.
I confide first in GOD!
My special friends!
Even mom and dad.

I've slowed down a lot for now I know.
That God's with me where ever I go.
If I take care of today—tomorrow will come.
The bad times will pass and the good times, fun!

Chuck Mc Cuen 5/14/89

SWEET SURRENDER

I stood at the doorway of life, steadfast and solemn.
Like an old Oak tree, bare limbs, in the brisk winter calm.
No direction left just scars from the storms—no hope of life.
No one could minister to me—not even the Sycamore, who seemed to know, I
    called her my wife.

I couldn't even talk to my neighbor, the big Elm.
Whose arms were raised, full of life, not brazed.
He stood tall in praise, of what, I don't know.
It was all just a haze, like he was aglow.

I couldn't move as my roots held firm.
I just stood there victim to the force of the cold evil breeze.
My heart had turned cold—I had lost all my leaves.
The fire in me died, though rigid, I fell to my knees.

I surrendered that cold winter day, as I prayed "God help me!" I
can't live any more this way.
Praise God, the Son shown, the rains gave birth.
New leaves sprouted as life began running again through my trunk.
The haze lifted ever so slowly—as if I were drunk.

Now today I don't worry when winter sets in, nor Pine for the past as the
    snow begins.
I now have faith, knowing He is within. That spring will come, I will grow
    again.
Either here with Him in me or somewhere else, which I've come to know.
I now stand tall, like an Oak should—In His Word, often aglow.

Chuck Mc Cuen   11/8/89

THE LAW

When God spoke, there was light.
Both for the day and for the night.
When God spoke there was land, there was sea.
When God spoke there was you, there was me.

Four Thousand years BC, God spoke but few heard.
Some neglected to listen, few headed His Word.
In the presence of Moses, God wrote out His law.
Pride, envy, greed and lust—many heard but few saw.

They were all punished in those days.
For the sins of their flesh and the walk of their ways.
It was God's law they were to live by, they did not heed.
Instead they worshiped idols, filled with lust, envy and greed.

But God in His Wisdom knew all that was to come.
The Spirit spoke through prophets and warned but many remained dumb.
Then in God's Glory, Christ Jesus was born.
Victory for the poor in heart and to evil a new thorn.

It was the birth, life, death and resurrection of Christ.
That He bore all of our sins and gave us new life.
Now we keep in step with the Spirit at a wonderful pace.
We now live in Christ Jesus, not under the law, but God's Grace!

Chuck Mc Cuen 8/29/91

WISDOM

What is a thought; where does it go?
What do I think and what do I know?
Who's talking? Oh! Those words in my head.
Analyze, formalize, speculate, speak until dead.

Can I be quiet, not think of one thing?
Just pray to God and see the unseen.
When the Holy Spirit speaks, how do I know?
Can I void myself of feelings except for the love of God?

Must my mind race through time-hither to there?
Sometimes in fear—often less care.
Or can I walk in faith, to know peace, love and joy.
To consider life as a gem—rather a toy.

Can I think about what I'm thinking?
Do I have a choice of my thoughts?
Only through Jesus, the Word of God.
With His death, resurrection, my soul He has bought.

I asked Jesus, "How much do you love me?"
"This much"—that's what He said.
Then He spread out His arms—said Father forgive them.
It's finished—then He was dead.

Thank God for the resurrection, what a miraculous feat.
For that was the victory—where Satan was beat.
With the Lord's Word, and forgiveness of sin.
Only my repentance will assure that I win.

My heart cries at my soul—don't be fooled—trust in God.
For Satan's still active, roaming about—not well.
But soon there will be heaven on earth.
Then Satan will be bound for eternity, forever in hell.

Chuck Mc Cuen 8/7/91

FOOTPRINTS

One night a man had a dream. He dreamed he was walking along the beach with the LORD .
Across the sky flashed scenes from his life. For each scene: he noticed two sets of footprints in the sand: one belonged to him, and the other to the LORD.

When the last scene of his life flashed before him, he looked back at the footprints in the sand. He noticed that many times along the path of his life there was only one set of footprints. He also noticed that it happened at the very lowest and saddest times in his life.

This really bothered him and he questioned the LORD about it. "LORD, you said that once I decided to follow You, you'd walk with me all the way. But I have noticed that during the most troublesome times in my life, there is only one set of footprints. I don't understand why when I needed you most you would leave me".

The LORD replied, "My precious, precious child. I love you and would never leave you. During your times of trial and suffering, when you see only one set of footprints, it was then that I carried you."

YESTERDAY–TODAY–TOMORROW

There are two days in every week about which we should not worry, two days which should be kept free from fear and apprehension.

One of those days is YESTERDAY with its mistakes and cares, its faults and blunders, its aches and pains. YESTERDAY has passed forever beyond our control.

All the money in the world cannot bring back YESTERDAY, we cannot undo a single act we performed, we cannot erase a single word we said .... YESTERDAY is gone.

The other day we should not worry about is TOMMOROW with its possible adversities, its burdens, its large promise and poor performance. TOMMOROW is always beyond our immediate control.

TOMMORROW'S sun will rise. Either in splendor or behind a mask of clouds–but it will rise. Until it does, we have no stake in TOMMOROW for it is yet unborn.

This leaves only one day ..... TODAY, Any man can fight the battle of just one day. It is only when you and I add burdens of those two awful eternities ..... YETERDAY and TOMORROW that we break down .....

It is not the experience of TODAY that drives men mad–it is remorse of bitterness for something which happened YESTERDAY and the dread of what TOMORROW may bring.

> God grant me the serenity to accept the things I cannot change!
> The courage to change the things I can!
> And the wisdom to know the difference!

Mat: 6-34   "Therefore do not worry about tomorrow, for tomorrow will worry about its own things. Sufficient for the day is its own trouble."

ATTITUDE

"The longer I live, the more I realize the impact of attitude on life. Attitude, to me, is more than facts. It's more important than the past, than education, than money, than circumstances, than failures, than successes, than what other people think or say to do. It is more important than appearance, giftedness, or skill. It will make or break a company, a church, a home. The remarkable thing is that we have a choice every day regarding, the attitude we will embrace for that day. We cannot change our past, we cannot change the fact that people will act in a certain way. We cannot change the inevitable. The only thing we can do is play on the one string we have, and that is our attitude. I am convinced that life is 10% what happens, and 90% how I react to those things. And so it is with you—we are all in charge of our attitudes."

Chuck Swindle

Psm. 40:1-5

1) I waited patiently for the Lord, and He inclined to me. And heard my cry.

2) He also brought me up out of a horrible pit. Out of the miry clay. And set my feet upon a rock. And established my steps.

3) He has put a new song in my mouth—Praise to our God; Many will see it and fear. And will trust in the Lord.

4) Blessed is that man who makes the Lord his trust. And does not respect the proud, nor such as turn aside to lies.

5) Many, O Lord my God, are Your wonderful works which you have done; And your thoughts toward us cannot be recounted to You in order; I would declare and speak of them. They are more that can be numbered.

JUST FOR TODAY

Just for today I will try to live through this day only, not to tackle my whole life problems at once. I can do things for 12 hours that would appall me if I had to keep them up for a time.

Just for today I will be happy. This assumes that what Abraham Lincoln said is true that "Most folks are about as happy as they make up their minds to be." Happiness is from within; it is not a matter of externals.

Just for today I will try to adjust myself to what is, and not try to adjust everything to my own desires. I will take my family, my business and my luck as they come and fit myself to them.

Just for today I will take care of my body. I will exercise it, care for it, nourish it, not abuse it or neglect it, so that it will be a perfect machine for my bidding.

Just for today I will try to strengthen my mind. I will learn something useful. I will not be a mental loafer. I will read something that requires effort, thought and concentration.

Just for today I will exercise my soul in three ways, I will do somebody a good turn and not get found out. I will do as least two-things I don't want to do, as William James suggests, just for exercise.

Just for today I will be agreeable, I will look as well as I can, dress as becomingly as possible, talk low, act courteously, be liberal with praise, criticize not at all, nor find fault with anything and not try to regulate nor improve anyone.

Just for today I will have a quiet half hour all by myself and relax. In this half hour I will think of God, so as to get a little more perspective to my life.

Just for today, I will be unafraid, especially I will not be afraid to be happy, to enjoy what is beautiful, to love, and to believe what I choose to love, loves me.

If you understand and trust… that is Wisdom. If you do not understand and still trust… That is Faith.

Heb: 11-1 "Now " faith is the substance of things hoped for, the evidence of things not seen."

11-6 But without faith it is impossible to please Him, for he who comes to God must believe that He is, and He is a rewarder of those who diligently seek Him.

ABOUT THE AUTHOR

My name is Chuck Mc Cuen; I'm sixty-six years old; soon to be sixty-seven, in Feb., 2008. I am married and we have two adult sons and several grandchildren by now, which are most enjoyable. I married, to me, the most beautiful woman who came from a very influential family, in the business world. My parents were Christians, there were four of us children growing up and are all still living. My father was also very well liked and respected in the community. They called dad "Coach". After graduating from college in the mid/late 1930's he taught on the High School level both Math and History and he coached every sport that the school offered only to later to become Athletic Director. When he retired the school built a new gymnasium and dedicated it to my father for all that he had contributed over the years. The name is in bold letters above the entrance and it says "Mc Cuen" Gymnasium. That is something that you do not see on a high school level, very often. As family we are very proud of our father and blessed that we were given the parents that we had. I graduated from High School in 1958 and wanted to see the World, I had enough of education and in my lopsided way of seeing things I didn't have the time or want to sit in a classroom and study anymore. Like I said; I wanted to see the World. There are, I believe, only four states in the United States that I have not visited yet and the military service took me to places like Madrid, Spain; Libya, North Africa; Saudi, Arabia and then to Peshawar, Pakistan. Today I wouldn't trade that exposure for anything. I would dearly love to go to Israel, to walk where the Lord did and see so that I can have a mental image to live with. I was very successful in the business world in spite of my problems. I am pleased with what I have accomplished and the positions that I was able to obtain with a high school education. Anymore; today my whole life is with the Lord. If you only knew what all that He has done for me, in forgiven me and teaching me; you would understand. The book will draw you a fairly good picture. The good news is that today I know that everything I have been through was pre-destined; it was that I can do that which He has called me to do, which is for an appointed time which is yet in the future. I ask that you buy and read this book, not for the money but so that you can either help yourself or someone else that you know or love. You do not want to miss out on the questions and the information contained within. It could determine your destiny in the life after this one.

To Whom it May Concern

Having enjoyed Chuck's retelling of his story, and having lived a lot of it as it happened, I am even further convinced Jesus Christ is alive and well.

If this work helps just one soul find the Master it will be worth all the effort.

I have seen Chuck's walk from a personal standpoint as his sponser in recovery from his battle with alcohol, and I know he walks the walk.

Read this book then make your judgement and decision. If you decide you want what Chuck has, just ask for it.

A side note, I may have hit a 5 wood out of bounds 3 times but never would I have hit a 7 wood that badly.

Charlie God loves you but we know you. Thank you.

Gordon Mills